of a single species can set off a chain reaction affecting many others. A little-known species may be an important link in a complicated chain of life.

Farmers, ranchers, and other people who make their living off the land have found that getting rid of one species to protect their own livestock (sheep, cattle, etc.) can create even worse problems than the ones they tried to solve. When a group of ranchers banded together and killed the wolves that were attacking their cattle and sheep, they found their successful hunt had upset the "balance of nature." With no wolves to control their numbers, rabbits overran the land and destroyed the valuable crops that fed livestock.

WHAT IS AN ENDANGERED SPECIES?

A *species* is a group of individual organisms that share a common pool of genetic material. Professional taxonomists classify the organic world into its basic species units, kinds of organisms distinguishable from other kinds, by criteria such as anatomy, biochemistry, color, breeding systems, and, sometimes, behavior.

Endangered species are those at risk of extinction from all or a significant portion of their natural Earth homes. Some of them are in so much danger that scientists and the U.S. government have made a list of them called the Endangered Species List (see Chapter VIII). A *threatened* species is one that is likely to become endangered in the foreseeable future. Scientists estimate that we lose hundreds, or even thousands, of species each year.

How Many Species Are Already Extinct?

Almost all professional football players are still alive. The same is probably true for nuclear physicists, city planners, and tax consultants.... Not so for species! There are millions of different species of animals and plants on earth — possibly as many as 40 million. But somewhere between five and fifty billion species have existed at one time or another. Thus, only about one in a

TABLE 1.1

Group	No. of described species
Bacteria and blue-green algae:	4,760
Fungi:	46,983
Algae:	26,900
Bryophytes (mosses and liverworts:)	17,000 (WCMC, 1988)
Gymnosperms (conifers):	750 (Raven *et al.*, 1986)
Angiosperms (flowering plants):	250,000 (Raven *et al.*, 1986)
Protozoans:	30,800
Sponges:	5,000
Corals & Jellyfish:	9,000
Roundworms & earthworms:	24,000
Crustaceans:	38,000
Insects:	751,000
Other arthropods and minor invertebrates:	132,461
Mollusks:	50,000
Starfish:	6,100
Fishes (Teleosts):	19,056
Amphibians:	4,184
Reptiles:	6,300
Birds:	9,198 (Clements, 1981)
Mammals:	4,170 (Honacki *et al.*, 1982)
Total	**1,435,662 species**

Reprinted with permission from *Conserving the World's Biological Diversity*, published by World Resources Institute, World Conservation Union, Conservation International, World Wildlife Fund, and the World Bank, Washington, DC, 1990

thousand species is still alive — a truly lousy survival record: 99.9 percent failure!

— David M. Raup, *Extinction — Bad Genes or Bad Luck?* 1991

Over the millions of years since life began on Earth, species have formed and then died out naturally. Plants and animals were becoming extinct all that time. Scientists know from their study of fossils that dinosaurs, mammoths, and many thousands of other animals and plants once lived on Earth. (Fossils are the remains or traces of prehistoric plants and animals buried in the earth and turned to rock.) Figure 1.1 shows the periods in which the dinosaurs lived and became extinct. As dinosaurs were replaced with other species, the overall numbers and types of animals did not change dramatically. But since human beings have taken over the planet, species have been dying out at a much faster rate. According to some experts,

3

TABLE 1.2

Listings and Recovery Plans as of December 31, 1997

GROUP	ENDANGERED U.S.	ENDANGERED FOREIGN	THREATENED U.S.	THREATENED FOREIGN	TOTAL LISTINGS	SPECIES W/ PLANS
MAMMALS	58	251	7	15	331	42
BIRDS	75	178	15	6	274	74
REPTILES	14	66	20	14	114	30
AMPHIBIANS	9	8	7	1	25	11
FISHES	67	11	41	0	119	78
SNAILS	15	1	7	0	23	19
CLAMS	56	2	6	0	64	45
CRUSTACEANS	16	0	3	0	19	7
INSECTS	28	4	9	0	41	21
ARACHNIDS	5	0	0	0	5	4
ANIMAL SUBTOTAL	343	521	115	36	1,015	331
FLOWERING PLANTS	525	1	113	0	639	390
CONIFERS	2	0	0	2	4	1
FERNS AND OTHERS	26	0	2	0	28	22
PLANT SUBTOTAL	553	1	115	2	671	413
GRAND TOTAL	896	522	230	38	1,686*	744**

TOTAL U.S. ENDANGERED: 896 (743 animals, 553 plants)
TOTAL U.S. THREATENED: 230 (115 animals, 115 plants)
TOTAL U.S. LISTED: 1126 (458 animals***, 668 plants)

*Separate populations of a species listed both as Endangered and Threatened are tallied once, for the endangered population only. Those species are the argali, chimpanzee, leopard, Stellar sea lion, gray wolf, piping plover, roseate tern, green sea turtle, saltwater crocodile, and olive ridley sea turtle.

For the purposes of the Endangered Species Act, the term "species" can mean a species, subspecies, or distinct vertebrate population. Several entries also represent entire genera or even families.
**There are 478 approved recovery plans. Some recovery plans cover more than one species, and a few species have separate plans covering different parts of their ranges. Recovery plans are drawn up only for listed species that occur in the United States.
***Five animal species have dual status in the U.S.

Source: *Endangered Species Bulletin*, U.S. Fish and Wildlife Service, January/February 1998

plant or animal species are disappearing at the rate of one per day.

The Sixth Extinction?

At least five times in the last 600 million years, planet-wide cataclysms, such as drastic climate change or colliding asteroids, have wiped out whole families of organisms. Because of such turnover, scientists believe that more than 95 percent of all species that have ever existed are extinct to-day. Researchers predict that as tropical ecosystems are converted to farms and pasture, that rate will approach several hundred extinctions per day in the next 20 to 30 years — millions of times higher than background levels. (See below.) The Worldwatch Institute, a think-tank devoted to environmental issues, believes that more species of flora and fauna may disappear in our lifetime than were lost in the mass extinction that included the disappearance of the dinosaur 65 million years ago.

ENDANGERED SPECIES — MUST THEY DISAPPEAR?

CHAPTER I   **Earth — A Living Planet** 2
What Is an Endangered Species? ... Why Save Endangered Species? ... Habitat Is Home ...
Evolution and Mass Extinctions ... How Do People Endanger Plants and Animals? ... The
Role of Population in Species Survival ... Redefining Diversity ... Factors That Contribute
to Species Endangerment ... Distribution of Species Loss

CHAPTER II   **How Environmental Factors Affect Species** 19
Climate and the Evolution of Species ... The World Climate ... Carbon Dioxide ... Effects of
Climate Change ... The Response of the Nations ... Acid Rain ... Sources of Sulfur and
Nitrogen in the Atmosphere ... Transport — The Link Between Emissions and Deposition ...
Contributing Factors ... Damage to Aquatic Systems ... Other Damage Caused by Acid Rain ...
The Politics of Acid Rain ... A Look to the Future

CHAPTER III   **The Condition of Plant Species** 36
The First Global Assessment of Plants — The *IUCN Red List* ... The American Landscape —
The First Complete Review ... How Global Warming Affects Plant Ecosystems ... Forests ...
Wetlands and Marine Ecosystems ... Plant Protection Under the Endangered Species Act ...
The Clinton Administration's Focus on Ecosystems, Not Species

CHAPTER IV   **Imperiled Aquatic Species** 52
Water Pollution — Many, Many Causes ... Dams — Unexpected Consequences ... Some
Examples of Endangered Water Species ... Enforcement of Laws Protecting Aquatic Species

CHAPTER V   **The Status of Bird Species** 77
What Are the Threats to Birds? ... The Bald Eagle ... Bye, Bye, Songbird? ... The Northern
Spotted Owl ... The Red-Cockaded Woodpecker ... The Peregrine Falcon ... The Great
White Whooping Crane ... The California Condor ... South American Flamingos

CHAPTER VI   **Vanishing Land Creatures — Mammals, Herpetofauna, Insects, and Primates** 90
Levels of Endangerment ... Who Cares About Bears? ... The Giant Panda — Loved To
Death? ... The Wolf ... The Big Cats ... The Black-Footed Ferret ... Butterflies and Moths ...
Amphibians ... Primates ... Symbols of the American West ... When Humans and Animals
Collide ... Animals Used for Research

CHAPTER VII   **Commercial Trade of Wild Animals** 110
The Great Whales ... Sharks ... Dolphins ... The Rhinoceros ... Reptiles ... Exotic Birds ...
Elephants ... The Fur Trade ... The Apes ... The Economists' Argument ... The Lacey Act ...
The Convention on the International Trade in Endangered Species ... The U.S. Government
Gets Involved ... NAFTA and GATT ... The World Trade Organization ... World Leaders in
Wildlife Trade

CHAPTER VIII   **Wildlife as Recreation** 130
Sports Involving Wildlife and Natural Resources ... Trends ... Expenditures ... Who Participates
in Wildlife Sports? ... Hunting ... Fishing ... Wildlife-Watching Activities ... Canned Hunting

CHAPTER IX   **The Road To Recovery — How Some Species Have Rebounded** 138
The History of the Protection of Species ... The Endangered Species Act ... Delisted and
Downlisted Species ... Habitat Conservation Plans ... Captive Breeding ... The National
Park System ... The National Wildlife Refuge System ... America's Wild Lands Under
Attack ... Zoos ... Federal Lands ... Ecosystem Conservation Replaces Species-By-Species
Conservation ... The United Nations' List of Protected Areas

CHAPTER X   **The Endangered Species Act Has Worked Well** 160

CHAPTER XI   **The Endangered Species Act Has Not Worked Well** 165

IMPORTANT NAMES AND ADDRESSES 170
RESOURCES 171
INDEX 172

INFORMATION PLUS®   **EDITORS:**
WYLIE, TEXAS 75098   **CORNELIA BLAIR, B.A., M.S.**
© 1992, 1994, 1996, 1998   **MARK A. SIEGEL, Ph.D.**
ALL RIGHTS RESERVED   **NANCY R. JACOBS, B.A., M.A.**

CHAPTER I

EARTH — A LIVING PLANET

*Homo sapiens is perceived to stand at the top of the pyramid of life,
but the pinnacle is a precarious station.*
— Patrick Leahy, U.S. Senator, 1978

Earth is a biosphere, a "living globe" — a network of plants and animals that depend on one another to live. Animals breathe in oxygen and breathe out carbon dioxide; plants take in carbon dioxide and give off oxygen. Plants and animals keep each other alive in other ways also. While some animals eat other animals, many animals eat plants, so even the meat eaters (carnivores) depend on plants to stay alive. In turn, the plants benefit from the animal droppings and from the decay of animal matter.

In one way or another, plants and animals live together in balance, in *habitats* (see below), forming *ecosystems*. The planet is richly supplied with living things, both animals and plants. Many species have not yet been identified or named. Some species have not even been discovered, but removal

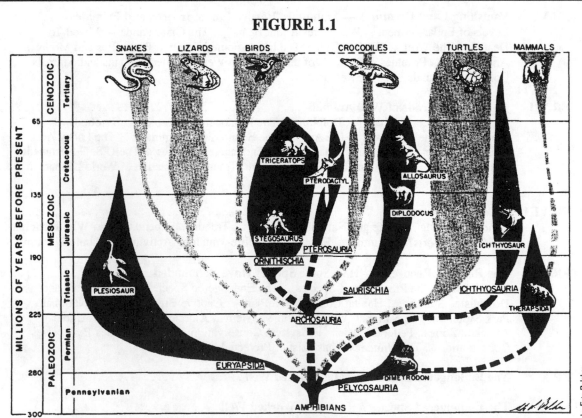

FIGURE 1.1

DINOSAURS APPEAR AND RECEDE

Ornithischia and Saurischia, the true dinosaurs, and other early reptiles faded out gradually as modern life forms evolved. Dashed lines indicated presumed lineages. Some scientists believe that birds are derived from Saurischian dinosaurs.

Source: *The Endangered Species Handbook*, Animal Welfare Institute, Washington, DC, 1990

2

Theories That Explain the Causes of Extinctions

Scientists debate the reasons for the recent extinctions of species. Most theories involve one of three hypotheses:

- Changing climate — A rapidly changing climate at the end of the last ice age transformed the habitat of species.

- Hunting to extinction — Newly arrived humans who hunted animals, which were easy prey due to their lack of fear of humans, in such large numbers that they were eventually too depleted to reproduce their populations.

- Pestilence — Animals were killed by diseases carried by rats, birds, parasites, and even humans, that were unknown to their immune systems.

How Many Are Threatened or Endangered?

The majority of species have not even been identified. While estimates of the number of species range between 5 and 100 million, most estimates are around 10 million. Of that number, only 1.4 million have been identified. Table 1.1 shows the numbers of known and estimated species on Earth. Mammals, including humans, make up only three-tenths of 1 percent of all known organisms.

Table 1.2 reports the number of species identified as threatened or endangered by the Endangered Species Act as of December 1997. The list includes a total of 1,686 species, 1,126 of them in the United States. (See Chapter IX for discussion of the Endangered Species Act and listing protocol.) In the United States, 753 species were endangered; 206 species were threatened. More than half (59 percent) the endangered or threatened species are plant forms. Among animal species, the greatest numbers are among fish, birds, and mammals. Since 1976, endangered and threatened species have been listed at an annual rate of 34 species; in the past 10 years, that rate has averaged more than 50 species per year.

In 1996, the Nature Conservancy, a private conservation group, studied more than 20,000 native American species and found that about one-third are rare or imperiled, a larger percentage than many scientists had expected. Of the 20,481 species studied, about two-thirds were secure, while 1.3 percent were extinct or possibly extinct, 6.5 percent were critically imperiled, 8.9 percent were imperiled, and 15 percent were considered vulnerable. The study, considered the most comprehensive assessment to date of the state of American flora (plant life) and fauna (animal life), reported that mammals and birds were doing relatively well compared with other groups. However, a high proportion of flowering plants and freshwater species like mussels, crayfish, and fish were in trouble. The destruction of habitat was seen as the main threat to species.

The Red List

Since 1960, the International Union for the Conservation of Nature (IUCN), based in Gland, Switzerland, has compiled *Red Data Books* for those species recognized as threatened. Worldwide, in 1996, some 698 mammals, 1047 birds, 191 reptiles, 63 amphibians, 762 fishes, and 2,250 invertebrates were listed as threatened. Furthermore, at least 60,000 plants — one in every 8 species and nearly 1 in 3 in the United States — were listed as threatened. These are, of course, only the ones that are known. The list has no official use but is considered an influential guide for conservation policy makers. The United States ranked first, by far, of nations in total numbers of plants at risk.

WHY SAVE ENDANGERED SPECIES?

The diversity of life forms, so numerous that we have yet to identify most of them, is the greatest wonder of this planet. — Edward Wilson, Biologist, Harvard University

One commonly given reason for protecting animal and plant species is that they give beauty, variety, and entertainment to the world. People also appreciate them for their scientific, educational, historical, and cultural value. But even more important is that all animals, plants, and even human beings are linked together in a "chain of life." Each species has a unique purpose, and if it dies out, the planet may not function as well. For example, some species serve as food for other species that will, in turn, starve without them. The loss of one species can cause a "chain reaction" throughout the ecosystem, and Earth's biodiversity is at great risk.

Aside from the economic or utilitarian reasons for preserving species, many people think that humanity has a moral responsibility to maintain the earth's biodiversity. They believe that every creature has an intrinsic right to exist and that humans, the animals with the greatest power to destroy the environment, have a moral obligation to protect other species. When species are lost, they believe, the quality of all life is diminished.

Biodiversity, a shortened form of the term *biological diversity*, refers to the full range of various plants and animals and their habitats that compose the biosphere that we call the planet Earth. Environmentalists began using the term during the 1980s, when biologists began to warn that human activities were causing the loss of plant and animal species.

Environmental Ethics

Many ethicists believe humans are concerned about environmental issues and nature for any of three reasons. First, nature benefits humans; it is useful — this is the *instrumental* good. Monetary price is normally the measure of instrumental value (what can this object do for me, and how much am I willing to pay for it?). Second, people may value nature as an object of knowledge and perception, an *aesthetic* good, that is based solely on the qualities of the object itself, as judged by an appreciative response of informed and discriminating observers. Third, humans may regard an object with love or affection, such as a person or an ideal (love of country, for example). This is a *moral* value.

Mark Sagoff, in *Zuckerman's Dilemma: A Plea for Environmental Ethics* (The Hastings Center,

1991), suggested that E. B. White's *Charlotte's Web* serves as an environmental parable for today. Reflecting on humankind's relationship with nature, one might value Wilbur the pig in three ways. His instrumental value lies in ham hocks and sausage. His aesthetic value earns him a ribbon at the county fair. His moral value is the value he has in and of himself, and Charlotte the spider loves him for it. Humans can value nature the way Charlotte valued Wilbur, or can, as the farmer Zuckerman did initially, see the natural world in terms of the pork chops it provides.

Monitors of the Environment

Coal miners once took canaries down the mineshafts with them as a means of checking the safety of the air in the tunnels underground. Dangerous gases can collect in the tunnels of coal mines. When that happens, the smallest spark can cause an explosion, trapping the workers underground, or the men could be killed by breathing poisonous fumes. Because the feared gas had no odor, miners could not detect the gas by smelling it. As long as the canary lived, the miners could trust the air to be clean; but if the bird died, the miners would know that the mine was unsafe and they would get out of the tunnels.

In the same way, some species are important to human beings because they warn us of dangers that we cannot see in the world. These are called "indicator species." The sudden deaths of Bald eagles and Peregrine falcons warned people about the dangers of DDT, a strong, once widely used pesticide that accumulates in body tissues. The disappearance of fish in various rivers, lakes, and seas alerted people to the presence of chemicals that can also harm human beings. Many scientists are concerned about what the disappearance of many amphibians, especially frogs, might mean to the future of the earth.

HABITAT IS HOME

To survive, animals and plants need healthful environments and places to raise their young and live in health and safety. These homes are called

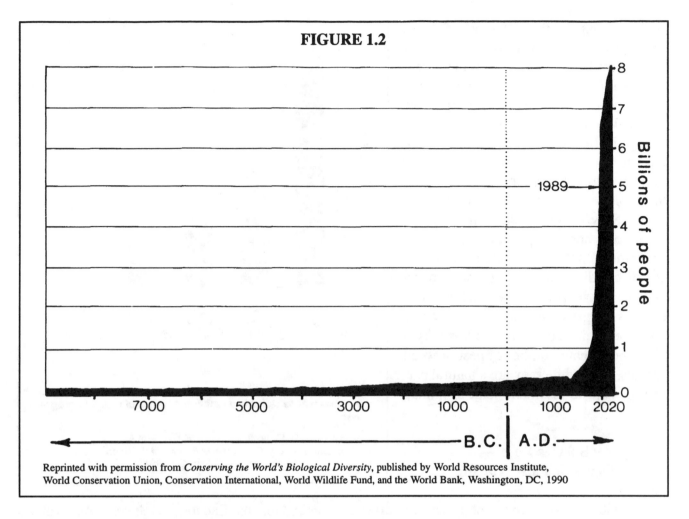

FIGURE 1.2

Billions of people

1989

B.C. | A.D.

7000 5000 3000 1000 1 1000 2020

Reprinted with permission from *Conserving the World's Biological Diversity*, published by World Resources Institute, World Conservation Union, Conservation International, World Wildlife Fund, and the World Bank, Washington, DC, 1990

habitats. A forest is habitat for deer; a swamp is habitat for alligators. If those habitats are lost, the species will die out. People sometimes destroy habitats by using the land for human needs, clearing the land of trees or filling swamps in order to build homes, roads, or shopping centers. They also poison habitats with chemicals and industrial waste. Every day, hundreds of animal and plant homes are lost. Saving habitats is necessary to save the life forms that inhabit them.

EVOLUTION AND MASS EXTINCTIONS

Today, even though obscure or little-known species are lost with little or no notice, we can document the date of loss of relatively well-known species to the nearest decade (e.g., the sea mink ... became extinct about 1880, sometimes to the year (e.g., the Guam flycatcher ... became extinct in 1985), or even to the day, in the case of
the last passenger pigeon, which died on September 1, 1914.
— National Research Council, Science and the Endangered Species Act, 1995

Widespread extinctions have occurred infrequently in Earth's history and have generally been due to major geological and astronomical events. Scientists call the disappearance of a few species per million years a "background rate." When that background rate doubles for many different groups of plants and animals at the same time, a *mass extinction* is taking place. Scientists generally believe that there have been five mass extinctions, known as the Big Five — one each in the Ordovician, Devonian, Permian, Triassic, and Cretaceous periods. The best documented mass extinction, because it was the most recent, occurred at the end of the Cretaceous period. Its rocks and fossils are the best preserved. In between those major mass extinctions, background extinctions have always occurred.

Many experts think the loss of diversity leads to problems beyond the loss of animal and plant variety. When local populations are wiped out, the genetic diversity within that species that provides the ability to adapt to environmental change is diminished. The links between the species are cut, resulting in a situation of "biotic impoverishment," where the habitat is less fertile and disease can thrive. Survivors of these extinctions are likely to be hardy, "opportunistic" organisms, those that can tolerate a wide variety of conditions, characteristics often associated with pests. Based on this, some experts suggest that as some species dwindle, their places may be taken by a disproportionate number of pest or weed species, that, while they are a natural part of life, will be less beneficial to human beings.

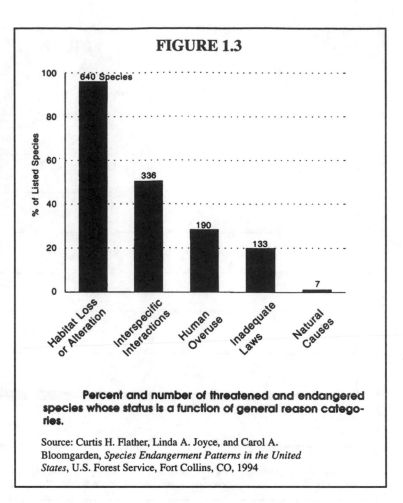

FIGURE 1.3

Percent and number of threatened and endangered species whose status is a function of general reason categories.

Source: Curtis H. Flather, Linda A. Joyce, and Carol A. Bloomgarden, *Species Endangerment Patterns in the United States*, U.S. Forest Service, Fort Collins, CO, 1994

Species Loss — Crisis or False Alarm?

As with many environmental questions, experts disagree about the seriousness of the threat to species diversity. Some observers believe the danger is unproven and claim that while wild habitats are disappearing because of human expansion, the seriousness of the extinction is exaggerated and unsupported by scientific evidence. They point to the fact that the total number of species and their geographic distribution are unknown. How, they ask, can forecasts be made based on such sketchy data?

Other observers contend that extinctions, even mass ones, are inevitable and occur as a result of great geological and astronomical events that man cannot affect. They do not believe that disruptions caused by human activity are enough to create the mega-extinction prophesied by people they consider "alarmists."

Furthermore, many critics of the environmental movement believe that the needs of humans are being made secondary to those of wildlife. They contend that the Endangered Species Act protects wildlife regardless of the economic cost to human beings. Sometimes that cost is jobs for people. They claim, for example, that the concern for the spotted owl of the Pacific Northwest forests has halted logging there, at some economic loss to communities and families in the area.

HOW DO PEOPLE ENDANGER PLANTS AND ANIMALS?

The American people must understand that all species, including human beings, are connected ... that the choice between people and animals, between the economy and endangered species, is a false one. [Americans] cannot eliminate the habitat of their fellow species and expect our own to survive.—
Mollie Beattie, Director, U.S. Fish and Wildlife Service, 1994

Many experts believe that people can no longer attribute the increasing loss of species to "natural" processes but must consider the effect of human activities on the environment. Human beings affect plant and animal life in two ways. First, in industrialized countries, people use up natural resources at a fast rate. Wildlife is considered a natural resource because the animal and plant kingdoms are part of the earth's natural environment. Second, the human population is growing rapidly, requiring more room, food, and water. Figure 1.2 shows the increased numbers of human beings over a thousand-year period. As a result, animal and plant species suffer from habitat destruction, commercial exploitation, disease, predation, pollution, and introduction of non-native species.

Animals need food and water, but some human activities make it hard for animals to find safe water and food, and many species cannot reproduce often enough to keep up their populations. In the past century, human beings have spread farms, cities, highways, and towns across the land, displacing plant life and driving the animals out of areas where they can feed.

Some animals die from poisoned air and water, and others die at the hands of hunters and trappers. Because people value their furs, hides, tusks, or horns, many wild animals are facing extinction today. Some people pay a lot of money for those trophies. Others like to own certain animals simply because they are rare, exotic, or financially valuable.

Many people who believe that animals are more than just another natural resource, but are also particularly valuable to the entire ecosystem of Earth, are trying to help save the animals. Many species that were becoming extremely rare have been helped by people, and their numbers are recovering, although it remains a constant struggle. Other species have been lost forever.

Hawaii is an example of an ecosystem unbalanced by human activities. In 1794, explorers from the West introduced cattle, horses, goats, and sheep to the islands. These animals multiplied and moved into the forests, destroying native plants through overgrazing and causing the loss of birds and other animals that had evolved over centuries in the delicate habitat. Human settlements and agriculture claimed further wildlife. Today, 29 of Hawaii's birds and its only two native mammals are listed as endangered, more than 800 of its native plants are at risk, and at least 65 species of animals and 45 plant species have disappeared forever.

Are Some Species More Important than Others?

Not all animals are in danger. Some, such as raccoons, white-tailed deer, cardinals, and coyotes are plentiful and healthy because they can get along well in a world full of human beings. Furthermore, people often seem to be more interested in saving certain endangered animals (such as whales, giant pandas, Bald eagles, and elephants) than in saving others. Other species, such as certain insects, reptiles, and fish, get much less attention, and often, less is done to prevent their extinction. Many experts believe that point of view is short-sighted because one species may have many other species depending on it for survival. Furthermore, a species' continued existence should not depend on how cuddly or appealing a species may appear to human beings.

THE ROLE OF POPULATION IN SPECIES SURVIVAL

While overpopulation in poor nations tends to keep them poverty-stricken, overpopulation in rich nations tends to undermine the life-support capacity of the entire planet.
— Paul Ehrlich, Stanford University, 1994

The world population has grown rapidly during the last half of the twentieth century. For centuries, deaths largely offset births, resulting in low growth. High birth rates in developing countries, coupled with a reduction in death rates and reduced infant mortality (an overall lengthening of the life

TABLE 1.3

Number of threatened and endangered species by specific reasons contributing to their endangerment. Specific reasons had to affect ≥15% of the species for speciose taxa (≥20 species listed), and 25% of the species in less speciose taxa.

All T&E (667 spp.)		Plants (285 spp.)		Fish (95 spp.)		Birds (85 spp.)	
256	Agricultural Development	110	Rural/Resid./Indust. Areas	49	Exotic/Introduced Species	52	Exotic/Introduced Species
234	Exotic/Introduced Species	104	Grazing	49	Water Diversion/ Drawdown	49	Predation
228	Rural/Resid./Indust. Areas	97	Heavy Equipment	44	Channel Modification	47	Agricultural Development
187	Grazing	90	Agricultural Development	42	Competition	45	Veg. Composition Changes
176	Low Gene Pool	84	Low Gene Pool	43	Environ. Contaminants/ Pollution	34	Forest Clearing
173	Predation	81	Highways/Railroads	41	Agricultural Development	31	Grazing
168	Veg. Composition Changes	76	Exotic/Introduced Species	37	Sedimentation	31	Rural/Resid./Indust. Areas
165	Heavy Equipment	69	Collecting	36	Predation	30	Forest Alteration
160	Competition	69	Recreational Areas	34	Reservoirs	28	Disease
157	Forest Clearing	69	Veg. Composition Changes	31	Erosion	25	Competition
147	Highways/Railroads	65	Competition	26	Groundwater Drawdown	24	Harassment/Indiscr. Killing
138	Erosion	62	Forest Clearing	25	Passage Barriers	19	Adverse Weather
136	Recreational Areas	56	Off-Road Vehicles	25	Water Temperature Fluctuation	19	Low Gene Pool
127	Channel Modification	54	Surface Mines	23	Bank Modification/ Devel.	18	Fire
124	Collecting	53	Erosion	22	Water Level Fluctuation	18	Food Supply Reduction
120	Forest Alteration	43	Forest Alteration	21	Hybridization	18	Parasites
115	Water Diversion/ Drawdown			20	Low Gene Pool	18	Wetland Filling
114	Surface Mines			19	Grazing	16	Pesticides
				17	Flooding	16	Recreational Areas
				17	Surface Mines	15	Shoreline Modif./Devel.
						14	Channel Modification
						14	Heavy Equipment
						14	Highways/Railroads
						14	Subsistence Hunting
						13	Erosion

Mammals (68 spp.)		Clams (42 spp.)		Reptiles (33 spp.)		Insects (22 spp.)	
25	Rural/Resid./Indust. Areas	36	Channel Modification	16	Predation	15	Rural/Resid./Indust. Areas
23	Agricultural Development	34	Sedimentation	14	Commercial Exploitation	10	Veg. Composition Changes
21	Forest Clearing	32	Environ. Contaminants/ Pollution	12	Exotic/Introduced Species	9	Grazing
19	Predation	24	Agricultural Development	12	Incidental Capture/ Killing	8	Agricultural Development
19	Recreational Areas	24	Reservoirs	11	Collecting	8	Exotic/Introduced Species
19	Veg. Composition Changes	24	Water Level Fluctuations	10	Rural/Resid./Indust. Areas	8	Heavy Equipment
17	Highways/Railroads	23	Herbicides	9	Agricultural Development	7	Highways/Railroads
16	Forest Alteration	23	Pesticides	9	Environ. Contaminants/ Pollution	7	Low Gene Pool
16	Heavy Equipment	23	Surface Mines	9	Forest Clearing	6	Fire Suppression
15	Food Supply Reduction	22	Passage Barriers	9	Harassment/Indiscr. Killing	6	Food Supply Reduction
14	Exotic/Introduced Species	20	Erosion	9	Shoreline Modif./Devel.	6	Recreational Areas
14	Harassment/Indiscr. Killing	19	Water Temperature Alteration	7	Channel Modification	5	Adverse Weather
14	Low Gene Pool	18	Inherent Reproductive Characteristics	7	Erosion	5	Collecting
14	Poaching	17	Dissolved Oxygen Reduction	7	Highways/Railroads	5	Surface Mines
13	Competition	17	Exotic/Introduced Species	7	Poaching	4	Fire
11	Incidental Capture/ Killing	17	Low Gene Pool	7	Recreational Areas	4	Off-Road Vehicles
10	Commercial Exploitation	13	Underground Mines	6	Adverse Weather	4	Pesticides
10	Grazing	9	Collecting	6	Grazing		
		8	Fertilizers	6	Inherent Reproductive Characteristics		
		7	Water Diversion/ Drawdown	6	Off-Road Vehicles		
				6	Subsistence Hunting		
				5	Fire Suppression		
				5	Forest Alteration		
				5	Reservoirs		
				5	Wetland Filling		

(continued)

TABLE 3.1 (Continued)

Snails (13 spp.)		Amphibians (11 spp.)		Crustaceans (10 spp.)		Arachnids (3 spp.)	
6	Collecting	7	Agricultural Development	8	Environ. Contaminants/ Pollution	3	Environ. Contaminants/ Pollution
6	Forest Alteration	7	Rural/Resid./Industr. Areas	5	Sedimentation	3	Exotic/Introduced Species
6	Forest Clearing	5	Highways/Railroads	4	Agricultural Development	3	Rural/Resid./Indust. Areas
5	Hiking/Camping	5	Low Gene Pools	4	Collecting		
5	Low Gene Pool	4	Grazing	4	Herbicides		
4	Grazing	3	Adverse Weather	4	Rural/Resid./Indust. Areas		
4	Highways/Railroads	3	Collecting	3	Flooding		
4	Predation	3	Food Supply Reduction	3	Forest Clearing		
4	Recreational Areas	3	Forest Clearing	3	Gas/Oil Development		
4	Rock Climbing	3	Groundwater Drawdown	3	Heavy Equipment		
4	Rural/Resid./Indust. Areas	3	Heavy Equipment	3	Highways/Railroads		
		3	Inherent Reproductive Charact.	3	Low Gene Pool		
		3	Predation	3	Predation		
		3	Veg. Composition Changes	3	Spelunking		
		3	Water Diversion/ Drawdown	3	Surface Drainage		
				3	Water Diversion/ Drawdown		

Source: Curtis H. Flather, Linda A. Joyce, and Carol A. Bloomgarden, *Species Endangerment Patterns in the United States*, U.S. Forest Service, Fort Collins, CO, 1994

span), dramatically increased population growth beginning around 1950. Between 1950 and 1990, the global population doubled from 2.5 billion to more than 5.5 billion people. Another billion people will be added by the end of the year 2000.

Population growth rates are now falling everywhere except in Africa, which continues to have the fastest growing continental population. The United Nations projects continuing slow declines in growth rates in all areas of the world due to declining fertility rates. Nevertheless, even if fertility *rates* decrease, population will continue to grow because people are living longer and there are simply more people who can reproduce.

The growing number of people increases demand on natural resources. More people require more food, fuel, clothing, and other necessities of life. All of these must be supplied from the planet's resources and from the sun's energy. These facts, combined with the realization that the earth's resources are limited, not infinite, pose serious questions about rapid population growth. Can the world's resources support its population and maintain the environment, or will human needs overwhelm the capacity of the earth?

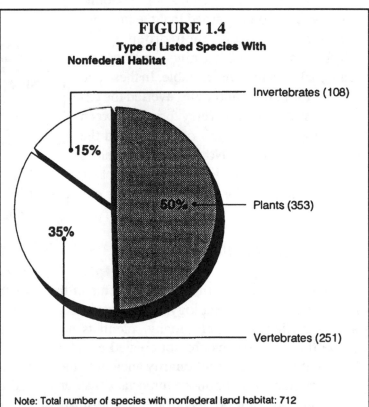

FIGURE 1.4

Type of Listed Species With Nonfederal Habitat

Invertebrates (108)

15%

50%

35%

Plants (353)

Vertebrates (251)

Note: Total number of species with nonfederal land habitat: 712

Source: *Endangered Species Act — Information on Species Protection on Nonfederal Lands*, General Accounting Office, Washington, DC, 1994

The answer is not clear and depends on assumptions about economic development, technology and progress, and human behavior. However, there is substantial evidence that population growth is pressing, or has exceeded, the capacity of natural resources in many areas. A country's population generally will stabilize as its economy develops and living standards rise. This "demographic shift" has already taken place in industrialized countries, where the fertility rate is generally at or below replacement level. This is unlikely to occur for some time in the developing world, although the fertility rate has also been dropping there.

Environmentalists warn that conservation, resource protection, and drastic measures to curb population may be required to avoid serious consequences. Other analysts do not share this rather fatalistic approach and point to the fear held at one time that as the world ran out of whale oil for lamps, great cities would be left in darkness. Others had predicted that a lack of coal would stop economic development. Some warned that the huge increases of horses and their droppings in American cities in the late nineteenth century would make them uninhabitable. In these and other cases, new technologies averted the expected disasters. Controversy thrives between those supporting the "era of limits" and the "no limits" advocates. Nonetheless, both sides agree that continued development must include wise consideration for resources and the environment.

REDEFINING DIVERSITY

Scientists today are throwing out some of the old assumptions about ecology. For example, contrary to traditional beliefs, many scientists now believe that "all species are not created equally." Those that are more evolutionarily ancient in their genetic content may be more important than any of the multitude of more recent species or subspecies. For example, the 10 species of cichlid fishes found in Madagascar that are believed to be the

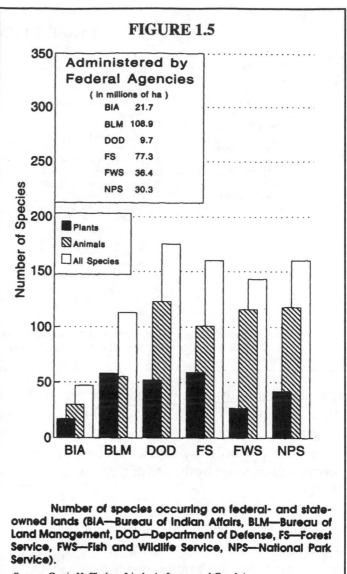

FIGURE 1.5

Administered by Federal Agencies
(in millions of ha)

BIA	21.7
BLM	108.9
DOD	9.7
FS	77.3
FWS	36.4
NPS	30.3

Plants ■
Animals ▨
All Species ☐

Number of species occurring on federal- and state-owned lands (BIA—Bureau of Indian Affairs, BLM—Bureau of Land Management, DOD—Department of Defense, FS—Forest Service, FWS—Fish and Wildlife Service, NPS—National Park Service).

Source: Curtis H. Flather, Linda A. Joyce, and Carol A. Bloomgarden, *Species Endangerment Patterns in the United States*, U.S. Forest Service, Fort Collins, CO, 1994

link between the founder cichlid and the thousands of cichlid species worldwide are thought to be very important genetically.

Another general rule of biodiversity, sometimes called the "law of southern assets," is that the Southern Hemisphere is more biologically wealthy, in general, than the Northern Hemisphere, largely because land there has been divided more times by changes in rivers, glaciers, and mountain growth, thereby subdividing populations of plants and animals. Also, areas at higher altitudes are generally less rich in species than locations at lower heights.

12

FIGURE 1.6
ALL TAXA

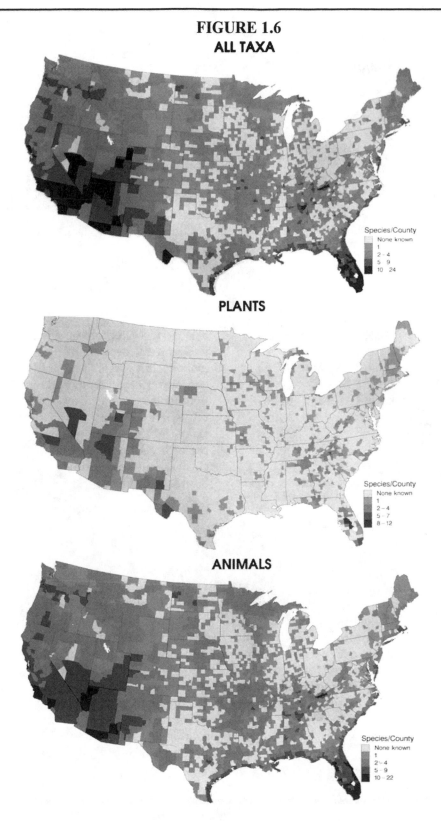

PLANTS

ANIMALS

Number of threatened and endangered species/county for the conterminous U.S.; all taxa (a), plants (b), and animals (c).

Source: Curtis H. Flather, Linda A. Joyce, and Carol A. Bloomgarden, *Species Endangerment Patterns in the United States*, U.S. Forest Service, Fort Collins, CO, 1994

FIGURE 1.7

MAMMALS

-BIRDS

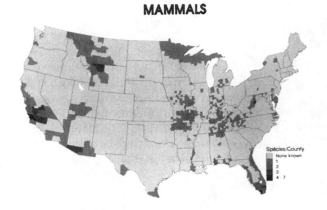
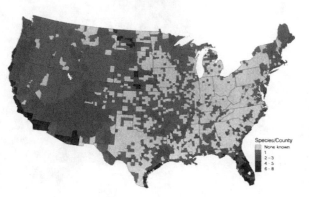

FISH

REPTILES

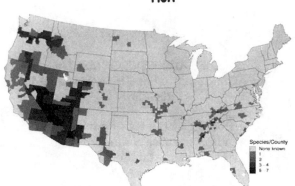
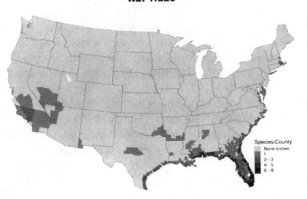

AMPHIBIANS

Number of threatened and endangered species/county by vertebrate taxa for the conterminous U.S.

Source: Curtis H. Flather, Linda A. Joyce, and Carol A. Bloomgarden, *Species Endangerment Patterns in the United States*, U.S. Forest Service, Fort Collins, CO, 1994

TABLE 1.4

Number of threatened or endangered species by specific reasons contributing to their endangerment within each region of high species endangerment. Specific reasons had to affect ≥ 25% of the species found in each region.

Southern Appalachia (39 spp.)

29	Environ. Contaminants/Pollution
26	Agricultural Development
25	Sedimentation
24	Channel Modification
24	Surface Mines
22	Reservoirs
20	Pesticides
18	Passage Barriers
18	Water Temperature Alteration
17	Herbicides
16	Dissolved Oxygen Reduction
16	Erosion
16	Exotic/Introduced Species
15	Inherent Reproductive Characteristics
15	Low Gene Pool
14	Forest Clearing
14	Water level Fluctuation
13	Collecting
13	Underground Mines

Peninsular Florida (64 spp.)

47	Rural/Resid./Indust. Areas
33	Forest Clearing
32	Agricultural Development
27	Fire Suppression.
19	Heavy Equipment
19	Veg. Composition Changes
18	Recreational Areas
17	Highways/Railroads
16	Competition

Eastern Gulf Coast (27 spp.)

11	Rural/Resid./Indust. Areas
11	Shoreline Modif./Devel.
10	Harassment/Indiscr. Killing
9	Recreational Areas
8	Adverse Weather
8	Commercial Exploitation
8	Erosion
8	Forest Alteration
8	Forest Clearing
8	Incidental Capture/Killing
8	Off-Road Vehicles
8	Predation
7	Agricultural Development
7	Channel Modification
7	Collecting
7	Environ. Contaminants/Pollution
7	Exotic/Introduced Species

Southern Desertic Basins, Plains, and Mountains (32 spp.)

13	Collecting
12	Recreational Areas
11	Grazing
11	Highways/Railroads
10	Commercial Exploitation
10	Heavy Equipment
10	Water Diversion/Drawdown
9	Competition
8	Exotic/Introduced Species

Arizona Basin (27 spp.)

15	Grazing
11	Erosion
10	Exotic/Introduced Species
10	Predation
10	Surface Mines
9	Heavy Equipment
8	Competition
8	Forest Alteration
8	Veg. Composition Changes
7	Agricultural Development
7	Flooding
7	Recreational Areas
7	Reservoirs

Colorado/Green River Plateaus (29 spp.)

12	Grazing
11	Collecting
10	Off-Road Vehicles
10	Surface Mines
8	Commercial Exploitation
8	Erosion
8	Gas/Oil Development
8	Water Diversion/Drawdown
7	Competition
7	Heavy Equipment

Central Desertic Basins and Plateaus (18 spp.)

9	Surface Mines
8	Gas/Oil Development
6	Water Diversion/Drawdown
5	Collecting
5	Grazing
5	Heavy Equipment
5	Recreational Areas
5	Transmission Lines/Towers

Southern Nevada/ Sonoran Basin (53 spp.)

36	Exotic/Introduced Species
32	Water Diversion/Drawdown
23	Grazing
22	Agricultural Development
21	Channel Modification
19	Competition
19	Groundwater Drawdown
19	Predation
19	Recreational Areas
18	Rural/Resid./Indust. Areas
17	Low Gene Pool
17	Off-Road Vehicles
17	Surface Mines
16	Heavy Equipment
16	Reservoirs
15	Veg. Composition Changes
14	Highways/Railroads

Central/Southern California (49 spp.)

25	Rural/Resid./Indust. Areas
24	Agricultural Development
24	Exotic/Introduced Species
24	Grazing
23	Predation
18	Heavy Equipment
18	Off-Road Vehicles
16	Highways/Railroads
13	Gas/Oil Development
13	Surface Mines

Northern California (32 spp.)

18	Agricultural Development
18	Heavy Equipment
17	Rural/Resid./Indust. Areas
16	Grazing
15	Highways/Railroads
12	Off-Road Vehicles
11	Exotic/Introduced Species
10	Low Gene Pool
10	Recreational Areas
9	Adverse Weather
9	Food Supply Reduction
9	Veg. Composition Changes

Source: Curtis H. Flather, Linda A. Joyce, and Carol A. Bloomgarden, *Species Endangerment Patterns in the United States*, U.S. Forest Service, Fort Collins, CO, 1994

More than a century ago, Charles Darwin wrote, in *The Origin of Species* (1859), that more diverse ecosystems would also be more productive. That theory was largely untested until recently, when scientists, heeding the warnings of an impending biodiversity crisis, began to consider the role biodiversity might play in the functioning of ecosystems. A major 1996 study, performed by a team of biologists at the University of Minnesota and the University of Toronto, confirmed Darwin's

TABLE 1.5

Taxonomic composition of high endangerment regions

	Southern Appalachia	Peninsular Florida	Eastern Gulf Coast	Southern Desertic Basins, Plains, and Mountains	Arizona Basin	Colorado/ Green River Plateaus	Central Desertic Basins and Plateaus	Southern Nevada/ Sonoran Basin	Central/ Southern California	Northern California
Mammals	3	10	4	1	4	1		3	8	3
Birds	1	10	7	5	6	4	3	6	11	7
Fish	6	1	1	6	9	6	4	23	6	1
Reptiles		11	8					2	4	1
Amphibians								1	1	
Vertebrates	10	32	20	12	19	11	7	35	30	12
Clams	17									
Snails		1		2		1				
Insects		1						1	5	7
Crustaceans	1	1		1						1
Invertebrates	18	3		3		1		1	5	8
Animals	28	35	20	15	19	12	7	36	35	20
Plants	11	29	7	17	8	17	11	17	14	12
Total	39	64	27	32	27	29	18	53	49	32
Endemics[1]										
Total	2	17	2	15	5	7	4	20	16	13
Plant	1	10		10	2	7	4	7	11	7

[1]Endemics refers to species whose range is thought to be restricted to a single county.

Source: Curtis H. Flather, Linda A. Joyce, and Carol A. Bloomgarden, *Species Endangerment Patterns in the United States*, U.S. Forest Service, Fort Collins, CO, 1994

claim — they found that the more species a plot of prairie grasses had, the more "biomass," or plant material, it produced and the better it retained nitrogen, its most crucial nutrient. The fewer the species, the sparser the growth and the greater the amount of nitrogen leaching out of upper soil layers.

When nitrogen leached down to where plants' roots could not reach it, sustained growth was less likely. Based on their observations, the scientists concluded that the more species on a plot of land, the more efficiently those many species, all slightly different, can utilize the resources present, thereby producing more actual plant mass.

FACTORS THAT CONTRIBUTE TO SPECIES ENDANGERMENT

The U.S. Forest Service, based on its major 1994 study of species loss in the United States, *Species Endangerment Patterns in the United States* (Fort Collins, Colorado, 1994), concluded that general factors believed to adversely affect species in the United States include habitat loss or al-

teration, human overuse, disease, predation, competition, natural causes, and inadequate laws concerning resource management. Habitat loss associated with land use is, by far, the single most important factor. More than 95 percent of the 667 species in the study database had experienced habitat loss or alteration. Interspecific interactions, such as disease, predation, or competition, adversely affected more than 50 percent of the species. (See Figure 1.3.)

The third most frequent factor contributing to species endangerment was human overuse associated with the harvest, collection, or commercial trade of species. Human overuse was most common in the endangerment of mammals and reptiles. Table 1.3 shows the specific reasons cited for the endangerment of the various species and how often each reason was cited.

DISTRIBUTION OF SPECIES LOSS

The U.S. Forest Service observed that endangered species are not evenly distributed across the United States. Instead, threatened and endangered

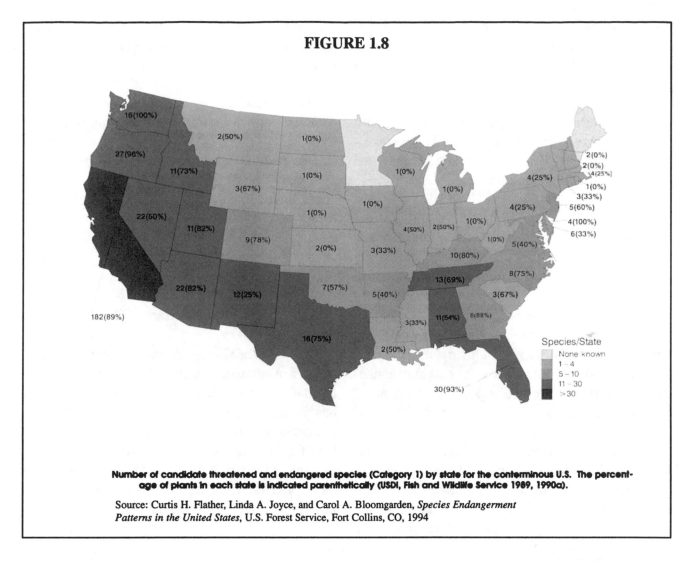

FIGURE 1.8

Number of candidate threatened and endangered species (Category 1) by state for the conterminous U.S. The percentage of plants in each state is indicated parenthetically (USDI, Fish and Wildlife Service 1989, 1990a).

Source: Curtis H. Flather, Linda A. Joyce, and Carol A. Bloomgarden, *Species Endangerment Patterns in the United States*, U.S. Forest Service, Fort Collins, CO, 1994

species show a strong nonrandom pattern related to geographical area.

Land Ownership Patterns of Listed Species

Most of the species protected under the Endangered Species Act have a major share of their habitat on nonfederal lands. Ninety percent of the listed species have over 60 percent of their total habitat on nonfederal lands. The species with habitat on nonfederal lands are approximately equally divided between plants and animals (vertebrates and invertebrates). (See Figure 1.4.)

The two agencies that account for the majority of federally owned lands, the U.S. Forest Service and the Bureau of Land Management, supported 24 percent and 17 percent of the endangered spe-

cies, respectively. Of the remaining federal agencies, the number of threatened and endangered species that occurred on Department of Defense lands was disproportionately high — 26 percent of the species on 3.4 percent of the federally administered land area. Figure 1.5 shows the number of endangered plant and animal species located on land administered by various federal agencies.

Regional Distribution of Listed Species

There are regions where the number of threatened and endangered species is relatively high. Southern Appalachia, Florida, and the arid Southwest support high numbers of endangered species. Figure 1.6 shows the distribution of listed plants and animals by county. Figure 1.7 shows the number of species per county by category of species.

17

Table 1.4 shows the number of endangered species by region and the specific reasons contributing to their endangerment

Among vertebrates, birds are the most widespread because they migrate. Fish species endangerment is generally concentrated in the southwestern United States. Very few amphibians are listed as threatened or endangered.

Florida, the eastern Gulf Coast, and Central/Southern California all listed urban development as the most common reason for species endangerment. Grazing was the most frequent reason in the Arizona Basin and in Colorado. Endangerment regions in the East were associated with intensive human land use activities, such as road building, conversion of coastal areas, industrial use, and construction. Catastrophic weather events and human-caused mortality were also important reasons along the Gulf Coast.

In the West, collecting rare plants, surface mining, oil and gas development, and water diversions were the most frequently cited causes for endangerment. Recreational activities, specifically off-road vehicles, were prominent factors common to several regions in the arid West. Table 1.5 breaks down the categories of endangered species by region.

The Forest Service study also analyzed those candidate species awaiting decisions under the Endangered Species Act. The Forest Service calculated that the Southwest and Southeast will remain areas where species endangerment will be concentrated in the future. Endangerment in California will become more serious. The number of endangered species in the Pacific Northwest, including Oregon, Washington, and Idaho, will likely increase. (See Figure 1.8.)

Crossing the Border — Canada

In 1998, the Canadian government listed 291 species of animals, birds, insects, and plants located in Canada as endangered. So far, however, it has passed no legislation to protect them. Environmental groups in Mexico and the United States have filed a complaint with the environmental commission of the North American Free Trade Agreement (NAFTA; Chapter VII) charging Canada with failing to protect its endangered species.

CHAPTER II

HOW ENVIRONMENTAL FACTORS AFFECT SPECIES*

Scientists have long recognized climate, especially temperature and precipitation, as one of the major ecological forces affecting the abundance, location, and ecological health of living organisms. This relationship is so strong that, in many cases, if biologists know what plants and animals are present in an area, they can approximate the climate of the area.
— Edward T. LaRoe, National Biological Service, 1995

Climate change and acidification of water and soil are among the most important factors determing the health status of plant and animal species. Although most scientists believe that mass extinctions are generally the consequences of geologic and climactic shifts caused by major astronomical events, there is little doubt that human activities including industrialization and the clearing of land have influenced or hastened climate change. Most researchers believe that such changes in the environment have endangered life forms on Earth. In 1998, astronauts revealed the surprising and frightening fact that from outer space they could see both the vivid colors of the *Aurora Borealis* and the fires in Mexico and Guatemala.

CLIMATE AND
THE EVOLUTION OF SPECIES

Piece-by-piece, researchers are discovering the geological and astronomical forces that have changed the planet's environment from hot to cold, wet to dry, and back again, over hundreds of millions of years. The scientists believe that dramatic climate change is nothing new for planet Earth. The environment that has existed over the past 10,000 years, during which human civilization developed, is a mere blip in a much bigger history of widely varying climate over many hundreds of millions of years. In fact, Earth's climate will most certainly continue to go through dramatic climactic changes — with or without the influence of human activity. Most evolutionists believe that if not for extreme climactic shifts some 65 million years ago, most of the animals on Earth today, including humans, would probably not be here.

Astronomical cycles have caused Earth's climate to fluctuate between long periods of cold lasting 50,000 to 80,000 years and shorter periods of warmth lasting about 10,000 years. In fact, some scientists believe that these rapid shifts between warm and cold were the driving force behind human evolution. Physiologically and socially, humans and other species have always had to change to cope with changing climate.

THE WORLD CLIMATE

Earth's climate is a delicate balance of energy inputs, chemical processes, and physical phenomena. Temperatures on Venus are too hot for the human body; on Mars, a person would instantly freeze to death. This difference in temperature is due to the varying composition of each planet's atmosphere. All three planets receive huge quanti-

---

*For a full discussion of the environment — global warming, air and water pollution, acid rain, and related legislation and remedies, see *The Environment — A Revolution in Attitudes*, Information Plus, Wylie, Texas, 1998.

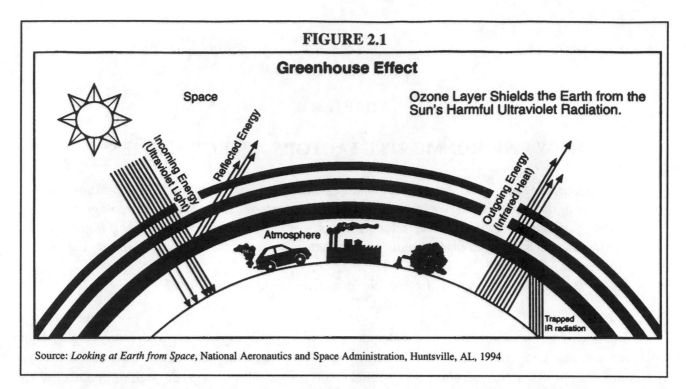

FIGURE 2.1

Greenhouse Effect

Space

Ozone Layer Shields the Earth from the Sun's Harmful Ultraviolet Radiation.

Incoming Energy (Ultraviolet Light)

Reflected Energy

Outgoing Energy (Infrared Heat)

Atmosphere

Trapped IR radiation

Source: *Looking at Earth from Space*, National Aeronautics and Space Administration, Huntsville, AL, 1994

ties of solar energy, but the amount radiated back into space in the form of heat depends on the atmospheric composition of the particular planet. Some gases, such as carbon dioxide and methane, absorb and maintain heat in the same way that glass traps heat in a greenhouse, allowing temperatures to build up and keeping the earth warm and habitable. That is why the increased buildup of carbon dioxide, methane, and other gases is often called the "greenhouse effect." (See Figure 2.1 for a diagram of the processes producing global warming and the greenhouse effect.)

The scorching heat of Venus is the result of an atmosphere composed largely of carbon dioxide. On the other hand, the atmosphere of Earth is nitrogen and oxygen-based and contains only 0.03 percent carbon dioxide. This percentage has varied little over the past million years, permitting a stable climate favorable to life. The blanket of air enveloping Earth moderates its temperature and sustains plant and animal life.

A Revolutionary Idea

Earth's atmosphere was first compared to a glass vessel in 1827 by the French mathematician Jean-Baptiste Fourier. In the 1850s, British physi-

cist John Tyndall tried to measure the heat-trapping properties of various components of the atmosphere. By the 1890s, some scientists had theorized that the great increase in combustion in the Industrial Revolution had the potential to change the atmosphere's percentage of carbon dioxide.

In 1896, the Swedish chemist Svante Arrhenius made the revolutionary suggestion that human activities could actually disrupt this delicate balance. He theorized that the rapid increase in the use of coal that came with the Industrial Revolution could increase carbon dioxide concentrations and cause a gradual rise in temperatures. For almost six decades, his theory stirred little interest.

In 1957, studies at the Scripps Institute of Oceanography in California suggested that, indeed, half the carbon dioxide released by industry was being permanently trapped in the atmosphere. The studies showed that atmospheric concentrations of carbon dioxide in the previous 30 years were greater than in the previous two centuries and that the gas had reached its highest level in 160,000 years.

Recent findings have provided more disturbing evidence. Scientists have detected increases in other, even more potent, greenhouse gases, notably chlorofluorocarbons (CFCs), methane, and nitrous oxide. The heat-trapping qualities of the combination of these gases had already been documented. Table 2.1 shows the activities that produce these gases. Figure 2.2 shows the increase in carbon dioxide, methane, nitrous oxide, and CFCs from the 1700s through the 1900s.

Global warming has only recently been recognized as an international problem. At the world's first ecological summit, the 1972 Stockholm Conference, climate change was not even listed among the threats to society.

Is Earth Getting Warmer?

Even experts are not sure. Whether the world has already experienced human-induced climate change remains a question. Scientists do know that humans are putting an increasing amount of gases, including carbon dioxide, into the atmosphere (Figure 2.3). These gases are building up and could possibly trap energy from the sun. No one, however, is certain how this accumulation affects Earth's climate.

A Record High in 1997

Three international agencies compile long-term data on surface temperatures — the British Meteorological Office in Bracknell, United Kingdom, the National Climatic Data Center in Asheville, North Carolina, and the NASA Goddard Institute for Space Studies in New York. Temperature measurements from these organizations reported that 1997 was the warmest year of the century and that the 1990s was the warmest decade since humans began measuring temperatures in the mid-nineteenth century. The average global surface temperature today is approximately 1 degree Fahrenheit warmer than it was a century ago. The rise has increased more rapidly in the past two decades. Dr. James Hansen, who heads NASA's Goddard Institute for Space Studies and an early believer that human activity is warming the earth, predicts a new record high temperature by 2000.

TABLE 2.1

GREENHOUSE GAS PROFILE

Greenhouse Gas	Sources	Lifespan	Current Contribution to Global Warming
Carbon dioxide (CO_2)	Fossil fuels, deforestation, soil destruction	500 years	49%
Methane (CH_4)	Cattle, biomass, rice paddies, gas leaks, mining, termites	7–10 years	18%
Nitrous oxide (N_2O)	Fossil fuels, soil cultivation, deforestation	140–190 years	6%
Chlorofluorocarbons (CFC 11 and 12)	Refrigeration, air conditioning, aerosols, foam blowing, solvents	65–110 years	15%
Ozone	Photochemical processes	Hours to days in upper troposphere (1 hour in upper stratosphere)	12%*
			100%

*Includes small contributions from other minor trace gases.

Source: Francesca Lyman et al., *The Greenhouse Trap: What We're Doing to the Atmosphere and How We Can Slow Global Warming*, Office of Technology Assessment, Washington, DC, 1991

Ten of the 14 years preceding 1991 were the warmest on record. Then came a two-year cooling period that computer models and climatologists attributed to the Mount Pinatubo volcanic eruption (see below). In 1994, the warming trend resumed, with Earth's average surface temperature approaching the record high of 60 degrees in 1990. In 1995, Earth's average temperature was 58.72 degrees Fahrenheit; in 1997, it was 62.45 degrees.

However, some scientists observe that major climate events should be viewed in terms of thousands of years, not just a century. Scientists have a record of only the past 104 years, which may indicate, but not prove, that a major change has occurred. Is it the greenhouse gases, or is it natural variability? While many experts believe it is not possible to conclude that the warming is caused

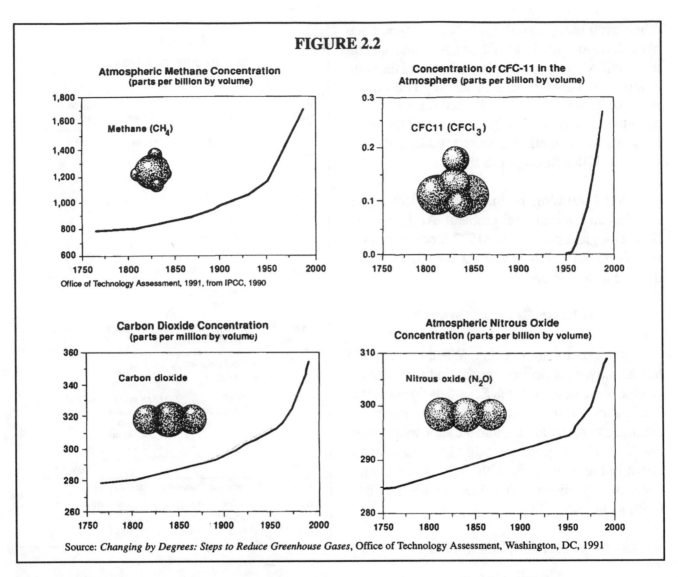

FIGURE 2.2

Atmospheric Methane Concentration (parts per billion by volume) — Methane (CH₄)

Office of Technology Assessment, 1991, from IPCC, 1990

Concentration of CFC-11 in the Atmosphere (parts per billion by volume) — CFC11 (CFCl₃)

Carbon Dioxide Concentration (parts per million by volume) — Carbon dioxide

Atmospheric Nitrous Oxide Concentration (parts per billion by volume) — Nitrous oxide (N₂O)

Source: *Changing by Degrees: Steps to Reduce Greenhouse Gases*, Office of Technology Assessment, Washington, DC, 1991

by greenhouse gases emitted by human activity, the temperature is roughly on a similar track of that predicted by computer models trying to predict the course of greenhouse warming. Climate models suggest the potential for a warming from 3 to 8 degrees over the next 100 years, warmer than Earth has been for millions of years.

In 1997, the U.S. Department of Energy reported that due to strong economic growth, the emissions of carbon dioxide and other heat-trapping greenhouse gases will grow faster in the next few years than previously expected. This will make it all the more difficult, if not impossible, for the United States to live up to President Clinton's proposal to cap emissions of these gases at 1990 levels over the next 10 to 15 years.

Further Signs

The Intergovernmental Panel on Climate Change (IPCC; see below) has noted several early signs of actual climate change. The average warm-season temperature in Alaska has risen nearly 3 degrees Fahrenheit in the last 50 years. Glaciers have generally receded and have become thinner on average by about 30 feet in the past 40 years. There is about 5 percent less sea ice in the Bering Sea than in the 1950s. Permafrost is thawing and, as it does, the ground is subsiding, opening holes in roads.

The thawing has produced landslides and erosion, threatening roads and bridges and causing local floods. Ice cellars in northern villages have thawed and become useless. More precipitation falls as rain than snow. The snow melts faster, causing more running and standing water. While this could be natural variability, it is the kind of change expected of global warming.

CARBON DIOXIDE

Carbon dioxide, a naturally occurring component of Earth's atmosphere, is generally considered the major cause of global warming. The burning of fossil fuels by industry and motor vehicles is the primary source of carbon dioxide in the atmosphere. (See Figure 2.4 for a diagram of the carbon dioxide cycle.) As populations and economies expand, they use ever-greater amounts of fossil fuels. The United States, with only 5 percent of the world's population, accounts for 25 percent of the world energy use, making it the most carbon-intensive country, with a rate of 5 tons per person.

Economic and political restructuring in the former Soviet Union and in Eastern Europe could increase their carbon emissions drastically. On the other hand, pollution control was of little or no importance in these areas, and a new recognition of the importance of protecting the environment could contain the growth of some pollution. Developing countries burn fossil fuels at far lower levels than developed nations, although emissions in these areas are expected to rise as development proceeds.

CHLOROFLUOROCARBONS

Most scientists believe that chlorofluorocarbons (CFCs), an important class of modern industrial chemicals, are responsible for much of the increased greenhouse effect experienced during the 1980s. The United States is the leading producer of CFCs. Because CFCs are also responsible for depletion of the ozone layer in the stratosphere, which shields the earth from deadly ultraviolet radiation, efforts to limit their use are better developed than for other greenhouse gases.

Beginning in the 1970s, the United States and many other nations banned the use of CFCs in aero-

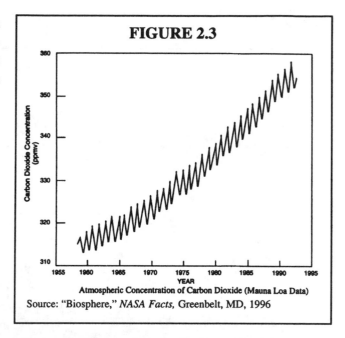

FIGURE 2.3

Atmospheric Concentration of Carbon Dioxide (Mauna Loa Data)

Source: "Biosphere," *NASA Facts*, Greenbelt, MD, 1996

sol sprays. In 1987, leaders of many world nations met in Montreal and agreed to cut output by 50 percent by the year 2000. In 1989, 82 nations signed the Helsinki Declaration, pledging to phase out five CFCs, and for the first time, a large number of developing countries were actively engaged in the agreement. The United States banned the use of CFCs in 1996.

THE EFFECTS OF CLIMATE WARMING

Rising Sea Level

Some observers compare global warming to nuclear war in its potential to disrupt human and environmental systems. If temperatures were to increase, substantial changes would occur on Earth's surface. If average temperatures rise 1.5 to 4.5 degrees Celsius by 2030, the global sea level would likely rise 20-140 centimeters (8 to 56 inches). The Climate Institute in Washington, DC, forecasts a rise of eight inches by 2030 and 26 inches by 2100. This increase in water level would be caused by the expansion of seawater as it is warmed and by the melting of glaciers and ice caps. Such a rise in sea level would have noticeable effects on shorelines around the world. The National Climatic Data Center reports that sea levels have risen by 10 inches in the past century.

FIGURE 2.4

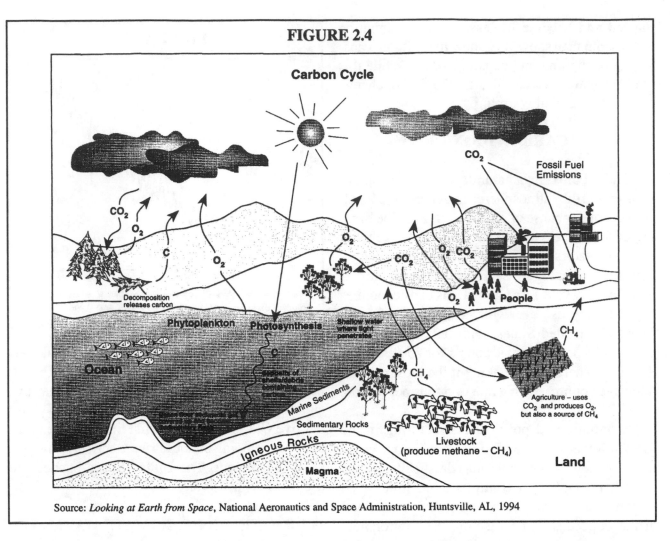

Source: *Looking at Earth from Space*, National Aeronautics and Space Administration, Huntsville, AL, 1994

More than half the U.S. population lives within 50 miles of a coastline. A rising sea level would narrow or destroy beaches, flood wetland areas, and submerge or force the costly fortification of shoreline property. If this rise occurs, coastal cities everywhere will be flooded. Some islands, such as the Philippines, have already seen encroachment. Residents of the Maldive Islands in the Indian Ocean, which lie approximately three feet above sea level, are already erecting artificial defenses — breakwaters formed by concrete — against rising seas.

Some 70 million people in low-lying areas of Bangladesh could be displaced by a one-meter (39.4 inches) rise. Such a rise would also threaten Tokyo, Osaka, and Nagoya in Japan, as well as many cities along the Chinese coast and the Atlantic and Gulf coasts of the United States. The rising waters would also intrude on inland rivers, threatening fresh water supplies. The salt level of groundwater will increase as saltwater intrudes on the freshwater aquifers (naturally occurring underground water reservoirs). Much of the increased rainfall would come not in steady, gentle rains favored by farmers, but from heavy storms and flooding. Higher water levels will increase storm damage. Some experts believe that trend is already happening.

The opposite problem — too little water — could worsen in arid areas such as the Middle East and parts of Africa. Most experts believe Africa would be the most vulnerable to climate change, because its economy depends largely on rain-fed agriculture, and many farmers are too poor and ill-equipped to adapt. Australia and Latin America would also be subject to drought.

Increased Heat

Throughout history, entire forests and ecosystems have migrated hundreds of miles in response to the warming and cooling of Earth's climate. Sugar maples, beeches, firs, and spruces that flourished in the Middle Atlantic states moved farther north as the world warmed after the last ice age, while oaks and hickories from farther south moved up to take their place. However, scientists have feared that natural communities might not be able to migrate fast enough to keep pace with the change if a global warming occurs as rapidly as many experts have predicted.

In 1998, Dr. Louis F. Pitelka, an ecologist at the University of Maryland, one of a number of scientists who have been studying the situation, found that the situation is much more complicated than previously thought. He reported that some trees may be able to migrate faster than some people have said, sufficient for plants to keep up with rapid climate change. At the same time, however, another factor may complicate the issue. Dr. Pitelka reported that hardy weeds that thrive in disturbed ground could race northward ahead of other species as the climate of northern temperate regions warm and dominate the environment. These interlopers could out-compete trees and other plants more valued by humans. Rapid climate change could result in "a complete rearrangement of biotic interactions," he concluded.

Warmer temperatures may also increase the evaporation rate, thereby increasing atmospheric water vapor and cloud cover, which in turn may affect regional rainfall patterns. A warmer climate will likely shift the rainbelt of the middle latitudes toward the poles, as water-laden air from the tropics travels further toward the poles before the moisture condenses as precipitation. This would also shift patterns of rainfall around the world.

Some experts suggest that the greenhouse effect and global warming are mild terms for a coming era that may be marked by heat waves that may make some regions virtually uninhabitable. Frequent droughts could plague North America and Asia, imperiling food production. Agriculture is particularly vulnerable to the effects of climate change. Wetter, more violent, weather is projected for other regions. Forests, which are adapted to a narrow temperature and moisture range, would be threatened by climate shifts.

The Effects of Increased Temperatures on Life Forms

Extra heat alone will be enough to kill some people, plants, and animals. Some human deaths will be attributed directly to the heat, as heat "strokes." Many heart attacks may be heat-induced. Air quality also deteriorates as temperatures rise. Hot, stagnant air contributes to the formation of ozone, the main component of smog, which damages human lungs. Poor air quality can aggravate asthma and other respiratory diseases. Increasing ultraviolet rays can increase the incidence of skin cancers, diminish the function of the human immune system, and cause eye problems. Higher temperatures and added rainfall could also create ideal conditions for a host of infectious diseases to spread through insects, parasites, or contaminated food. (Table 2.2 shows predictions for weather in

---

TABLE 2.2

THE WEATHER FORECAST FOR 2050

Powerful computer models can give climatologists a glimpse of future weather changes that the greenhouse effect might bring. Current models can only partly mimic Earth's many systems and cycles, but climate researchers have predicted that global temperatures could rise as much as 8 degrees Fahrenheit by the middle of the next century. Even a change of only 4 degrees would affect weather appreciably, according to a NASA computer. The model's forecast for 2050 is "hot and dry" for many U.S. cities.

City	Days over 90° F Today	Days over 90° F 2050	Days over 100° F Today	Days over 100° F 2050
Washington, DC	36	87	1	12
Omaha, NE	37	86	3	21
New York, NY	15	48	0	4
Chicago, IL	16	56	0	6
Denver, CO	33	86	0	16
Los Angeles, CA	5	27	1	4
Memphis, TN	65	145	4	42
Dallas, TX	100	162	19	78

Source: Francesca Lyman et al., *The Greenhouse Trap: What We're Doing to the Atmosphere and How We Can Slow Global Warming*, Office of Technology Assessment, Washington, DC, 1991

some leading U.S. cities based on National Aeronautical and Space Administration computer calculations.)

Decreased Biological (Species) Diversity

Biological diversity would suffer from global warming. Loss of forests, tundra, and wetlands would irrevocably damage ecosystems. Many species will likely not be able to migrate rapidly enough to cope with climate change. Some plants and animals, like the monarch butterflies and the Alps' edelweiss flower, that live in precise, narrow bands of temperature and humidity, may find their habitats wiped out altogether. Rising seas would cover mangrove swamps, causing the loss of many species including the Bengal tiger. Plants and animals of the far north, like the Polar bear and the walrus, would die out for lack of a cold environment.

The U.S. Forest Service believes that Eastern hemlock, yellow birch, beech, and sugar maple forests would gradually shift their ranges northward by 300 to 600 miles, but would be severely limited by the warming and would largely die out, along with the wildlife they shelter. Studies by the World Wildlife Fund International report that more than half the world's parks and reserves could be threatened by climate change. These include the Florida Everglades, Yellowstone National Park, the Great Smoky Mountains, and Redwood National Park in California. In 1988, the EPA warned, "If current trends continue, it is likely that climate may change too quickly for many natural systems to adapt." Figure 2.5 shows the proportion of species that would be out of their climate area if the temperature rises 5.4 degrees Fahrenheit (3 degrees Centigrade).

ACID RAIN

What Is Acid Rain?

Acid rain is any form of precipitation that contains a greater than normal amount of acid (having a pH of 5.5 or below; see below). Acid rain was

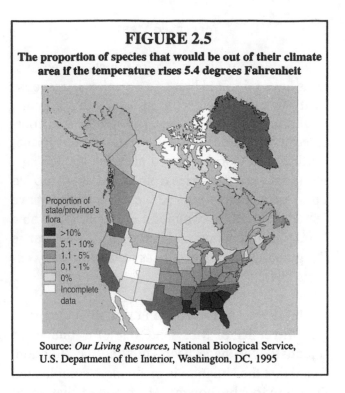

FIGURE 2.5

The proportion of species that would be out of their climate area if the temperature rises 5.4 degrees Fahrenheit

Proportion of state/province's flora
- >10%
- 5.1 - 10%
- 1.1 - 5%
- 0.1 - 1%
- 0%
- Incomplete data

Source: *Our Living Resources,* National Biological Service, U.S. Department of the Interior, Washington, DC, 1995

discovered in 1852 by Angus Smith, although his work received little recognition. Acid precipitation was rediscovered in the mid-1950s by scientists in the United States, United Kingdom, and the Scandinavian countries.

In nature, the combination of rain and oxides is part of a natural balance that nourishes plants and aquatic life. Fossil fuel-burning industrial plants and automobiles emit chemicals such as sulfur dioxide and nitrogen oxides. When the sulfur dioxide and nitrogen oxides combine with moisture in the atmosphere, they form sulfuric acid and nitric acid and eventually fall to the earth as acidic rain, snow, fog, or dust, in many cases creating dangerously high levels of acidic impurities in water, soil and plants.

Acid deposits, both dry and in precipitation (acid rain), are the most common human-produced causes of water acidification. During a spring snowmelt, for example, runoff containing large amounts of acidic particles accumulated over the winter can flow into a lake or river, causing acid shock to its aquatic inhabitants. High levels of acidity can also cause the release of aluminum and manganese particles stored in a lake or river bottom.

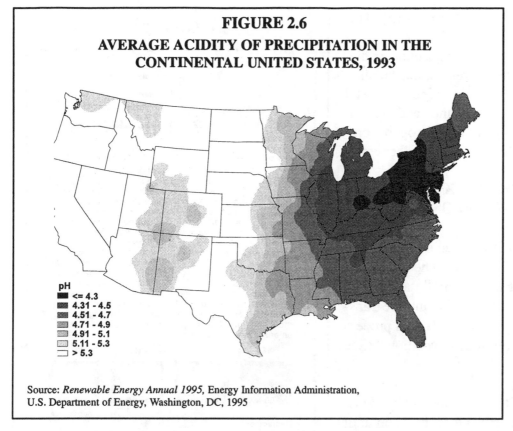

FIGURE 2.6

AVERAGE ACIDITY OF PRECIPITATION IN THE CONTINENTAL UNITED STATES, 1993

pH
■ <= 4.3
■ 4.31 - 4.5
■ 4.51 - 4.7
▨ 4.71 - 4.9
▨ 4.91 - 5.1
▨ 5.11 - 5.3
☐ > 5.3

Source: *Renewable Energy Annual 1995*, Energy Information Administration, U.S. Department of Energy, Washington, DC, 1995

through the atmosphere. Although pH levels vary considerably from one body of water to another, a "normal" pH value for the lakes and rivers in the United States is approximately 6. Acid rain generally has a pH of about 4, although it may be weaker.

The pH scale is a logarithmic measure. This means that every pH drop of 1 is a tenfold increase. Therefore, a decrease from pH 6 to pH 5 is a tenfold increase in acidity; a drop from pH 6 to pH 4 is a hundredfold increase in acidity; and a drop from pH 6 to pH 3 is a thousandfold increase. (See Figure 2.7.)

In the states bordering and east of the Mississippi River — about 17,000 lakes and 112,000 miles of streams — an estimated 25 percent of the land contains soil and bedrock that allow acidity to travel through underground water to lakes and streams. Approximately half of these bodies of water have such a limited ability to neutralize acid that acid-laden pollutants will eventually cause acidification. (See Figure 2.6 for average acidity of precipitation in the United States.)

Measuring Acid Rain

The acidity of any solution is measured on a pH (potential hydrogen) scale, numbered from 0 to 14 with a pH value of 7 considered neutral. Values which are higher than 7 are considered more alkaline or basic (the pH of baking soda is 8); values which are lower than 7 are considered acidic (the pH of lemon juice is 2).

Pure, distilled water would have a pH level of 7. Rainfall, which normally has a pH value of 5.65, is not pure because it accumulates sulfur oxides (SOx) and nitrogen oxides (NOx) as it passes

SOURCES OF SULFUR AND NITROGEN IN THE ATMOSPHERE

Natural Causes

Natural causes of sulfate or sulfides (sulfur in combination with other substances) in the atmosphere include ocean spray, volcanic emissions, and readily oxidized hydrogen sulfide released from the decomposition of organic matter found in the earth. Natural sources of nitrogen include nitrogen oxides produced by micro-organisms in soils, by lightning during thunderstorms, and by forest fires. An estimated one-third of the sulfur and nitrogen emissions in the United States comes from these natural sources.

Man-made Sources

Most man-made emissions of sulfur oxides (SOx) and nitrogen oxides (NOx) are the result of burning fossil fuels (oil and gas) for energy. This includes fossil-fueled electric utilities and industrial plants, motor vehicles using gasoline or diesel fuel, and commercial or residential heating. Non-energy sources of emissions include metal smelters that emit sulfur compounds and agricultural fertilizers, which produce nitrogen compounds that are carried by the wind to other areas.

TRANSPORT — THE LINK BETWEEN EMISSIONS AND DEPOSITION

Transport systems distribute acid emissions in definite patterns across the planet. The movement of air masses transport emitted pollutants many miles during which time these pollutants are transformed into sulfuric and nitric acid. This process is known as "transport and transformation." (See Figure 2.8.)

The acidification of the environment by industrial pollutants was primarily a local problem until well into the twentieth century, when taller smokestacks capable of dispersing pollutants over larger areas came into widespread use.

In the United States, a typical transport pattern occurs from the Ohio River Valley to the northeastern United States and southeastern Canada, since prevailing winds tend to move from west to east and from south to north. About one-third of the total sulfur compounds deposited over the eastern United States originate from sources more than 300 miles away.

The lakes and forests in and near the Adirondack Mountains in upstate New York are an example of what occurs in areas that do not have carbonate rock to quickly neutralize the acid. Approximately half of the lakes above 2,000 feet have a pH of less than 5.0, and 90 percent of these lakes contain no aquatic life.

In Europe, a typical transport pattern carries pollutants from the smokestacks of the United Kingdom over Sweden. In southwestern Germany, at least half the trees of the famed Black Forest are

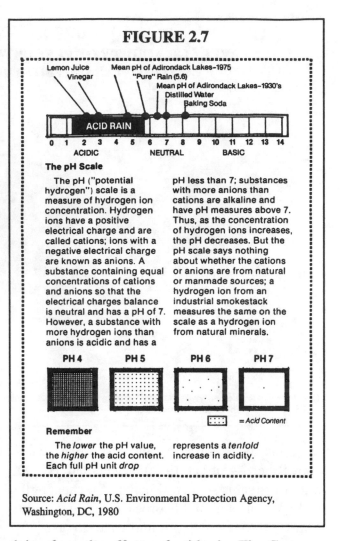

FIGURE 2.7

The pH Scale

The pH ("potential hydrogen") scale is a measure of hydrogen ion concentration. Hydrogen ions have a positive electrical charge and are called cations; ions with a negative electrical charge are known as anions. A substance containing equal concentrations of cations and anions so that the electrical charges balance is neutral and has a pH of 7. However, a substance with more hydrogen ions than anions is acidic and has a pH less than 7; substances with more anions than cations are alkaline and have pH measures above 7. Thus, as the concentration of hydrogen ions increases, the pH decreases. But the pH scale says nothing about whether the cations or anions are from natural or manmade sources; a hydrogen ion from an industrial smokestack measures the same on the scale as a hydrogen ion from natural minerals.

Remember

The *lower* the pH value, the *higher* the acid content. Each full pH unit *drop* represents a *tenfold* increase in acidity.

Source: *Acid Rain*, U.S. Environmental Protection Agency, Washington, DC, 1980

dying from the effects of acid rain. The Germans have coined a word for the phenomenon, "waldsterben," meaning "forest death." In Asia, air masses transport pollution from China toward Japan.

CONTRIBUTING FACTORS

Several factors contribute to the impact of acid rain on an area. Figure 2.9 is an illustration of how sulfur dioxide and nitrogen oxides carried in acid rain can affect the soil, vegetation, and aquatic life of a region.

Climate

In drier climates, such as the western United States, windblown alkaline dust blows freely and tends to neutralize atmospheric activity. On the other hand, in more humid climates, such as along

FIGURE 2.8

Transported Air Pollutants: Emissions to Effects

The transported air pollutants considered in this study result from emissions of three pollutants: sulfur dioxide, nitrogen oxides, and hydrocarbons. As these pollutants are carried away from their sources, they form a complex "pollutant mix" leading to acid deposition, ozone, and airborne fine particles. These transported air pollutants pose risks to surface waters, forests, crops, materials, visibility, and human health.

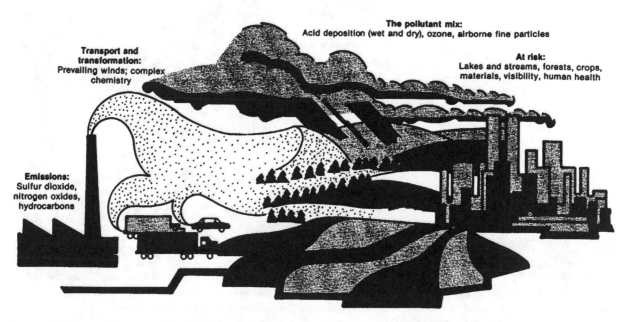

The pollutant mix:
Acid deposition (wet and dry), ozone, airborne fine particles

Transport and transformation:
Prevailing winds; complex chemistry

At risk:
Lakes and streams, forests, crops, materials, visibility, human health

Emissions:
Sulfur dioxide, nitrogen oxides, hydrocarbons

Source: *Acid Rain and Transported Air Pollutants: Implications for Public Policy*, Office of Technology Assessment, Congress of the United States, Washington, DC, 1984

the eastern seaboard where there is less dust, precipitation is more acidic. The season of the year also determines the extent of acid rain damage. For instance, acids will have a more harmful effect if rainfall occurs during periods when fish are spawning or seeds are germinating.

Topography/Geology

Areas most sensitive to acid rain contain hard, crystalline bedrock and very thin surface soils. When no alkaline buffering particles are in the soil, rainfall directly affects surface waters, such as mountain streams. In contrast, a thick soil covering or soil with a high buffering capacity, such as flat land, neutralizes acid rain better. Lakes tend to be most susceptible to acid rain because of low alkaline content in lakebeds. Lake depth, its watershed (the area draining into the lake), and the amount of time the water has been in the lake are also factors.

Human Activity

Human living habits produce substances that form acid in the environment. When fossil fuel is burned in urban areas by automobiles or through residential or industrial energy use, it releases pollutants into the air that eventually form acid rain. In agricultural areas, windblown chemicals are absorbed by the soil.

Nitrogen pollution of the waters had been blamed primarily on surface runoff from fertilizer, animal wastes, sewage, and industrial wastes. It is now believed that airborne nitrates produced by human activities account for one-fourth of all nitrogen, the second most prevalent cause after the runoff from fertilizers. Not only has the Chesapeake Bay area been affected, but preliminary findings from the Long Island Sound and the lower Neuse River in North Carolina indicate airborne nitrates have also caused similar problems in those eastern estuaries.

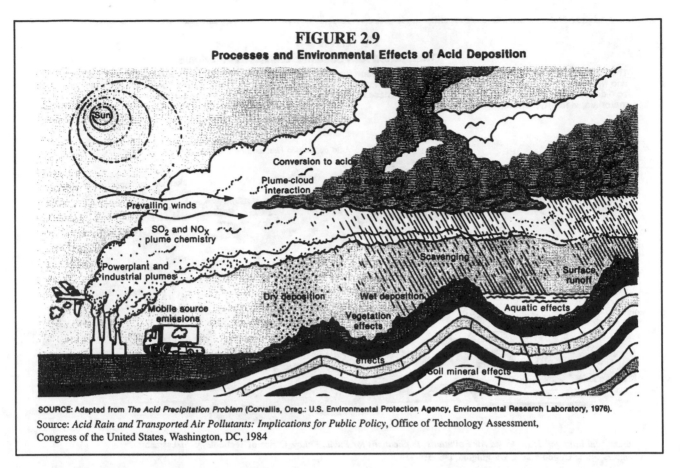

FIGURE 2.9
Processes and Environmental Effects of Acid Deposition

SOURCE: Adapted from *The Acid Precipitation Problem* (Corvallis, Oreg.: U.S. Environmental Protection Agency, Environmental Research Laboratory, 1976).

Source: *Acid Rain and Transported Air Pollutants: Implications for Public Policy*, Office of Technology Assessment, Congress of the United States, Washington, DC, 1984

DAMAGE CAUSED BY ACID RAIN

Aquatic Life

Research in the United States, Canada, and Scandinavia has shown that acidity affects the physiology, reproduction, food resources, and habitat of aquatic species. Low pH levels kill fish eggs, frog eggs, and fish food organisms. The degree of damage depends on the buffering capacity of the watershed soil; the higher the alkalinity, the more slowly the lakes and streams will acidify. Aquatic species decrease in numbers with increased acidity. The death of fish in acidified freshwater lakes and streams has been intensely studied. In the past 15 years, aquatic life has increasingly suffered because of

• Sudden, short-term shifts in pH levels resulting in acid shock for the fish population, such as spring snowmelts that release acidic materials accumulated during the winter. At pH levels below 4.9, damage occurs to fish eggs. At acid levels below 4.5, some species of fish die; below 3.5, most fish die within hours. (See Table 2.3.)

• Gradual decreases of pH levels over time, affecting fish reproduction and spawning.

Experiments conducted by the University of New Hampshire suggest that Atlantic salmon are unable to find their home streams and rivers because of acid rain. Moderate levels of acidity in water can confuse a salmon's sense of smell, which it uses to find the stream it came from. In addition, excessive acid levels in female fish cause low amounts of calcium, which prevent the production of eggs. Even if eggs are produced, their development is often abnormal. Over time, the fish population decreases, and the remaining fish population becomes older and larger.

In acidic waters, some reductions in sensitive species are partially offset by increases in more acid-tolerant species. This may result in little change in the total number of organisms even though the number of species may change. Acid-

30

ity also increases the availability and toxicity of other metals, such as mercury, that may be present in the ecosystem. Several studies have revealed high mercury concentrations in fish from acidified regions, which harmful to aquatic species and birds and humans that feed on the fish.

In colder parts of the country, pollutants become concentrated in upper layers of the snowpack. When the spring thaw begins or when rainstorms sweep the area, the residual acid is washed into streams and lakes. Six mountainous streams in New York, North Carolina, Pennsylvania, Tennessee, and Arkansas have shown increased acidity during rainstorms and snowmelts of between 3 to 20 times the previous level. Because many species of fish hatch in the spring, even small increases in acidity can harm or kill the new life, and, if the levels are high enough, even the adult fish can die. Temporary increases in acidity also affect insects and other invertebrates, such as snails and crayfish, which the fish feed on. (For more information on aquatic species, see Chapter IV.)

To prevent loss of fisheries and aquatic species in some severely acidic locations, limestone, a neutralizing agent, is sometimes added to reduce acidity levels. Legislation to reduce emissions that form acid rain has been enacted in both the United States and Canada. There is evidence that acidic deposition in some areas has started to decline and that water quality has improved. Monitoring over the last decade at 81 selected sites in the Northeast and upper Midwest has shown that most of the lakes and streams measured had decreases in sulfate levels that coincide with a general decline in national emissions of sulfur dioxides.

Trees

The effect of acid rain on trees is influenced by many factors. Some trees adapt to environmental stress better than others; therefore, the type of

TABLE 2.3

Generalized short-term effects of acidity upon fish (from Wellburn, 1988)

pH range	Effect
6.5–9	No effect
6.0–6.4	Unlikely to be harmful except when carbon dioxide levels are very high (> 1000 mg l^{-1})
5.0–5.9	Not especially harmful except when carbon dioxide levels are high (>20 mg l^{-1}) or ferric ions are present
4.5–4.9	Harmful to the eggs of salmon and trout species (salmonids) and to adult fish when levels of Ca^{2+}, Na^+ and Cl^- are low
4.0–4.4	Harmful to adult fish of many types which have not been progressively acclimated to low pH
3.5–3.9	Lethal to salmonids, although acclimated roach can survive for longer
3.0–3.4	Most fish are killed within hours at these levels

Source: C.F. Mason, *Biology of Freshwater Pollution*, Longman Scientific & Technical, Wiley and Sons, NY, 1991

tree, its height, and its leaf structure (deciduous or evergreen) influence how well it will adapt to acid rain. Acid rain may affect trees in at least two ways. In areas with high evaporation rates, acids will concentrate on leaf surfaces; in regions where a dense leaf canopy does not exist, more acid may seep into the earth to affect the soil at the base of the tree.

Scientists have only recently begun to study the effects of acid fog on trees. In fog conditions, the concentration of acid and sulfate in the droplets is much greater than in rainfall. In areas of frequent fog, such as London, significant damage has occurred to trees and other vegetation because the fog condenses directly on the leaves.

A 1994 joint report of the European Commission and the United Nations Economic Commission for Europe (UNECE) surveyed 102,300 trees at 26,000 sampling plots in 35 European countries and found that almost one-quarter of the trees in Europe were defoliated by more than 25 percent. The report showed that forest damage is a problem in virtually all European countries. The most severely affected country was the Czech Republic, where 53 percent of all trees suffered moderate or severe defoliation or have died. The least affected was Portugal, where 7.3 percent of trees were damaged.

Thomas Cahill and Robert A. Eldred, scientists at the University of California at Davis, in a 10-year survey of air quality in 12 national parks, concluded from more than 12,000 measurements of air samples that levels of sulfate in the air over national parks increased by nearly 40 percent from 1982 to 1992, suggesting that more stringent controls may be needed. The Great Smoky Mountains National Park, which extends from North Carolina to Tennessee, experienced the largest increase, 39 percent. Other parks showing increases were Shenandoah National Park, Glacier National Park, Bryce Canyon National Park, Big Bend National Park, Grand Canyon National Park, Yosemite National Park, and Guadalupe Mountains National Park.

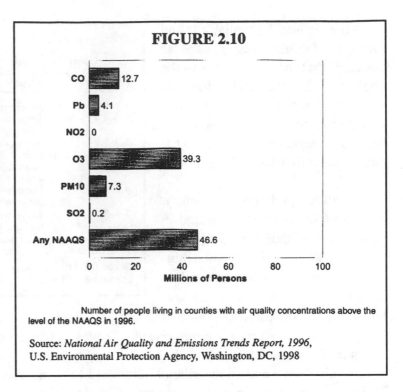

FIGURE 2.10

Number of people living in counties with air quality concentrations above the level of the NAAQS in 1996.

Source: *National Air Quality and Emissions Trends Report, 1996,* U.S. Environmental Protection Agency, Washington, DC, 1998

Soil and Vegetation

Acid precipitation can cause leafy plants, such as lettuce, to hold increased amounts of potentially toxic substances, such as the mineral cadmium. Research has also found a decrease in carbohydrate production in the photosynthesis process of some plants exposed to acid conditions. Some researchers believe that acid rain disrupts soil regeneration, which is the recycling of chemical and mineral nutrients through plants and animals back to the earth. They also believe acids suppress the decay of organic matter. Valuable nutrients like calcium and magnesium are normally bound to soil particles and are, therefore, protected from being rapidly washed into groundwater. Acid rain, however, may accelerate the process of breaking these bonds to rob the soil of these nutrients. (For more information on plant life, see Chapter III.)

Research is underway to determine whether acid rain could ultimately lead to a permanent reduction in tree growth, food crop production, and soil quality. Effects on soils, forests, and crops are difficult to measure because of the numerous species of plants and animals, the slow rate at which ecological changes occur, and the complex interrelationships between plants and their environment.

A national survey of soils conducted for the government of the United Kingdom by the Institute of Terrestrial Ecology in Britain in 1994 pinpointed the "critical loads" of acid fallout for the main types of soil in England. Maps of ecological damage to British soils showed the worst-hit areas to be in southern England, including the New Forest in Hampshire and Ashdown Forest in Sussex. Britain is already committed by a European directive to reduce its emissions of sulfur dioxide from power stations to 60 percent below the 1980 level by the year 2003.

Birds

Increased freshwater acidity harms some species of migratory birds. Experts believe the dramatic decline of the North American black duck population since the 1950s is due to decreased food supplies in the acidified wetlands. The U.S. Fish and Wildlife Service reports that ducklings on man-made wetlands in Maryland are three times more likely to die before adulthood if raised in acidic waters.

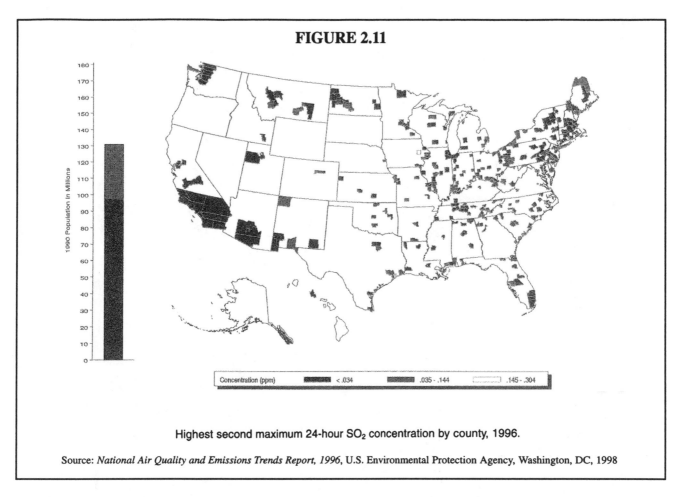

FIGURE 2.11

Highest second maximum 24-hour SO₂ concentration by county, 1996.

Source: *National Air Quality and Emissions Trends Report, 1996*, U.S. Environmental Protection Agency, Washington, DC, 1998

Acid rain leaches calcium out of the soil and robs snails of the calcium they need to form shells. Because titmice and other species of songbirds get most of their calcium from the shells of snails, the birds are perishing. The eggs they lay are defective — thin and fragile. The chicks do not hatch or have bone malformations and die. (For more information on birds, see Chapter V.)

HOW BAD IS ACID RAIN?

National Acid Precipitation Assessment Program (NAPAP)

In 1980, Congress created the National Acid Precipitation Assessment Program (NAPAP) to study the acid rain phenomenon and assess the damage it caused. Two thousand scientists worked with an elaborate multi-million-dollar computer model in an eight-year, $570-million undertaking. In 1988, NAPAP produced an overwhelming 6,000-page report on its findings. The report found that acid rain had adversely affected aquatic life in about 10 percent of eastern lakes and streams and contributed to the decline of red spruce at high elevations by reducing that species' cold tolerance. It also reported that acid rain had contributed to the erosion and corrosion of buildings and materials and reduced visibility throughout the Northeast and in parts of the West. Although the incidence of serious acidification was more limited than originally feared, the Adirondacks area of New York was one region showing significant damage from acid.

Progress Report

United States Geological Service (USGS) measurements taken in 1993 showed that sulfates in rainwater tested at 26 of 33 test sites across the United States, had declined significantly since 1980. Also, acidity of the rainwater had decreased at most sites; at 9 of the 33 selected locations, the pH rose significantly. The USGS attributed the im-

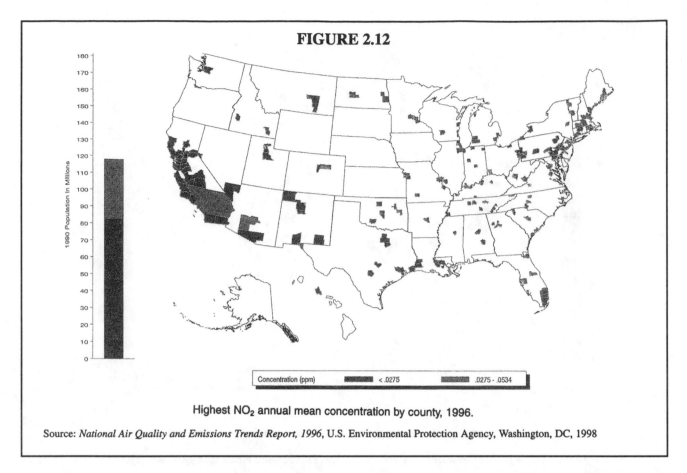

FIGURE 2.12

Concentration (ppm)   < .0275   .0275 - .0534

Highest NO_2 annual mean concentration by county, 1996.

Source: *National Air Quality and Emissions Trends Report, 1996*, U.S. Environmental Protection Agency, Washington, DC, 1998

provement to the standards put in place by the Clean Air Act of 1970 (PL 91-604) and subsequent amendments. Derek Winstanley, director of NAPAP in Washington, DC, observed that, "If we didn't start to see an increase in pH as we reduce sulfur dioxide emissions, we'd begin to wonder if we had an effective program in place here. This gives us confidence that things are working in the direction that I would hope."

In its 1996 *National Air Quality and Emissions Trends Report*, the EPA found that 200,000 persons lived in counties with sulfur dioxide (SO_2) concentrations above the 1996 standards. Because nitrogen oxides have declined to acceptable levels, no persons lived in areas where nitrogen oxides exceeded desired standards. (See Figure 2.10.) Figures 2.11 and 2.12 show those areas of the United States where concentrations of sulfur dioxide and nitrogen dioxide were highest.

The U.S. Geological Survey's *National Water Quality Inventory* found that, in 1994, 26 states reported that of the 5,933 lakes assessed for acid-

ity, 9 percent exhibited acidity and 16 percent were threatened by acidity. Roughly one-quarter of the lakes threatened by acidity were in New York.

THE POLITICS OF ACID RAIN

The early acid rain debate centered almost exclusively in the eastern portion of the United States and Canada. The controversy was often defined as a problem of property rights. The highly valued production of electricity in coal-fired utilities in the Ohio River Valley caused acid rain to fall on land in the Northeast and Canada. An important part of the acid rain controversy in the 1980s was the adversarial relationship between U.S. and Canadian federal governments over emission controls of SO_2 and NO_2. More of these pollutants crossed the border into Canada than the reverse. Canadian officials very quickly came to a consensus over the need for more stringent controls, whereas in the United States this consensus was lacking.

Throughout the 1980s, the major lawsuits involving acid rain all came from eastern states, and

34

the states that passed their own acid rain legislation were from the eastern part of the United States. There has been a clear difference in the intensity of interest between the eastern and western states regarding acid rain.

Legislative attempts to restrict emissions of pollutants were often defeated after strong lobbying by the coal industry and utility companies. Those industries advocated further research for pollution-control technology rather than placing restrictions on utility company emissions.

The Dispute with Canada

For more than a decade and a half, the United States and Canada disagreed about acid rain. In 1978, Canada and the United States established a Bilateral Research Consultation Group on the Long-Range Transport of Air Pollution to promote the exchange of research on acid rain. Two years later, the two neighbors signed a Memorandum of Intent to develop an agreement to control air pollution and try to resolve the acid rain problem.

However, the agreement resolved neither the air pollution nor the acid rain problems — the United States refused to commit to the stringent controls to which the Canadians were willing to subscribe. Many Canadians believed the United States did not take the problem as seriously as its northern neighbor and was less committed to finding a solution.

Former Canadian Prime Minister Brian Mulroney had insisted for several years that only mandatory controls on sulfur dioxide emission would resolve the problem. State visits between United States and Canadian leaders failed to produce a solution to the problem of Midwestern power plant emissions which, the Canadians claim, produced half the acid rain which was ruining their lakes, forests, and buildings. John Roberts, Minister of the Environment during the Pierre Trudeau government, accused the United States of "environmental aggression" against Canada.

The Canadian government, gravely disappointed with the lack of action on the part of the U.S. government, took matters into its own hands. Thousands of its eastern provinces' lakes were too acidic for fish life, and the salmon runs of Nova Scotia were disappearing. Canada not only took steps to halve its own sulfur dioxide emissions, but began media campaigns aimed at educating American tourists about acid rain and enlisting their support in fighting emission control.

By 1985, with the U.S.-Canada relationship strained considerably, the Ronald Reagan Administration appeared to take a conciliatory step by acknowledging, in the vague Report of the Special Envoys, the seriousness of acid rain. But official agreement did not come until 1990 during the George Bush Administration, when Congress renewed the Clean Air Act (PL 91-604). A long-awaited bilateral accord on acid rain was signed in Ottawa in 1991. After more than 12 years of conflict, the acid rain dispute between the United States and Canada ended.

A LOOK TO THE FUTURE

Damage to plants and aquatic animals from energy generation, auto exhaust, and manufacturing is one result of America's growing energy consumption and industrialization. Coal use is projected to increase as an industrial fuel, and this may cause an increase in sulfur dioxide emissions.

Future long-term exposure to increased amounts of acid rain is a major environmental concern. Once the waters and soil of any ecosystem have been overly acidified, a return to "normal" may never be possible. The natural resilience of the ecosystem can become depleted, causing losses not only of animal species but also agricultural productivity and forests.

CHAPTER III

THE CONDITION OF PLANT SPECIES

When scenes of severe floods appear on television screens, few people living comfortably in urban areas see the linkages between floods downstream and deforestation upstream. When markets are full with a wide range of food material, we tend to forget that we live on this earth as guests of the green plants that convert sunlight, nutrients, and water into food. If green plants cease to exist, animals cannot exist.
— Dr. M. S. Swaminathan, President, International Union for Conservation of Nature and Natural Resources (IUCN), 1990

Plant life makes up approximately half of the identified life forms on Earth, and endangered plant species are almost half of the species listed as endangered. When plant life is depleted, animal habitats are disrupted — animal species that live in concert with plants or that depend on plants for food and breeding areas become threatened. Many plants are victims of land and agricultural development. In addition, collectors or dealers often illegally seek rare, showy, or unusual plants.

A wide variety of environmental factors allowed specimens of most of the world's major plant formations to flourish in one region or another of America before settlement by Europeans. According to botanists, arctic ecosystems account for 19 percent of the continent; northern coniferous forests, 28 percent; grasslands, 21 to 25 percent; eastern deciduous forests, 11 percent; and coastal plain ecosystems, 3 percent. Desert ecosystems are 5 percent; western mountain coniferous forests, 7 percent; tidal wetlands, 1 percent; Mediterranean scrub lands and woodlands (for example, in California), 1 percent; and beach vegetation, less than 1 percent.

Species diversity generally decreases with distance from the equator. Like other temperate and arctic areas, North America has fewer plant types than even small tropical countries. The North American continent has 211 flowering plant families, according to one listing, while the small country of Costa Rica has 214. Among comparable temperate regions, however, North America is richer than all but China, which has 260 plant families.

The density of plant families within North America also generally diminishes with increasing distance from the tropics. The richest assemblages of flowering plants are in Florida and Texas. Close behind is New York. Despite its distance from the tropics, New York's size, moist climate, coastal area, and great range of habitats make it relatively rich in the number of species.

The impact of weeds, defined as plant species that aggressively take over areas that become impoverished, is particularly evident in the middle of the continent, the region where natural plant habitats have been most extensively reduced. Botanists and conservationists believe that habitat elimination and the crowding out of native species by uncontrolled growth have put many plant species on the road to extinction.

An estimated 40 percent of plants, algae, and photosynthetic bacteria is directly consumed, diverted, or wasted as a result of human activities. This estimate indicates the powerful ecological influence of human beings on Earth. For many centuries, humans have altered landscapes through deforestation, fire, and agriculture.

THE FIRST GLOBAL ASSESSMENT OF PLANTS — *THE IUCN RED LIST*

The numbers are staggering, not only because they are exceedingly large, but because we are talking about the organisms on which all animal life depends. Plants clothe us, feed us and our domesticated animals, and provide us with most of our medicines, yet our knowledge of their status is woefully inadequate. This needs to change. We need to invest in botany. We cannot afford to neglect the fate of the world's plants.
— David Brackett, chairman, IUCN, 1997

In 1997, the International Union for Conservation of Nature and Natural Resources (IUCN) published the first-ever comprehensive global listing of threatened plants on a global scale. The study, *The 1997 IUCN Red List of Threatened Plants*, was the result of 20 years of study by botanists, conservation organizations, botanical gardens, and museums from around the world. The most startling finding was that 12.5 percent, one out of every eight, of the world's plant species is at risk of extinction. In the United States, 29 percent of the nation's 16,000 plant species are at risk of extinction. Other findings included:

- Of the estimated 270,000 known species of vascular plants (ferns, conifers, and flowering plants, not including mosses, lichens, and algae) in 369 plant families in 200 countries, 33,798 species are at risk of extinction.

- Of the plant species at risk, 91 percent are found only in a single country, making such species more vulnerable and limiting options for their protection.

- Many plant species known to have medicinal value are at risk of disappearing. For example, 75 percent of the yew family, a source of cancer-fighting compounds, are threatened. Twelve percent of the willow family, from which aspirin is derived, is threatened.

- About 32.5 percent of the dipterocarps, a family of trees that includes valuable timber species in Asia, are threatened.

- The loss of each species causes a loss of access to critical genetic material that may have contributed to producing stronger, healthier crops for human and animal consumption.

- Close relatives to many familiar plants are at risk of extinction, including 14 percent of the rose family and 32 percent of lilies and irises.

- Numerous species whose value has not yet been studied are also at risk.

According to the report, the main reasons for the rapid loss of plant life are the loss of habitat and the introduction of alien, non-native plant species. Seven of the top 10 areas listed according to percentage of threatened flora are islands: St. Helena (41.2 percent), Mauritius (39.2 percent), Seychelles (31.2 percent), Jamaica (22.5 percent), French Polynesia (19.5 percent), Pitcairn (18.4 percent), and Reunion (18.1 percent). The United States (29 percent), Turkey (21.7 percent), and Spain (19.5 percent) completed the top ten.

The participating scientists have acknowledged several limitations of the study. *The Red List* reflects distinctly regional bias — the assessments from North America, Australia, and Southern Africa were more comprehensive than other regions. They report that the rest of Africa, Asia, the Caribbean, and South America, when fully studied, will undoubtedly be found to have more threatened plants than documented in the study. The scientists also believe that this is a very conservative estimate.

THE AMERICAN LANDSCAPE
— THE FIRST COMPLETE REVIEW

In 1995, the first full review of the health of the American landscape, "Endangered Ecosystems of the United States — a Preliminary Assessment of Loss and Degradation," concluded that vast stretches of natural habitat, once amounting to at least half the area of the 48 contiguous states, have declined to the point of endangerment. Although individual species had been studied previously, the health of the larger ecosystems had never before been considered. The report was released by the National Biological Service (NBS), an Interior Department research organization created by U.S. Secretary Bruce Babbitt in 1993.* The study was based on an extensive, year-long survey of the scientific literature of conservation agencies and professionals and of databases maintained by the states.

The study found that scores of ecosystems of varying types and sizes have declined on a grand but largely unrecognized scale. The study reported that ecosystems can be impoverished in two ways. The most obvious is quantitative — the conversion of a native prairie to a parking lot. Quantitative losses can often be measured by a decline in the areal extent of an ecosystem (area that can be mapped). The second kind of loss is qualitative and involves a change or degradation in the structure, function, or composition of an ecosystem.

Fifty-eight percent of the ecosystems that have declined by over 70 percent are terrestrial, 32 percent are wetland, and 10 percent are aquatic. Forests, grasslands, barrens, and savannas dominated the list, especially in the critically endangered category. (See Figure 3.1.) The greatest number of estimates and the greatest extent of losses are in the Northeast, South, Midwest, and California (Figure 3.2) and may reflect the more intensive land uses in these regions. The researchers found endangered ecosystems in all major regions of the United States except in Alaska.

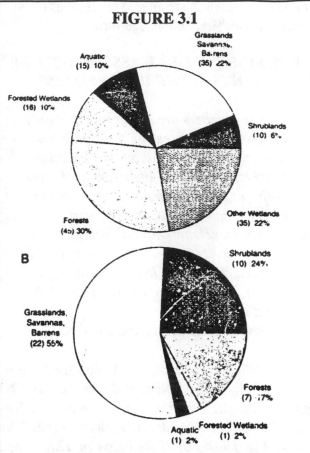

FIGURE 3.1

(A) Distribution of critically endangered, endangered, and threatened ecosystem types (Appendix B) in six general categories. To include general wetland-loss statistics, which are usually organized by state, a number was added in the wetland category for each state with declines of more than 70%. The greatest number of reported declines is among forest and wetland habitats and communities. (B) For ecosystems that have declined by more than 98% (i.e., critically endangered), the greatest losses are among grassland, savanna, and barrens communities.

Source: *Endangered Ecosystems of the United States — A Preliminary Assessment of Loss and Degradations*, U.S. National Biological Service, Laurel, MD, 1995

Among the largest imperiled ecosystems are the tallgrass prairies and oak savannas that characterized the Midwest before Europeans came to America, along with the deciduous forests of the eastern United States and more than 60 million acres of longleaf pine forests that formerly blanketed much of the southeastern coastal plain. (Longleaf pine was once the dominant vegetation type in the coastal plains, covering 40 percent of the region.)

---

* In 1996, the NBS was integrated into the United States Geological Service (USGS) as the Biological Resources Division (BRD).

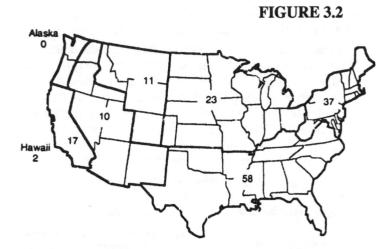

FIGURE 3.2

Distribution of critically endangered, endangered, and threatened ecosystem types by geographic region (defined ad hoc for this study; Appendix B). Each region received a point when types overlapped regions. Regions with fewer types are not necessarily in better condition because numbers reflect sampling and reporting biases in the literature and in heritage programs.

Source: *Endangered Ecosystems of the United States — A Preliminary Assessment of Loss and Degradations*, U.S. National Biological Service, Laurel, MD, 1995

All of these, the study reported, are among 32 ecosystems considered "critically endangered." Fifty-eight areas have declined by 85 to 98 percent and are classified as "endangered" and 38 others have declined by 70 to 84 percent and are listed as "threatened." The 128 imperiled areas are concentrated most heavily in the eastern half of the country. Some ecosystems, such as the Midwestern grasslands, have nearly been destroyed by the conversion to agriculture. Others suffer what the study terms degradation. Table 3.1 lists the critically endangered, endangered, and threatened ecosystems of the United States.

As ecosystems shrink, the study found, the species that live in them become imperiled as well. The longleaf pine ecosystem of the southern coastal plain, for instance, is now home to 27 species on the endangered list and another 99 proposed for listing. The study reports "a striking picture of endangerment." This concept of viewing the environment in terms of ecosystems is a recently introduced policy of the (Bill) Clinton Administration (see below and also Chapter IX).

HOW GLOBAL WARMING AFFECTS PLANT ECOSYSTEMS*

The World Wildlife Fund International ranks three categories of ecosystems threatened by global warming:

1. Front-line ecosystems, which experience a near-term threat. These include coral reefs, mangroves, and arctic seas where the ecosystem would be changed by melting ice.

2. Highly vulnerable ecosystems, including mountain ecosystems, coastal wetlands threatened by rising seas, Arctic tundra, and sub-Arctic and temperate-zone tropical forests.

3. High-risk ecosystems that are likely in jeopardy but where impact is not yet clear. These include savannas and tropical forests.

The species most likely to prosper in a warming world are those already common and able to adapt to a wide range of environments, including weeds, pests, and many disease-carrying vermin. Significant losses would be expected among rare species and among those species adapted to special niches. More than half the world's parks and reserves could be threatened by climate change, including the Florida Everglades, Yellowstone National Park, the Great Smoky Mountains, and Redwood National Park in California.

*For a full discussion of global warming, see Chapter II.

FORESTS

Not only are forests a source of timber, they perform a wide range of social and ecological functions. They provide a livelihood and home for forest dwellers. They protect and enrich soils, regulate the hydrologic cycle, affect local and regional climate through evaporation and storing of water, and help stabilize the global climate by processing carbon dioxide. They provide habitat for half of all known plant and animal species, are the main source of industrial wood and domestic heating, and are used for recreation.

Forests play a crucial role in the global cycling of carbon. The earth's vegetation stores 2 trillion tons of carbon, roughly triple the amount stored in the atmosphere. When trees are cleared, the carbon they contain is oxidized and released to the air, adding to the amount of carbon dioxide in the atmosphere. This release occurs either rapidly if the trees are burned or slowly if they decay naturally. The Worldwatch Institute, an environmental advocacy estimates that deforestation and the burning of fossil fuels have raised the level of carbon dioxide in the atmosphere by 24 percent since industrialization. While the clearing for agriculture in North America and Europe has largely stopped, tropical forests now produce the bulk of carbon dioxide added to the atmosphere by land-use changes.

Deforestation is caused by farmers, ranchers, logging and mining companies, and fuel wood collectors. Forests are attractive and accessible sources of natural wealth, but they are not unlimited. Governments have often encouraged settlements through cheap credit, land grants, and the building of roads and services, which inevitably threaten the forests. Some governments, however, are starting to reverse these policies.

In 1997 and 1998, fires set by humans and accelerated by drought spread throughout Southeast

---

TABLE 3.1

Critically endangered, endangered, and threatened ecosystems of the United States. Decline refers to destruction, conversion to other land uses, or significant degradation of ecological structure, function, or composition since European settlement. Estimates (see references in Appendix A) are from quantitative studies and qualitative assessments.

Critically Endangered (>98% decline) Ecosystems

Old-growth and other virgin stands in the eastern deciduous forest biome.

Spruce–fir (*Picea rubens–Abies fraseri*) forest in the southern Appalachians.

Red pine (*Pinus resinosa*) and white pine (*Pinus strobus*) forests (mature and old-growth) in Michigan.

Longleaf pine (*Pinus palustris*) forests and savannas in the southeastern coastal plain.

Slash pine (*Pinus elliottii*) rockland habitat in South Florida.

Loblolly pine–shortleaf pine (*Pinus taeda–Pinus echinata*) hardwood forests in the West Gulf Coastal Plain.

Arundinaria gigantea canebrakes in the Southeast.

Tallgrass prairie east of the Missouri River and on mesic sites across range.

Bluegrass savanna-woodland and prairies in Kentucky.

Black Belt prairies in Alabama and Mississippi and in the Jackson Prairie in Mississippi.

Ungrazed dry prairie in Florida.

Oak (*Quercus* spp.) savanna in the Midwest.

Wet and mesic coastal prairies in Louisiana.

Lakeplain wet prairie in Michigan.

Sedge (*Carex* spp. and others) meadows in Wisconsin.

Hempstead Plains grasslands on Long Island, New York.

Lake sand beaches in Vermont.

Serpentine barrens, maritime heathland, and pitch pine (*Pinus rigida*)-heath barrens in New York.

Prairies (all types) and oak savannas in the Willamette Valley and in the foothills of the Coast Range, Oregon.

Palouse prairie (Idaho, Oregon, and Washington and in similar communities in Montana).

Native grasslands (all types) in California.

Alkali sink scrub in southern California.

Coastal strand in southern California.

Ungrazed sagebrush steppe in the Intermountain West.

Basin big sagebrush (*Artenisia tridentata*) in the Snake River Plain of Idaho.

Atlantic white-cedar (*Chamaecyparis thyoides*) stands in the Great Dismal Swamp of Virginia and in North Carolina and possibly across the entire range.

Streams in the Mississippi Alluvial Plain.

Endangered (85–98% decline)

Old-growth and other virgin forests in regions and in states other than in those already listed, except in Alaska.

Mesic limestone forest and barrier island beaches in Maryland.

Continued on following page.

Asia and in Central America and Mexico, claiming lives and threatening the health of thousands of people around the globe. In an effort to cut timber and sell it, farmers have created some of the worst deforestation problems in history.

The Role of Forests in Climate Change

The increasing levels of carbon dioxide in the atmosphere, generally caused by industrialization, might conceivably be tolerated in Earth's normal carbon dioxide cycle were it not for the additional complicating factor of deforestation. The burning of the Amazon rain forests and other forests has had a twofold effect — the release of large amounts of carbon dioxide into the atmosphere from the fires and the loss of the trees that help neutralize the carbon dioxide in the atmosphere. Scientists, however, do not agree about the extent to which forests can soak up excess carbon dioxide.

Scientists at the Environmental Defense Fund (EDF) believe that an additional 10 million acres of forest would absorb all the carbon dioxide emitted by power plants to be built in the next decade. Unfortunately, forest acreage is not increasing, and deforestation is proceeding at the rate of 41 million acres a year. The Worldwatch Institute re-

ported, in *Taking a Stand: Cultivating a New Relationship with the World's Forests* (1998), that between 1980 and 1995 alone, at least 200 million hectares (a hectare equals 2.471 acres) of forests — an area larger than Mexico — vanished.

Recent studies indicate that unlike trees used in scientific research that are well fertilized and irrigated in controlled studies, trees under natural conditions appear unable to effectively respond to

---

TABLE 3.1 (Continued)

Coastal plain Atlantic white-cedar swamp, maritime oak–holly (*Quercus* spp.–*Ilex* spp.) forest, maritime redcedar (*Juniperus virginiana*) forest, marl fen, marl pond shore, and oak openings in New York.

Coastal heathland in southern New England and on Long Island.

Pine–oak–heath sandplain woods and lake sand beach in Vermont.

Floodplain forests in New Hampshire.

Red spruce (*Picea rubens*) forests in the central Appalachians (West Virginia).

Upland hardwoods in the Coastal Plain of Tennessee.

Lowland forest in southeastern Missouri.

High-quality oak–hickory (*Quercus* spp.–*Carya* spp.) forest on the Cumberland Plateau and on the Highland Rim of Tennessee.

Limestone redcedar (*Juniperus virginianus*) glades in Tennessee.

Wet longleaf pine savanna and eastern upland longleaf pine forest in Louisiana.

Calcareous prairie, Fleming glade, shortleaf pine/oak–hickory forest, mixed hardwood–loblolly pine forest, eastern xeric sandhill woodland, and stream terrace sandy woodland/savanna in Louisiana.

Slash pine (*Pinus elliottii*) forests in southwestern Florida.

Red pine and white pine forests in Minnesota.

Coastal redwood (*Sequoia sempervirens*) forests in California.

Old-growth ponderosa pine (*Pinus ponderosa*) forests in the northern Rocky Mountains, Intermountain West, and eastside Cascades Mountains.

Riparian forests in California, Arizona, and New Mexico.

Coastal sage scrub (especially maritime) and coastal mixed chaparral in southern California.

Dry forest on main islands of Hawaii.

All types of native habitats in the lower delta of the Rio Grande River, Texas.

Tallgrass prairie (all types combined).

Native shrub and grassland steppe in Oregon and in Washington.

Low elevation grasslands in Montana.

Gulf Coast pitcher plant (*Sarracenia* spp.) bogs.

Pocosins (evergreen shrub bogs) and ultramafic soligenous wetlands in Virginia.

Mountain bogs (southern Appalachian bogs and swamp forest–bog complex) in Tennessee and in North Carolina.

Upland wetlands on the Highland Rim of Tennessee.

Saline wetlands in eastern Nebraska.

Wetlands (all types combined) in south-central California, Illinois, Indiana, Iowa, Missouri, Nebraska, and Ohio.

Marshes in the Carson-Truckee area of western Nevada.

Low-elevation wetlands in Idaho.

Woody hardwood draws, glacial pothole ponds, and peatlands in Montana.

Vernal pools in the Central Valley and in southern California.

Marshes in the Coos Bay area of Oregon.

Freshwater marsh and coastal salt marsh in Southern California.

Seasonal wetlands of the San Francisco Bay, California.

Large streams and rivers in all major regions.

Aquatic mussel (Unionidae) beds in Tennessee.

Submersed aquatic vegetation in the Chesapeake Bay, in Maryland, and in Virginia.

Mangrove swamps and salt marsh along the Indian River lagoon, Florida.

Seagrass meadows in Galveston Bay, Texas.

Continued on following page.

---

higher levels of atmospheric carbon dioxide because of limits on other nutrients. Most of the world's trees are not being irrigated and fertilized, and scientists believe that a significant increase in carbon dioxide absorption will only be accomplished by the relatively small number of trees in cultivation.

Natural trees exposed to increased carbon dioxide grew smaller leaves and more numerous fine roots, but there was no increase in the size of the trunks and branches where carbon dioxide can be more permanently stored. Scientists also predict that Earth's warming may speed up the decay of organic matter in soils, adding extra carbon dioxide and methane to the atmosphere.

Predicted Impact of Global Warming on Forest Ecosystems

Scientists believe that the effects of warming on forest ecosystems will become apparent over decades. The U.S. Forest Service reports that, based on the known impact of climate change on forests in the past, eastern hemlock, yellow birch, beech, and sugar maple would gradually shift their ranges northward by 300 to 600 miles if, as some scientists predict, carbon dioxide concentrations in the air double in the next century.

Seedlings at the southern limits of the trees' ranges would disappear first. Most adult trees would continue to live for several decades, although growth rates would decline. But when they died, no others of their species would replace them. Eventually, all four species would die out, and with them, most of the animal species that live in these forests.

TABLE 3.1 (Continued)

Threatened (70–84% decline)

Nationwide riparian forests (other than in already listed regions), including southern bottomland hardwood forests.

Xeric habitats (scrub, scrubby flatwoods, sandhills) on the Lake Wales Ridge, Florida.

Tropical hardwood hammocks on the central Florida keys.

Northern hardwood forest, aspen (*Populus* spp.) parkland. and jack pine (*Pinus banksiana*) forests in Minnesota.

Saline prairie, western upland longleaf pine forest, live oak–pine–magnolia (*Quercus virginiana-Pinus* spp.–*Magnolia* spp.) forest, western xeric sandhill woodland, slash pine-pond baldcypress-hardwood (*Pinus elliottii-Taxodium ascendens*) forest, wet and mesic spruce–pine (*P. glabra*)–hardwood flatwoods, wet mixed hardwood–loblolly pine (*Pinus taeda*) flatwoods, and flatwoods ponds in Louisiana.

Alvar grassland, calcareous pavement barrens, dwarf pine ridges, mountain spruce–fir forest, inland Atlantic whitecedar swamp, freshwater tidal swamp, inland salt marsh, patterned peatland, perched bog, pitch pine–blueberry (*Pinus rigida-Vaccinium* spp.) peat swamp, coastal plain poor fens, rich graminoid fen, rich sloping fen, and riverside ice meadow in New York.

Maritime-like forests in the Clearwater Basin of Idaho.

Woodland and chaparral on Santa Catalina Island.

Southern tamarack (*Larix laricina*) swamp in Michigan.

Wetlands (all kinds) in Arkansas, Connecticut, Kentucky, and Maryland.

Marshes in the Puget Sound region, Washington.

Cienegas (marshes) in Arizona.

Coastal wetlands in California.

Source: *Endangered Ecosystems of the United States — A Preliminary Assessment of Loss and Degradations*, U.S. National Biological Service, Laurel, MD, 1995

The Role of Logging in Deforestation

Many observers claim that the forests of the Northwest United States are being depleted by "clear-cutting" practices — the method of logging in which all trees in an area are cut, as opposed to "selective management" techniques, in which certain trees are removed from an area. The lumber industry continues to battle with environmentalists and the U.S. Forest Service over the right to clear-cut ancient forests, including redwoods and national forests. The Natural Resources Defense Council reports that the "old growth" forests (stable stands of old, large trees) of North America store more carbon, acre for acre, than any other ecosystem on the earth.

NASA scientists report that satellite pictures show a serious level of damage to the evergreen forests of the Pacific Northwest. They attribute the damage to clear-cutting and say that the region has been so fragmented by clear-cutting that the overall health of the forests are at risk. Many observers believe that the biggest threat from this logging technique is the loss of diversity of species in the area. In an effort to counteract tree loss, forests are often "replanted" or replaced. Experts contend, however, that when a natural forest is replanted with commercially valuable trees after clear-cutting, the plot becomes a tree farm, not a forest, and the biological interaction is damaged.

Fragmentation of Forests in the Northeast

Roads, power lines, encroaching industry, vacation homes, and urban expansion have claimed much of the forested land in the Northeast. Old trees, where they are replaced by younger vegetation, are replaced by different species. Chestnuts, elms, sugar and red maples, beech, flowering dogwood, hemlock, sycamore, balsam fir, and white ash are disappearing in favor of ailanthus, Japanese honeysuckle, bittersweet, Norway maple, and the cork trees, ornamental exotics used for urban planting that have "escaped" to the wild.

But more importantly, acreage of vegetation is often cut up into fragments smaller than 50 acres. Fragmentation isolates plant and animal populations, so that each species is more vulnerable to local extinction. That creates lots of forest "edges" — places where non-native species invade the forests and displace native ones. At the forest's edge, trees are more susceptible to weather and to being eaten by game animals like deer. The more forest edges there are, the smaller the range of deep-forest creatures. For example, songbirds like the wood thrush and the promontory warbler are being pushed aside by aggressive bluejays and parasitic cowbirds.

Pollution and the Forests

William H. Smith, in *Chemical and Engineering News* ("Air Pollution and Forest Damage," November 1991), concluded that regional air pollution is a serious anthropogenic (man-made) stress that threatens temperate forest ecosystems. The most dangerous impact on forests comes from ozone, heavy metals, and acid deposition. Numerous studies suggest that photosynthesis and growth decline significantly after one or two weeks of ozone at levels of 50 to 70 parts per billion (ppb), over twice the normal background level of 20 to 30 ppb. Ozone levels are highest on the West Coast (California, Nevada, Utah, and Arizona) and the East Coast south of Pennsylvania.

In 1995, researchers at the Oak Ridge National Laboratory in Tennessee determined, in a 1988 to 1992 study of the loblolly pine, a widespread timber species, that the ground level ozone levels that frequently occur in the eastern United States caused growth to slow, especially under drier soil conditions. The loblolly pine, covering approximately 60 million acres, contributes billions of dollars to the economy of the South.

Timber Theft — Money Growing on Trees

As timber prices have risen, so has a new brand of larceny. Unscrupulous loggers are increasingly learning there is profit to be made from the theft and sale of stolen trees. For example, the Texas Forest Service reports that tree theft is occurring in unprecedented rates in the forests of East Texas, and undoubtedly other places as well. In 1994, the Forest Service received dozens of reports of tree theft, although actual numbers were unknown due to the nature of the crime. Since the victims of the thefts are usually absentee landlords (readily identifiable through county tax records), the crime may go undetected for years. In addition, many victims, believing there is little hope of recovery, do not report the crime.

Louisiana reports losses of between $12 and $15 million worth of trees annually. With a single tree worth anywhere from $30 to $150 and a truckload of logs fetching more than $1,000, thieves have developed a lucrative business. Timber theft is a crime that is easy to commit, hard to detect, and difficult to prosecute.

A New Forest Industry — Wildcrafting

Harvesting the riches of forests without cutting the trees is an industry that brings in hundreds of millions of dollars annually. *Wildcrafting*, a skill that goes back to the hunters and gatherers at the dawn of civilization, has been resurrected since the government and courts curtailed logging on public land in the early 1990s. Although it is no replacement for the financial rewards of timber, wildcrafting is a modest economic "life preserver" for some of the rural unemployed, particularly in the Northwest.

The market for forest products other than trees has mushroomed by nearly 20 percent annually over the past several years, the growth fueled partly by the exploding popularity of alternative medicine and herbal remedies. Industry experts project U.S. sale of medicinal herbs, which totaled $1.5 billion in 1995, could reach $5 billion in 2000.

In 1995, American exports of commercial moss and lichen alone amounted to $14 million, according to U.S. Forest Service scientists, who classify wildcrafting under the category "non-timber forest products." Ferns and shrubs for floral arrangements, Christmas greens, foods like mushrooms, and more than 100 medicinal herbs are also collected.

Medicinal herbs include mullein, used as an asthma reliever; ginseng, which is sold to boost vitality and can bring hundreds of dollars per pound; lemon balm, used in spices and teas; and fragrant herbs for organic soaps or lotions. More than 50 types of herbs have been marketed from forest gathering. Some mosses, such as usnea, a natural antibiotic, are believed to be medicinal; others are used for floral arrangements. Mushrooms — matsutakes, chanterelles, and morels — bring good prices. Burls, hardy woody growths on trees, which become unusually attractive when sanded and polished, can be used for furniture, cabinets, and trims.

The U.S. Forest Service, which requires that wildcrafters on public lands have permits, is still studying how much of the forest products can be harvested without harm. Some forest rangers and environmentalists worry that forest products may be overharvested, causing habitat damage, or that trampling will damage the forest floor. "It's the direction we're going in, and we'll manage the forests more holistically, moving away from a lum-

ber monoculture," said ecologist Yvonne Everett. "It's going to be very, very important to forest communities."

Sunken Treasure

From the Civil War to World War I, when lumberjacks largely stripped the woods of Wisconsin, logs were often stored in floating masses on Lake Superior. Many of the logs sank, and it was cheaper and easier to cut down more trees than to retrieve the sunken logs. Now, however, the scarcity of old lumber has made these logs sunken treasure.

In 1997, the U.S. Army Corps of Engineers and Wisconsin officials approved underwater logging in certain parts of Lake Superior. Company owners noted that millions of ancient logs could be recovered from the bottom of lakes, rivers, and oceans around the world. After a drying process that takes several weeks, the old wood sells for much higher prices than new wood, sometimes 10 times as much. This old wood is much less likely to be marred by knots than new wood, comparable to the material used by the Italian Antonio Stradivari, who built the world's finest violins in the seventeenth and eighteenth centuries. (Because of the extreme age of old growth wood, it has very few knots.)

Medicinal Plants from Forests

Worldwide, medications derived from plants are worth $40 billion annually. Most medicines originally came from wild plants, including major painkillers, birth-control agents, and malaria drugs. Between 25 and 40 percent of all medical prescriptions in the United States contain active ingredients from plants. Table 3.2 shows some of the medications derived from plant species. Medically useful species are used in the treatment of cancer, HIV/AIDS, circulatory disorders, bacterial infections, anxiety, and inflammatory diseases and for the prevention of organ rejection in transplants.

Among drugs derived from plants are vincristine and vinblastine for cancer and quinine, the oldest malaria medicine. The Madagascar periwinkle, a small flowering plant that grows in a country that has lost 80 percent of its vegetation, provides two potent compounds used in the treatment of Hodgkin's Disease and produces a 99 percent remission in patients with acute lymphocytic leukemia. Sales of the two drugs exceed $180 million a year. Diosgenin, a key ingredient of contraceptive pills, comes from the yam.

The Pacific yew, a "trash" evergreen that grows in the old-growth forests of the Pacific Northwest, is often cleared to make way for plant species profitable to the timber industry. Research in recent years revealed that the yew contains compounds effective in treating ovarian and other cancers, compounds that may save thousands of lives and be worth millions of dollars. The halting of logging in the Pacific Northwest by the Endangered Species Act has protected the habitat of both the spotted owl and the Pacific yew. (See also Chapter V.)

Scientists report that the harvesting of medicinal plants from tropical forests could be more lucrative than clearing the land for farming or growing timber. Conservationists argue that tropical forests should be preserved because they contain undiscovered plants that could be worth billions of dollars if developed into drugs. But that abstract argument for preservation, which might not pay off for many decades, is of little interest to a farmer who needs to feed his family.

An international team of 500 researchers participating in the "Global Biodiversity Strategy"

believes that the extinction of species will deprive future generations of new medicines and new strains of food crops. With as many as 50 plant species disappearing daily, the researchers calculate that the planet's diversity could be reduced by 10 percent by the year 2015.

TABLE 3.2
SELECTED EXAMPLES OF SPECIES MEDICALLY USEFUL SPECIES

species	drug & use
CANCER	
Madagascar periwinkle	vincristine & vinblastine: childhood (lymphocytic) leukemia & Hodgkin's disease
Pacific yew	taxol: ovarian, breast
HIV/AIDS	
Cameroon vine	michellamine B
tree in Malaysia	calanolides
tree in Samoa	prostatin
bush in Australia	conocurvone
mulberry trees	Butyl-DNJ (analogue of natural compound)
HEART/CIRCULATORY	
foxglove	digitalis: regulates contractions
ergot (fungus of wheat)	atenolol & metoprolol: blocks adrenaline (especially in coronary disease)
Strophanthus gratus & Strophanthus kombe	cardiac glycoside, G-strophanthin, K-strophanthin: treatment of acute heart failure hypotension during surgery
snake venom	captopril & enalapril -- reduces blood pressure
fungal metabolite	lovastatin -- used to reduce cholesterol levels byblocking its biosynthesis
INFECTIOUS	
molds	avermectins: worm killers
molds	penicillin
sewer microbes	cephalosporin; developed into cefaclor, ceftriaxone, & cefoxitin -- produces antibiotics
IMMUNOSUPPRESSANTS (used in organ transplants)	
molds	cyclosporin
molds	FK 506
PARKINSON'S DISEASE	
Atropa acuminata, Atropa belladonna	hyosyamine: treatment of Parkinson's disease, epilepsy, and gastric ulcers
TRANQUILIZERS	
Indian snake root	reserpine: muscle relaxant, antianxiety; developed alprazolam
ANTI-INFLAMMATORY	
ergot (fungus on wheat)	anti-histimines Terphenadine (H1): used to treat allergies & motion sickness; ranitidine & cimetidine (H2) used to treat gastric ulcers

Source: Endangered Species Coalition, Washington, DC, 1993

Pharmaceutical Prospecting

In 1990, the National Institute for Biodiversity in Costa Rica entered into a landmark deal with Merck, a pharmaceutical company, with the Institute providing rights to drug exploration and Merck providing the money for conservation and research. The agreement became a model for other tropical nations and companies, but until 1996, no such arrangements were attempted in the United States.

In 1996, the idea caught the attention of conservationists in the United States. Some drug manufacturers are now supporting a 270-acre pharmaceutical preserve in upstate New York, the first preserve outside the tropics that is set aside specifically for chemical prospecting. Scientists already have discovered there the mold that produces cyclosporin, which is used to prevent the rejection of transplanted organs.

But Are These Drugs Economical?

Tropical forests have produced at least 47 major pharmaceutical drugs, and some scientists estimate that several hundred more are undiscovered somewhere in the tropical forests. Dr. James Tiedje, director of the National Science Foundation Center for Microbial Ecology at Michigan State University, reported in 1996 that a single gram of temperate forest soil could harbor as many as 10,000 species of bacteria. Yet, worldwide, only 4,000 species have actually been studied and identified by scientists, and even fewer have been screened to see if they contain chemicals that can be used for drugs. Some researchers believe social institutions should be put in place to slow deforestation and protect biodiversity.

Dr. Robert Mendelsohn, an economist at Yale University, and Dr. Michael Balick, director of the Institute of Economic Botany at the New York Botanical Garden in the Bronx, estimate that, collectively, the undiscovered drugs would be worth $147 billion to society. The researchers take into account the costs of research and development, manufacturing, marketing, and taxes, making clear the difficulty of finding a useful drug in the forests. Past research reveals that 1 in 50,000 to 1 in one million screening tests leads to a commercially useful drug. The researchers made their calculations using the more conservative figure, estimating that the potential value to society of drugs derived from the rain forest is $48 per two and a half acres, too little for a company to profitably develop.

The pharmaceutical industry counters that the potential drugs could treat diseases for which there is currently little or no therapy. In addition, many products were found not in plants but in fungi, bacteria, and other organisms in the forests.

Dr. Mendelsohn suggested that drug companies pay countries for rights to search their rain forests for medicines, thereby providing economic incentives for the countries not to develop these areas, something already done by at least one major pharmaceutical firm. He also recommended that the federal government subsidize drug research because new drugs have greater potential value to society as a whole than to an individual company.

Tropical Forests

Deforestation will be stopped only when the natural forest is economically more valuable for the people who live in and around the forests than alternative uses for the same land.
—The Intergovernmental Panel on Climate Change, 1990

Tropical forests are the world's most biologically rich habitats, but they are also the most critically endangered. The United Nations reports that tropical forests and woodlands are falling faster than ever — about 41 million acres a year, 50 percent higher than in the early 1980s. The major underlying causes of deforestation and species extinction are underdevelopment, unemployment, and poverty among the growing populations of tropical countries.

Peasant farmers clear forests to create meager cropland, which is often useless after three years of conversion. Nations sometimes turn forests into quick cash to pay debts by cutting down trees to sell for lumber. Logging and the conversion of forest land to unsustainable (short-term) agricultural use has resulted in the destruction of the land, declining fisheries, erosion, and flooding. Observers predict that the resultant loss of habitats will contribute to the disruption of regional weather patterns and global climate changes, as well as eliminate plant and animal species that may serve medical, industrial, and agricultural purposes.

Tropical forests are storehouses of biological diversity. They cover less than 1 percent of the earth, but they are home to 50 to 90 percent of the world's species. Among tropical areas, the losses are greatest in West Africa, Central America, Mexico, Southeast Asia, and Madagascar.

Many countries lack the experts and technology needed to manage their forests. Methods of monitoring forest loss also need to be improved, since figures on deforestation are largely estimates. Nonetheless, it is apparent that deforestation is proceeding at a rapid pace, with conservative estimates suggesting rates as high as 6.5 percent per year (in Africa's Ivory Coast) and averaging 0.6 percent per year for all tropical countries. At this rate, which incorporates reforestation and natural regrowth, all tropical forests could be cleared within 177 years. Given the growth in human population and economic activity in developing countries, the rate of deforestation is more likely to increase than to stabilize.

The Amazon

The Amazon rain forest is the most widely known of Earth's tropical forests. Controversy regarding not only those forests but others, such as Africa's Ivory Coast, centers on the environmentalists' (often from the developed countries) interest in stabilizing the environment and the developing world's basic need for fuel and livelihood. The developing nations claim to have a more immediate need, and they resent the industrialized world's disdain of practices that they, themselves, followed in building their own nations. These poorer, developing countries also wonder how they can be expected to pay for the cleanup of a world that they did not contaminate.

Based on satellite photographs taken over the Amazon, researchers believe that as much as 10 percent of the Amazon forest has been destroyed, mainly through "slash and burn" methods of clearing land that are used to convert the forest land to farming use. Unfortunately for the farmers, the soil rarely contains the nutrients necessary for successful farming, and the land's productivity usually decreases within a few years. Farmers must often abandon the fields and move on.

WETLANDS AND MARINE ECOSYSTEMS

Since the first European settlers came to North America, we've lost more than 50 percent of our wetlands. And we're continuing to lose more than 300,000 acres of wetlands every year. That's an area the size of more than 200,000 football fields.
— World Wildlife Fund

Wetlands are transitional areas between land and water bodies, where water periodically floods the land or saturates the soil. The term "wetlands" includes wet environments such as marshes, swamps, and bogs. They may be covered in shallow water most of the year or be wet only seasonally. Plants and animals found in wetlands are uniquely adapted to these wet conditions. Wetlands are found in most states, from arctic tundra wetlands in Alaska, to peat bogs in the Appalachians, to riparian (riverbank) wetlands in the arid West. (See Figure 3.3.) Table 3.3 shows the locations of various wetland types in the United States.

A wide variety of wetlands have formed across the country due to regional differences in climate, geology, soils, vegetation, and other factors. Although there are many types of wetlands, they are broadly divided into *non-tidal* and *tidal* wetlands.

Non-tidal wetlands account for most of the wetlands in the United States and are found throughout the nation's interior. Tidal wetlands are found along the nation's coastline.

In the past, wetlands were often regarded as swamps — sources of mosquitoes, flies, disease, and unpleasant odors. Wetlands were commonly drained or filled (converted) for other uses or used as dumping grounds. As a result, more than half of America's original wetlands have vanished (Figure 3.4).

Today, wetlands are known to serve a variety of important ecological functions. They provide critical habitats for fish and wildlife, purify polluted water, and check the destructive power of floods and storms. Wetlands also provide recreational opportunities such as fishing, hunting, photography, and wildlife observation. For more information on wetlands, see *Water — No Longer Taken for Granted*, Information Plus, Wylie, Texas, 1997.

The Florida Everglades

The Everglades are a vast freshwater marsh covering approximately 5,000 square miles of south Florida. A wilderness of swamp, savanna, and virgin forest covered primarily in saw grass, it is one of the wildest and most inaccessible areas in the United States. The Everglades were formed by centuries of overflow from Lake Okeechobee. The highest land in the Everglades is only seven feet above sea level.

In many parts of the Everglades in central and southern Florida, the water is clouded with cattail debris believed to be a symptom of disruption in the Everglades' fragile food chain. The cattails have died because of agricultural pollution, and their decaying foliage has caused a lack of sunlight for algae, which anchor the ecosystem. Environmentalists contend that a decline in quality and quantity of water entering the area is slowly degrading the Everglades. Government-sponsored improvements have focused primarily on a system

FIGURE 3.3

WETLANDS IN THE AMERICAN WEST

of pollution credits (see Chapter II) in an effort to control phosphorous levels of the water.

In 1997, the Florida State Supreme Court ruled that all polluters, not just sugar growers, should be held responsible for the pollution and cleanup costs. For many years, environmentalists have argued that fertilizer-laced runoff water from farms has damaged the Everglades by polluting the water and encouraging rampant growth of vegetation that chokes the wetlands. Sugar is the third-largest cash crop in Florida, after citrus and tomatoes, accounting for 10 percent of farm revenue.

Mangroves

Mangroves are maritime groves of small trees continually forming at the point where land and sea meet. These mangroves are an important part of the coastal ecosystem, serving as habitat for in-

TABLE 3.3

Locations of Various Wetland Types in the United States

Wetland type	Primary regions	States
Inland freshwater marsh	Dakota-Minnesota drift and lake bed (8); Upper Midwest (9); and Gulf Coastal Flats (4)	North Dakota, South Dakota, Nebraska, Minnesota, Florida
Inland saline marshes	Intermontane (12); Pacific Mountains (13)	Oregon, Nevada, Utah, California
Bogs	Upper Midwest (9); Gulf-Atlantic Rolling Plain (5); Gulf Coastal Flat (4); and Atlantic Coastal Flats (3)	Wisconsin, Minnesota, Michigan, Maine, Florida, North Carolina
Tundra	Central Highland and Basin; Arctic Lowland; and Pacific Mountains	Alaska
Shrub swamps	Upper Midwest (9); Gulf Coastal Flats (4)	Minnesota, Wisconsin, Michigan, Florida, Georgia, South Carolina, North Carolina, Louisiana
Wooded swamps	Upper Midwest (9); Gulf Coastal Flats (4); Atlantic Coastal Flats (3); and Lower Mississippi Alluvial Plain (6)	Minnesota, Wisconsin, Michigan, Florida, Georgia, South Carolina, North Carolina, Louisiana
Bottom land hardwood	Lower Mississippi Alluvial Plain (6); Atlantic Coastal Flats (3); Gulf-Atlantic Rolling Plain (5); and Gulf Coastal Flats (4)	Louisiana, Mississippi, Arkansas, Missouri, Tennessee, Alabama, Florida, Georgia, South Carolina, North Carolina, Texas
Coastal salt marshes	Atlantic Coastal Zone (1); Gulf Coastal Zone (2); Eastern Highlands (7); Pacific Moutains (13)	All Coastal States, but particularly the Mid- and South Atlantic and Gulf Coast States
Mangrove swamps	Gulf Coastal Zone (2)	Florida and Louisiana
Tidal freshwater wetlands	Atlantic Coastal Zone (1) and Flats (3); Gulf Coastal Zone (2) and Flats (4)	Louisiana, Texas, North Carolina, Virginia, Maryland, Delaware, New Jersey, Georgia, South Carolina

SOURCE: This table is based on maps from Samuel P. Shaw and C. Gordon Fredine, "Wetlands of the United States: Their Extent and Their Value to Waterfowl and Other Wildlife," Fish and Wildlife Service, U.S. Department of the Interior, Circular 39, 1956.

Source: *Wetlands: Their Use and Regulation*, Office of Technology Assessment, Washington, DC, 1984

numerable species of birds, fish, and other marine life. They provide food and wood for local communities, stabilize the coastline, and provide a barrier against the sea during storms. (See Figure 3.5.)

Mangroves once lined about one-quarter of the world's tropical coasts. Now, according to the World Resources Institute, an environmental advocacy group, less than half remain. Indonesia, a country of more than 13,000 islands, has the most mangrove forest land of any country.

Mangroves are disappearing because, throughout history, people often regarded them as sinister, malarial wastelands. The writer John Steinbeck wrote, "In the mangroves it was like stalking, quiet murder. The roots gave off clicking sounds, and the odor was disgusting. We felt that we were watching something horrible. No one likes the mangroves." Government officials around the world have tended to feel the same way, seemingly happy to support projects that cash in on the apparently worthless swampland.

Tracts of mangroves have been sold to logging companies to make paper pulp, pest-proof timber, and chip board for coastal development. Mangroves have been commonly replaced with salt water ponds where shrimp are raised commercially. Herbicides were dumped on an estimated 124,000 hectares of mangrove in South Vietnam during the Vietnam War, and these areas remain, for the most part, still barren. Once the trees are cleared, they do not grow back, and, within a few years, the land usually becomes barren — true wasteland.

PLANT PROTECTION UNDER THE ENDANGERED SPECIES ACT

The Endangered Species act of 1973 (ESA, PL 93-205) restricts the sale in interstate commerce or the import or export of endangered plants, just as it does endangered animals. Over 100 listed plants found on Bureau of Land Management lands and national forests are protected by the law from deliberate destruction or vandalism. Plants also receive protection under consultation requirements of the ESA. All federal agencies must consult with the Fish and Wildlife Service (FWS) to conserve listed species and to ensure that permits are not granted that would jeopardize any listed species or modify habitats.

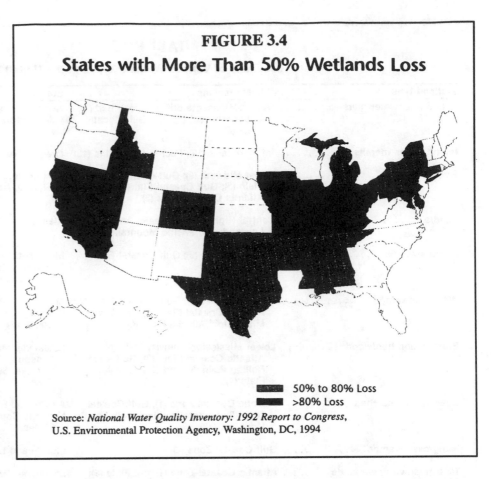

FIGURE 3.4

States with More Than 50% Wetlands Loss

50% to 80% Loss
>80% Loss

Source: *National Water Quality Inventory: 1992 Report to Congress,* U.S. Environmental Protection Agency, Washington, DC, 1994

Nonetheless, many environmentalists believe that, under the ESA, plants receive less protection than animals. The ESA imposes no restriction on private landowners whose property provides habitat for endangered plant species — only lands under federal jurisdictions are governed. The one exception is that plants on private lands are protected if a state law exists regarding them (such as state laws protecting some state flowers). Critics complain that the FWS has been slow to list plant species, and hundreds of plant species first proposed in 1976 are still waiting to be listed as imperiled.

Although threatened plants are supposed to be guarded every bit as much as endangered animal species, they are frequently not protected because the Fish and Wildlife Service has not issued regulations implementing the law. Damage to habitats supporting plants is not addressed with the same seriousness as with animal species. The FWS virtually never designates "critical habitat" for a plant species.

Furthermore, the FWS has rarely bought National Wildlife refuges to protect plant species and has consistently shortchanged plants when funding programs to restore them to healthy population levels. Of the money spent on endangered species, about half generally goes to just a handful of the species listed under the ESA — all animals. Plant species typically receive less than 3 percent of the total. About 15 percent of the plants — twice the proportion of animals — receive no funding. In addition, if the ESA is amended, as some people have proposed, to drop protection for species found in only one state, nearly half the plant species would lose protection under the law. In the current budget-cutting climate of the Congress, funding for endangered species protection, especially for plant species, has become increasingly difficult to achieve.

50

The ESA encourages federal cooperation with the states in conserving endangered and threatened species. Under Section 6, matching grants are given to those states that have enacted a compatible conservation program. Congress has appropriated so little money to Section 6 that most states and species receive little benefit.

THE CLINTON ADMINISTRATION'S FOCUS ON ECOSYSTEMS, NOT SPECIES

FIGURE 3.5
MANGROVE

Red mangroves, Everglades National Park, FL   NPS Photo

The concept of protecting whole ecosystems, rather than a single endangered species, is embodied in a number of laws governing federal lands. This holistic concept has also been promoted as the Clinton Administration's central strategy for keeping species off the endangered list while accommodating private economic interests, such as developers. An application of the holistic approach occurred in 1996, when Secretary of the Interior Bruce Babbitt and the U.S. Bureau of Reclamation initiated the release of water from Glen Canyon Dam of the Colorado River at the Grand Canyon. Scientists believed that restoring the water to riverbeds would reverse changes that have occurred since the dam was built in 1963, stirring up and redistributing nutrient-rich sediment onto canyon shores, allowing vegetation to take root, attracting birds and fish — rebuilding the entire ecosystem.

The ecosystem concept, however, is under sharp attack by conservatives who see it not only as a threat to private property, but also fear that the act of identifying habitats to be protected could reduce property values. (For more information on this approach, see Chapter IX.)

"A Better Way of Doing Business"

The Clinton policy of ecosystems was drawn into negotiations between Southern California developers and environmentalists. At issue were hundreds of thousands of biologically rich acres lying between Los Angeles and Mexico. The land was home to uncounted species of plants and animals. Developers wanted to build there, while federal regulators wanted to protect the land. Haggling over small parcels of land had cost time and money and led to frustration on both sides.

A compromise permitted developers to develop large parcels of land in exchange for setting aside other large, unfragmented, accessible regions as conservation areas. In addition, the developers were released from any further liability under the Endangered Species Act — a "no surprises" guarantee officially given by the Fish and Wildlife Service.

A similar agreement was reached in the Texas Hill Country. The Balcones Canyonlands Conservation Plan set aside 111,428 acres for ecosystem enhancement, while allowing uncontested development of many thousands of acres of land in the central Texas corridor.

CHAPTER IV

IMPERILED AQUATIC SPECIES

Creatures that live in lakes, rivers, and oceans are endangered when their environment and habitat — water, beaches, and wetlands — become unhealthy or disrupted. Those animals include fish, crustaceans (shellfish), and water-dwelling mammals, such as whales and porpoises. While some of these animals, such as whales, are also hunted for trade (see Chapter VII), most water inhabitants are endangered because pollution or acid rain has contaminated the water or because habitats have been affected by the development of the land or seashores.

Fish occur in nearly all permanent water environments, from the deepest ocean to remote alpine lakes or desert springs. They are the most diverse vertebrate group; scientists have officially cataloged nearly 24,000 fish species, about equal to all other vertebrates combined. Less than 10 percent of those species have been assessed for their conservation status. The world's fish offer the best measure of the state of biological diversity in aquatic communities. (See Chapter II for a discussion of acid rain.)

LEVEL OF ENDANGERMENT

Fish

According to the International Union for Conservation of Nature and Natural Resources (IUCN), in its *1996 Red List of Threatened Animals*, one-third of all fish species worldwide are already threatened with extinction. The IUCN reported that at least 60 percent of threatened freshwater fish species are in decline because of habitat alteration.

In the United States, according to the U.S. Fish and Wildlife Service's (FWS) Endangered Species List (December 31, 1997), 67 fish species were endangered, and 41 were threatened. (See Table 1.2, Chapter I.)

The causes of fish endangerment — habitat loss, exotic species, and exploitation — are generally the same as those afflicting other species. These sources of endangerment appear, however, to be more pervasive in aquatic ecosystems. The IUCN reports that areas of greatest endangerment tend to be large rivers heavily disturbed by human activity, such as the Missouri, Columbia, and Yangtze rivers, and unique habitats that hold endemic (native) fish species. Saltwater areas of greatest loss include coral reefs, estuaries, and other shallow, near-shore habitats. Many fish species also face a high degree of exploitation from commercial fisheries.

The world's coral reefs, second only to the world's tropical rainforests in species diversity, are being destroyed just as rapidly as those forests. Reefs hold over 1 million species of plants and animals. The IUCN found that thirty percent of coral reefs worldwide are in critical condition, with 10 percent already destroyed. In 1997, researchers at the Florida Keys National Marine Sanctuary reported that unidentified diseases had affected coral at 94 of 160 monitoring stations in the 2,800-square-mile coral reef sanctuary. In addition, divers and scientists have seen an increase in recent years in coral bleaching, a whitening of the usually colorful coral reefs.

Invasive (exotic) species are most likely to harm isolated, freshwater lakes and rivers. Some 34 percent of threatened freshwater fish face pressure from introduced species. None have been more devastated than the cichlids of Africa's lake Victoria (see below), the world's second-largest freshwater lake.

Snails, Clams, Crustaceans, and Marine Mammals

According to the FWS, in 1997, 15 U.S. snail species were endangered, and seven were threatened. Among clams, 56 species were endangered, and another six were threatened. Sixteen crustacean species were endangered, and three were threatened. (See Table 1.2.) Many species of marine mammals are also threatened.

WATER POLLUTION — MANY, MANY CAUSES

Humans burn fuels, produce wastes, and use fertilizers, pesticides, and other chemicals. These by-products of industrialization end up in the environment — in the air and in the water. The condition of water-dwellers is often a good measure of the condition of the environment; their presence and health indicate when something may be wrong in their habitat and with the world.

The Mediterranean Sea

Like Lake Erie a generation ago, the Mediterranean Sea, located between southern Europe, western Asia, and northern Africa, had become a dumping ground for chemicals, raw sewage, and litter. Many beaches near major cities have been closed.

In 1994, hundreds of dead dolphins washed up on the Mediterranean beaches, killed by a virus linked to water pollution. Scientists pointed to these dead dolphins as an indication of what may happen in the future to other sea animals and humans if the Mediterranean is not cleaned up soon. "It is important to watch what is happening to these mammals," said Dr. Gabriel Gabrielidis, coordinator of the United Nations Mediterranean Action Plan. "They are indicators of what happens in the environment. They may be telling us that there is a point when *we* will get sick."

Oil Spills

When oil is pumped from the ground for energy use, it must then be distributed to the area where it is needed by pipeline, by trucks, or by tanker ships on the oceans. Unfortunately, transporting large amounts of oil by "super tankers" is sometimes dangerous. When an accident occurs and oil is spilled into the oceans, it floats on the surface, cutting off oxygen from the sea life below and covering and killing animals, birds, and fish.

In 1989, the tanker *Exxon Valdez* ran aground on the pristine Alaskan coastline, spilling 11 million gallons of oil into the bay and killing millions of animals and plants and resulting in massive and expensive cleanup efforts. In addition, many of the measures used to clean up the spill (spraying the beaches with hot water) also proved to be damaging. In 1994, a federal jury assessed the highest punitive damage award in history — $5 billion — against Exxon for causing the spill. Juries had previously levied criminal fines, settlements, and oil cleanup costs of $3.5 billion against Exxon for its role in the spill.

Larger oil spills than the *Valdez* have occurred before and since that time, but the incident alerted many people to the dangers and the damage that can be done to unspoiled waters and marine habitats. The spill led to discussion about added safety measures for tankers, which are bigger than ever before. In 1945, the largest tanker held 16,500 tons of oil. Today, super tankers the length of several football fields carry more than 550,000 tons. These super tankers are harder to steer and likely to spill more oil if damaged. As a result of the *Valdez* spill, tankers are now built with double hulls to prevent spills.

The U.S. National Research Council estimates that approximately 8.4 billion gallons of oil enter marine waters each year, not from major oil spills,

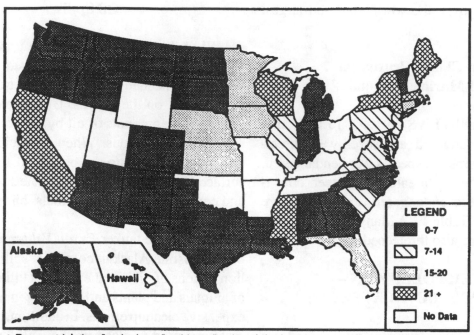

FIGURE 4.1

NUMBERS OF PESTICIDES FOUND IN GROUND WATER AS A RESULT OF AGRICULTURAL PRACTICE

LEGEND
- 0-7
- 7-14
- 15-20
- 21 +
- No Data

• Figures contain both confirmed and unconfirmed data attributed to agricultural uses.

Source: *Progress in Ground-Water Protection and Restoration*, U.S. Environmental Protection Agency, Washington, DC, 1990

but from street runoff, industrial liquid wastes, and intentional discharge from ships flushing their oil tanks. The agency indicated concern for areas that are habitually exposed to oil pollution, such as harbors or waters located near developed areas, since as little as one part of oil per million parts of water can be detrimental to the reproduction and growth of fish, crustaceans, and plankton.

Pesticides — An Ancient Remedy

Pesticides are chemicals used to kill insects that feed on crops and vegetation. The first documented use of pesticides was by the ancient Greeks. Pliny the Elder (A.D. 23-79) reported using common compounds such as arsenic, sulfur, caustic soda, and olive oil to protect crops. The Chinese later used similar substances to retard insects and fungi. In the 1800s, Europeans used heavy metal salts such as copper sulfate and iron sulfate as weed killers.

The invention of DDT (dichloro-diphenyl-trichloroethane, a powerful insecticide) in 1939 marked a revolution in the war against pests. DDT was effective, relatively cheap, and apparently safe for people — certainly a miracle chemical. Its discoverer, Paul Muller, received a Nobel Prize for its discovery. DDT promised a world with unprecedented crop yields and without insects. Farmers began using DDT and other pesticides, herbicides, and fungicides intensively and began to accept chemicals as essential to agriculture.

Farmers today apply about one pound of pesticide per year for every person on Earth, 75 percent of it in industrial countries. Much of this pesticide seeps into the ground as runoff from watering or rain. Figure 4.1 shows the extent of the seepage of pesticides into the groundwater in the United States. The number of pesticides found in California, Mississippi, Wisconsin, New York, Massachusetts, and Maine are particularly high.

In the United States, pesticide use in agriculture nearly tripled after 1965, held steady through the 1980s, and declined slightly in 1993 (Figure 4.2). Despite a number of problems associated with the chemicals used, pesticide use continues to grow. Unlike most chemicals, pesticides are purposely designed to kill or alter living organisms. According to the United Nations World Health Organization (WHO), poisonings from pesticides affect around 1 million people per year. Of these, three-quarters suffer health problems such as dermatitis, nervous system disorders, and cancer. An estimated 4,000 to 19,000 people die annually as a result of pesticide poisoning.

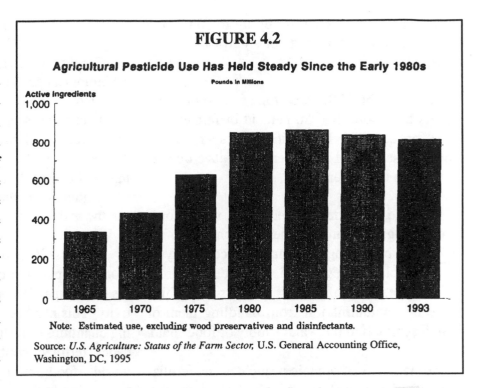

FIGURE 4.2

Agricultural Pesticide Use Has Held Steady Since the Early 1980s

Pounds in Millions

Note: Estimated use, excluding wood preservatives and disinfectants.

Source: *U.S. Agriculture: Status of the Farm Sector,* U.S. General Accounting Office, Washington, DC, 1995

In recent years, improved safety testing has led to tougher standards for the new generation of pesticides. The best of the new pesticides can be used in minute quantities and show few signs of causing health problems. They are, however, more expensive. Many farmers continue to use the older pesticides, especially in developing countries. While DDT is now banned in most industrialized countries, it is still used in many developing nations. Even the new formulations are not entirely safe, especially for wildlife. The U.S. Fish and Wildlife Service reports that pesticides harm about 20 percent of the country's endangered and threatened animal and plant species.

A major problem with the use of pesticides is that they create the need for more and different chemicals. The development of a strain of insect resistant to a pesticide is virtually automatic, because those insects that survive are unaffected by that chemical and will breed offspring that are also immune — "superbugs." At first, insecticides cause crop losses to fall, but over time, the pests rebound. Worldwide, the number of pests resistant to chemicals continues to climb.

New Methods

As an alternative to pesticide use and abuse, many scientists encourage the practice of Integrated Pest Management (IPM), a system that combines biological controls (like natural predators of pests), cultural practices (planting rotation and diversification), and genetic manipulation (pest-resistant crop varieties) with a modest use of chemicals. Rather than attempting the impossible task of eliminating pests, the goal is to strike a sustainable, profitable balance.

For a variety of reasons, farmers have been slow to adopt the new methods. First, some banks and lending institutions require farmers to use pesticides to qualify for crop loans. Second, pesticide companies spend heavily on advertising and lobbying. Third, in developing countries, funds and expertise are lacking. Finally, government subsidies and pricing policies encourage pesticide use. Nonetheless, sustainable agriculture is gaining ground, and researchers estimate that U.S. farmers could cut their pesticide use by up to 50 percent and still not lower harvests or significantly raise costs.

In 1996, the U.S. Department of Agriculture reports that more than 50 percent of farmers use some form of IPM. The United States aims to extend the use of IPM to 75 percent of its crop area by the turn of the century.

Organic pesticides and fertilizers, which come from biological sources rather than chemical factories, are beginning to compete successfully in the marketplace. These products include pyrethrum and neem, extracts of flower and tree seeds, which cause no contamination from handling them or from leaching into the water supply or food chain.

Some critics of organic pesticides and fertilizers contend that low levels of chemicals in groundwater should be acceptable. They also argue that some areas should be designated for agribusiness and allowed to become polluted. They emphasize the uncertainty of the health risk calculations, especially since tests have not been done on humans, but only on animals. Pesticide supporters wield a great deal of influence in Congress and have, in the past, successfully halted much groundwater legislation, although the Farm Bill of 1990 (PL 101-624) signaled a greater willingness to control chemical seepage into water supplies.

The discovery of banned pesticides in underground drinking water many years after they had been outlawed challenged long-held notions about agricultural chemicals. Farmers had thought that pesticides either evaporated or degraded into harmless substances. Now farmers are facing the possibility that they may have poisoned their own drinking water. Many experts predict that this is the tip of the iceberg. Further evidence of the spread of pesticides into the air, water, and food chains are being found. The Environmental Protection Agency (EPA) currently lists 55 possible carcinogens being used on U.S. food crops.

Fertilizers

Fertilizers are chemicals, or sometimes, natural biological products, that people apply to crops and plants to increase their growth. Both types of substances may seep into the water cycle and eventually reach animal species and even humans. These chemicals are often poisonous to living things. In 1962, Rachel Carson, in *Silent Spring*, called attention to the fact that chemicals were killing the nation's wildlife.

With less land to bring under the plow and the world's population expanding, the world's farmers have expanded output by raising land productivity. This has been done by using ever-increasing quantities of fertilizer. For more than three decades, fertilizer contributed to the increase in the world's food production. Fertilizer use and food production both grew at the rate of 7 percent per year from 1950 to 1984. Since 1984, however, that increase has dropped to less than 2 percent annually. As the world adds 90 million people per year, the need for food supplies expands.

From 1950 to 1989, world fertilizer use climbed to a new high almost every year, peaking at 146 million tons in 1989. Fertilizer use then fell for five years, followed by a two-year rise. Most of the growth was in China. Although fertilizer is used on all crops, about 60 percent is used to produce grain.

In the United States, fertilizer use peaked in 1981 at approximately 22 million tons. In 1996, Americans used 21 million tons of fertilizer. Farmers have found that the "little bit" extra that they might once have used is lost in nutrient runoff, which creates stream pollution in agricultural areas. The major factor, however, is the decreasing response of crops to fertilizer. During the 1960s, an additional ton of fertilizer applied on a farm in the U.S. cornbelt boosted output by 20 tons. Today, another ton may boost output by only a few tons. Crops are apparently approaching the limits of photosynthetic efficiency.

Mercury Poisoning

Wildlife and human beings are at risk from mercury poisoning from water in lakes and oceans. During the 1990s, scientists began reporting widespread mercury contamination in fish. They found elevated concentrations of mercury in fish inhabiting remote lakes that were previously considered unpolluted. The U.S. Environmental Protection Agency (EPA), in its *National Water Quality Inventory* (1998), reported that, in 1996, mercury was the cause of 1,675 fish and wildlife consumption advisories, by far the greatest number of advisories in the United States (Figure 4.3).

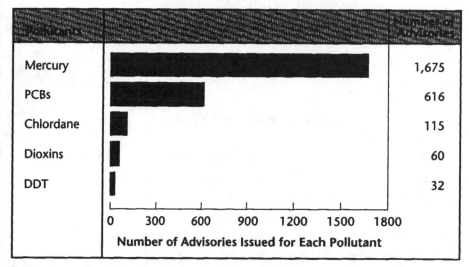

FIGURE 4.3
Pollutants Causing Fish and Wildlife Consumption Advisories

Pollutants		Number of Advisories
Mercury		1,675
PCBs		616
Chlordane		115
Dioxins		60
DDT		32

Number of Advisories Issued for Each Pollutant

Source: *National Water Quality Inventory — 1996 Report to Congress,* U.S. Environmental Protection Agency, Washington, DC, 1998

Mercury poisoning can cause brain damage, and many states have warned people to stop eating fish caught from lakes in their states because of the mercury content of the water. Scientists believe the main source of mercury pollution is rainwater carrying mercury from coal-burning power plants, incinerators that burn garbage, and smelters that make metals. Mercury poisoning is also a problem in Brazil, where gold miners pour mercury directly into the water as part of a process to find gold.

For several years, the U.S. Food and Drug Administration (FDA) has advised Americans to eat swordfish no more than once a week (once a month for pregnant women) to limit the level of exposure to mercury.

Ocean Dumping

The coast, that bright thin edge of the continent where you can sit with your back to the crowds and gaze into seemingly infinite space, is now a theater of discovery.... Survival on land and in the sea depends on a functioning coast.
— Anne Simon, *The Thin Edge*, 1978

Many cities, such as New York City, once loaded their sludge and debris on barges, took them out to sea, and dumped it into the ocean. The federal government banned this practice in 1992. Some scientists thought garbage could safely be dumped into the oceans, believing the oceans were large enough to absorb the sludge without harmful effects. Other scientists thought it would eventually lead to the pollution of the ocean.

Unseen Problems with Clean Harbors

In a few cases, environmental progress can prove to be a double-edged sword, with costs as well as benefits. Mariners once called New York City a "clean harbor," but they did not mean you could drink the water. New York was a "clean harbor" because water pollution was so severe that it killed any organisms attached to the hulls of their ships so the hulls were stripped of all organic life after a stay in New York harbor. Now the waters around New York are truly much cleaner, and voracious mollusks and crustaceans have returned and are devouring the waterfront. In fact, officials fear that they may lose many of the wooden bulkheads and piers that line the waterfront unless they protect the timbers from the insatiable creatures known as bore worms.

Ozone Depletion and the Marine Food Chain

The thinning of the atmospheric ozone layer has allowed ultraviolet radiation to penetrate into the ocean in some portions of the planet, causing sizable reductions in the oceanic food web. Marine ecologists also believe that rising radiation levels have caused genetic damage to phytoplankton, essential marine organisms. The most severe damage appears to be in the waters off Antarctica where depleted phytoplankton (minute plant forms), which is food for larger fish species, may signal the loss of other species higher in the food chain.

Up the Food Chain

Small fish and zooplankton (microscopic grazers) consume vast quantities of phytoplankton. In doing so, any toxic chemicals accumulated by the phytoplankton are passed to the fish. These concentrations are increased at every level of the food chain, a process called *biomagnification*. Biomagnification of pollutants in the food chain is a major concern, not only for fish, but also for the birds and humans that eat fish. (Figure 4.4 shows the food chain in a marine environment.)

Fish Consumption Advisories

States and tribes issue fish and wildlife advisories to protect the public from ingesting harmful quantities of toxic pollutants in contaminated fish. In general, advisories recommend that people limit the quantity and frequency of consumption of fish harvested from contaminated waterbodies. Advisories may completely ban consumption in severely

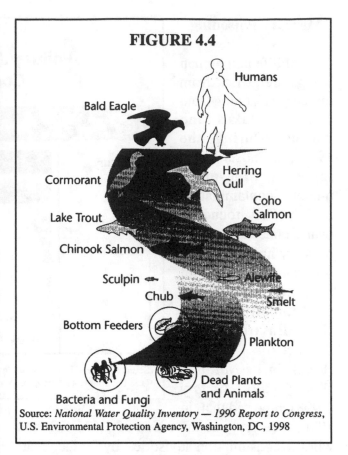

FIGURE 4.4

Humans
Bald Eagle
Cormorant
Herring Gull
Coho Salmon
Lake Trout
Chinook Salmon
Sculpin
Alewife
Chub
Smelt
Bottom Feeders
Plankton
Dead Plants and Animals
Bacteria and Fungi

Source: *National Water Quality Inventory — 1996 Report to Congress*, U.S. Environmental Protection Agency, Washington, DC, 1998

polluted waters or limit consumption to a minimum number of meals. The 1996 EPA listing of fish advisories listed 2,196 advisories in effect in 47 states (Figure 4.5). Most (76 percent) of the advisories were due to mercury. The other pollutants most commonly detected in fish samples were polychlorinated biphenyls (PCBs), chlordane, dioxins, and DDT. (See Figure 4.3.)

The Impact of Ocean Debris on Aquatic Life

Ocean debris comes from many sources (Figure 4.6), and it affects marine and human life. Scattered records of interactions between marine debris and wildlife date back several decades before the 1970s. Entangled northern fur seals were spotted as early as the 1930s. By the 1960s, various seabirds were found to have plastic in their stomachs. The problems were not fully recognized, however, until later, when floating plastic particles were found throughout the North Atlantic and North Pacific Oceans.

Waterborne litter entangles wildlife, masquerades as a food source, smothers beach and bottom-dwelling plants, and provides a surface for epiphytes (small organisms) to travel to foreign shores, perhaps with ecological consequences. Table 4.1 shows cases of entanglement and ingestion by wildlife worldwide. A total of 255 species are documented to have become entangled or to have ingested marine debris.

DAMAGE FROM INTRODUCED SPECIES

As raw materials are increasingly being traded between countries, such as the export of raw logs, you have a lot of opportunities for things to come in.
— Dr. Bruce Stein, consultant, the Nature Conservancy, 1996

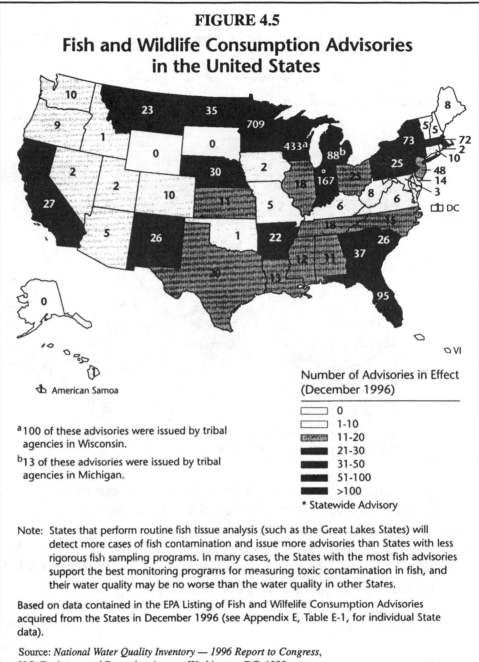

FIGURE 4.5
Fish and Wildlife Consumption Advisories in the United States

American Samoa

Number of Advisories in Effect (December 1996)

- 0
- 1-10
- 11-20
- 21-30
- 31-50
- 51-100
- >100
- * Statewide Advisory

[a] 100 of these advisories were issued by tribal agencies in Wisconsin.

[b] 13 of these advisories were issued by tribal agencies in Michigan.

Note: States that perform routine fish tissue analysis (such as the Great Lakes States) will detect more cases of fish contamination and issue more advisories than States with less rigorous fish sampling programs. In many cases, the States with the most fish advisories support the best monitoring programs for measuring toxic contamination in fish, and their water quality may be no worse than the water quality in other States.

Based on data contained in the EPA Listing of Fish and Wilfelife Consumption Advisories acquired from the States in December 1996 (see Appendix E, Table E-1, for individual State data).

Source: *National Water Quality Inventory — 1996 Report to Congress*, U.S. Environmental Protection Agency, Washington, DC, 1998

Some species of plants and animals have been imported from other countries, very often unintentionally. Many synonyms are used to describe these foreign species: alien, exotic, non-native, and nonindigenous. Once these introduced species become established, they are virtually impossible to get rid of. Furthermore, they often prey on native species.

In 1996, the Nature Conservancy reported that about 42 percent of the U.S. species listed as threatened or endangered owe at least part of their decline to nonindigenous species. For 18 percent, exotic species is the main threat to their survival. According to the FWS, at least 2,300 species of animals have come here from other places. The United States also has an estimated 4,000 non-native plant species.

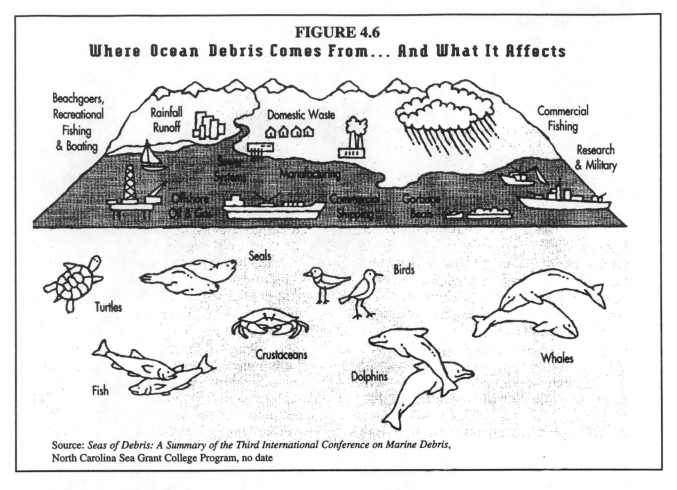

FIGURE 4.6
Where Ocean Debris Comes From... And What It Affects

Beachgoers, Recreational Fishing & Boating

Rainfall Runoff

Domestic Waste

Commercial Fishing

Research & Military

Sewage Systems

Manufacturing

Offshore Oil & Gas

Containerized Shipping

Garbage Boats

Turtles

Seals

Birds

Whales

Crustaceans

Dolphins

Fish

Source: *Seas of Debris: A Summary of the Third International Conference on Marine Debris*, North Carolina Sea Grant College Program, no date

Fire ants and kudzu, two unwanted imports, have not only survived in the southern United States; they have thrived. Africanized honeybees, sometimes called "killer bees," were taken from Africa to Brazil to breed hybrids species of bees. Several of the bees escaped and have been expanding their range northward at an average rate of 200 to 300 miles per year.

In the state of Georgia, Asian eels, brought from Southeast Asia or Australia, where they are delicacies, have adapted and reproduced. The three-foot-long, flesh-eating eels prey on fish found in lakes and rivers near the Chattahoochee River, such as largemouth bass and crawfish. The eels have gills but can breathe air and can worm their way across stretches of dry ground to get from one body or water to another. They have few predators, and humans have found no effective way to kill them. Biologists fear they will upset the balance between predators and prey. If they reach the Chattahoochee, it may be only a matter of time before they spread through rivers from Georgia to Florida and Alabama.

DAMS —
UNEXPECTED CONSEQUENCES

Mightiest thing ever built by a man.
— Folksinger Woody Guthrie, about the Grand Coulee Dam

Some 100,000 dams regulate America's rivers and creeks (Figure 4.7); 5,550 are more than 50 feet high. Nationwide, reservoirs encompass an area equivalent to New Hampshire and Vermont combined. Of the major (more than 600 miles in length) rivers in the lower 48 states, only the Yellowstone River still flows freely. "It's hard to find a river without a dam or one that hasn't been channelized," observes Arthur Benke, University of Alabama freshwater ecologist. America is second only to China in the usage of dams. World-wide, dams collectively store 15 percent of Earth's annual renewable water supply. Globally, water demand has more than tripled since mid-century, and the rising demand has been met by building even more and larger water supply projects.

Being a world leader in dams was a point of pride during the golden age of dam building, a fifty-year flurry of construction ending in approximately 1980. The construction of the massive Hoover Dam on the lower Colorado River in the 1930s began an engineering frenzy that would continue for several decades. The Army Corps of Engineers built most of the multi-state projects in the early years for flood control; more recent projects served narrower interests such as communities of farmers, small towns, or developers who wanted floodplain land.

Dams epitomized progress, Yankee ingenuity, and humankind's mastery of nature. According to a children's book from the 1960s, dams made rivers "behave." Dams have been placed on every type and size of flowing water, from intermittent headwater streams to the Mississippi. In North America, more than 200 major dams were completed each year between 1962 and 1968. The very success of the dam-building endeavor accounted, in part, for its decline; by 1980 nearly all the nation's best suited sites — and many dubious ones — had been dammed.

Three other factors, however, accounted for most of the decline: public resistance to the enormous costs, a growing belief that politicians were foolishly spending taxpayers' monies on "pork barrel" (local) projects such as dams, and a developing public awareness of the profound environmental degradation that dams can cause. Daniel P. Beard, Commissioner of the U.S. Bureau of Reclamation, observed, "It is a serious mistake for any

TABLE 4.1

Documented Worldwide Marine Debris Entanglement and Ingestion

Species Group	Total No. of Species Worldwide	No. and Percentage of Species with Entanglement Records No.	%	No. and Percentage of Species with Ingestion Records No.	%	Species with Entanglement and/or Ingestion Records No.	%
• Sea Turtles	7	6	86	6	86	6	86
• Seabirds	312	51	16	99	32	128	41
Penguins	16	6	38	0	0	6	38
Grebes	19	2	10	0	0	2	10
Albatrosses, Petrels and Shearwaters	99	10	10	57	58	58	59
Pelicans, Boobies, Gannets, Cormorants, Frigatebirds, Tropicbirds	51	10	20	6	12	14	27
Shorebirds, Skuas, Gulls, Terns, Auks	122	23	19	36	30	48	39
• Other Birds	-	5	-	0	-	5	-
• Marine Mammals	115	31	27	24	21	47	41
Baleen Whales	10	6	60	2	20	6	60
Toothed Whales	65	4	6	19	29	20	31
Fur Seals and Sea Lions	14	11	79	1	7	11	79
True Seals	19	8	42	1	5	8	42
Manatees and Dugongs	4	1	25	1	25	1	25
Sea Otters	1	1	100	0	0	1	100
• Fish	-	34	-	33	-	60	-
• Crustaceans	-	8	-	0	-	8	-
• Squid	-	0	-	1	-	1	-
SPECIES TOTAL	-	135	-	163	-	255	-

Source: *Seas of Debris: A Summary of the Third International Conference on Marine Debris*, North Carolina Sea Grant College Program, no date

region in the world to use what we did on the Colorado and Columbia Rivers as examples."

Where Have All the Rivers Gone?

Dams provide a source of energy generation; flood control; irrigation; recreation for pleasure boaters, skiers, and anglers; and locks for the passage of barges and commercial shipping vessels. But dams have altered the rivers, the land abutting them, the waterbodies they join, and the aquatic life throughout, resulting in profound changes in the water systems of the United States and the world.

Many regions have now fallen into a zero-sum game in which increasing the water supply to one user means taking it away from another. More water devoted to human activities means serious and potentially irreversible harm to natural systems. Most scientists believe that the manipulation of river systems has wreaked havoc on the aquatic environment and on biological diversity. The American Fisheries Society lists 364 species or subspecies of fish that are threatened or endangered because of habitat destruction.

Only recently has much attention been paid to the effects of diminished river flows on deltas and estuaries. When rivers are dammed and water flow is stopped or reduced, wetlands dry up, species die, and nutrient loads delivered by rivers into seas are altered, with many consequences. Some rivers, including the large Colorado River, no longer reach the sea at all, except in years of very high precipitation. Keeping enough water in rivers is especially difficult in the arid West. Dams also can contribute to the decline of local economies, cause the resettlement of millions of people, and increase health risks.

FIGURE 4.7

Grand Coulee Dam on the Columbia River. Franklin D. Roosevelt Lake holds nearly 2.8 cubic miles of water.

Source: *Water of the World*, U.S. Department of the Interior/ U.S. Geological Survey, Washington, DC, no date

In March 1996, the U.S. Bureau of Reclamation made a first step to restoring some of the damage done by dams when they opened the gates to the Glen Canyon Dam of the Colorado River at the Grand Canyon. Scientists believed that restoring the water to riverbeds would reverse changes that have occurred since the dam was built in 1963. Scientists hoped the week-long flood would stir up and redistribute nutrient-rich sediment onto canyon shores, allowing vegetation to take root, attracting birds and fish. The flood appears to be having the desired effect of creating new beaches and sand deposits in the Grand Canyon.

Tearing Down Dams?

In November 1997, for the first time in U.S. history, the Federal Energy Regulatory Commission ordered Edwards Dam removed from the Kennebac River in Augusta, Maine, to restore the

FIGURE 4.8

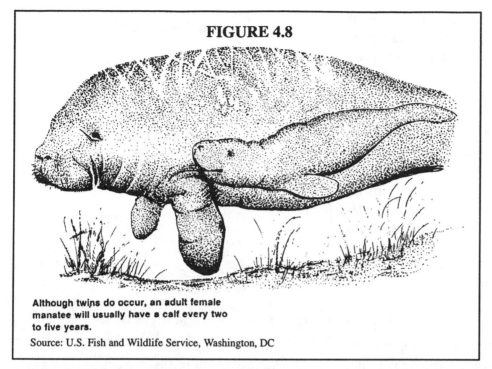

Although twins do occur, an adult female manatee will usually have a calf every two to five years.

Source: U.S. Fish and Wildlife Service, Washington, DC

habitat of sea-run fish. The federal order is expected to increase pressure across the country, particularly in the salmon-depleted rivers of the Pacific Northwest, for removal of dams even larger and more productive than Edwards. The commission gave the dam's owner a year to file a plan to tear down the 160-year-old dam, which produces one percent of Maine's electricity. The owner, Edwards Manufacturing, has appealed the decision. Congress passed a law in 1986 requiring the federal commission to balance power generation and environmental protection when it licenses hydroelectric dams. About 550 dams across the country are up for relicensing within the next 15 years.

Foreign Interest in Dams

As the era of big dams fades in North America, construction is increasing in Asia, fueled by growing demand for electricity and irrigation, the same factors that caused Americans to build dams. China accounts for more than one-fourth of the big dams under construction, while China, Japan, South Korea, and India together account for more than half. During the 1990s, ever-larger dams were being built. In 1992, 60 percent of the dams being built were more than 99 feet high, compared with only 21 percent of existing dams in 1986. The largest dams were being built in Japan, China, and Turkey. For more information on dams, see *The Environment — A Revolution in Attitudes*, Information Plus, Wylie, Texas, 1998.

SOME EXAMPLES OF ENDANGERED WATER SPECIES

Manatees

The last remaining manatees swim in the clear springs and lakes of Florida. These mammals, often called "sea cows," can grow to be 2,000 pounds and bear only one baby every three to five years (Figure 4.8). They swim just below the surface of the water and feed on vegetation. In the summer they migrate north, generally no farther than the North Carolina coast. In 1995, however, a manatee nicknamed "Chessie" made it as far as Chesapeake Bay before biologists, concerned about his health in cooler waters, had him airlifted back to Florida.

Unlike most animals that are threatened by other predators, manatees have no natural predators. The only real danger to them comes from humans — manatees are being killed primarily by motorboats. Because of their large size, they often cannot move out of the way of the boats fast enough to avoid being hit. Most manatees have scars on their backs from motorboat propellers, and many more are killed. Individual manatees are recognized largely through these unique scar patterns caused by boat strikes. National Biological Service personnel have catalogued almost 1,000 recognizable manatees and maintained their sighting histories in a computer-based system.

Because manatees do not produce young very often, they cannot replace the number of manatees being killed. Biologists estimate there are about 1,800 manatees remaining. Environmentalists are trying to keep the manatees safe from boaters, and some areas of Florida have been declared boat-free areas, while some other places require boaters to lower their speeds in order to protect the manatees. Figure 4.9 shows the number of manatee deaths attributable to motor boats from 1976 to 1993 and the number of vessels. In addition, in 1995, approximately 10 percent of Florida's manatees died suddenly from unexplained causes. Biologists believe the deaths may be attributable to an as-yet-unidentified virus.

Sea Turtles

Sea turtles have existed virtually unchanged for the past 200 million years, swimming in tropical waters, feeding on mollusks, vegetation, and crustaceans. These air-breathing reptiles are excellent swimmers and sometimes swim thousands of miles between their feeding and nesting or wintering areas (Figure 4.10). Six species of sea turtles regularly spend all or part of their lives off the U.S. coasts and in U.S. territorial waters. Some of the largest varieties may weigh hundreds of pounds. Loggerhead turtles are slow to mature and must be 20 to 30 years old before they can reproduce. Each year they lay their eggs in sandy beaches. The destruction of the beaches put all species of sea turtles found in U.S. waters under the Endangered Species Act (PL 93-205) as either threatened or endangered. Table 4.2 shows the condition of U.S. turtle species.

The building of recreational resorts and houses on the nation's beaches has been destroying the egg-laying ground for the young turtles. Furthermore, the temperature of its nest determines the sex of a baby turtle, and small temperature differences can alter the ratio of males to females. For example, among the Kemp's Ridley turtle, the most endangered species, there were 42,000 nesting females in 1947. Today, about 3,000 adults exist. Hatchery-born sea turtles cannot survive and reproduce in the wild, so natural habitats must be restored if the animal is to survive.

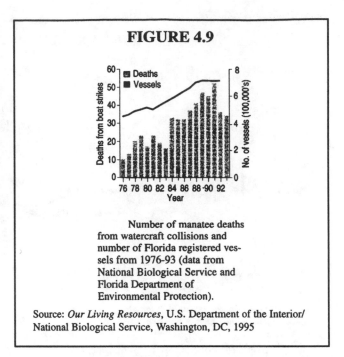

FIGURE 4.9

Number of manatee deaths from watercraft collisions and number of Florida registered vessels from 1976-93 (data from National Biological Service and Florida Department of Environmental Protection).

Source: *Our Living Resources*, U.S. Department of the Interior/ National Biological Service, Washington, DC, 1995

In addition, many turtles are caught in shrimp nets from fishing boats working in the Gulf of Mexico and the Caribbean. In 1990, the National Academy of Sciences reported that shrimp trawling was the greatest cause of death for sea turtles in U.S. waters, estimating that 55,000 animals die every year. In 1981, a device called a "turtle extruder" was invented that allows sea turtles to escape shrimp nets. Biologists attribute the gradual increase in the number of Ridley turtles in the last decade primarily to the use of turtle extruder devices.

In 1994, biologists reported a dramatic increase in the deaths of sea turtles off Texas beaches. Sixty-six turtles washed up on Texas shores in just one month, 40 of them Kemp's Ridley turtles. Scientists do not know whether their deaths were related to a surge in dolphin deaths along the same coast.

In January 1996, federal courts ruled that the Commerce Department must enforce provisions mandated by the Endangered Species Act to require nations that export shrimp to the United States to reduce sea turtle deaths by 97 percent through use of turtle excluder devices. The law had been suspended by the Bush Administration, which complained that the law would hurt commerce with countries that exported shrimp to the United States. The devices are already required on U.S. commercial fleets.

In addition to using turtle excluders when catching shrimp, humans can protect the turtles by restricting the dredging of channels and beachfront areas, especially during nesting and hatching seasons from May through October. Researchers with the U.S. Department of the Interior's Mineral Management Service have discovered that oil rigs off the Texas Gulf coast attract sea turtles. In 1993, oil company officials reported that sea turtles swam near offshore rigs, feeding off crabs, flying fish, and shrimp that were attracted to platform lights. In such cases, man-made shelters seem to have replaced lost habitat. In fact, that same year, a retired airplane hull was sunk off the Florida coast in hopes that it would become encrusted with marine life and provide an ecosystem approximating natural coral reefs. Studies of the hull show that this is occurring.

In April 1998, the World Trade Organization (WTO), an international trade body, ruled that the United States was wrong to prohibit shrimp imports from countries that do not use turtle excluder devices. The United States imports most of the shrimp that Americans consume, and by American law, buys only from countries that use the devices or fish in waters where turtles are not usually found. Most experts consider the ruling as a sign that when free trade conflicts with environmental protection, the WTO is unlikely to favor environmental protection over trade.

Seals and Sea Lions

Most sea lions and seals (Figure 4.11) live in the Gulf of Alaska and near the Aleutian Islands. Some breed and bear young as far south as California and then migrate north and westward twice a year to cooler waters, where fish are more plentiful. They are carnivorous, feeding on fish in deep waters and swimming great distances, 11,000 miles for females and 13,000 miles for males. Sea lions

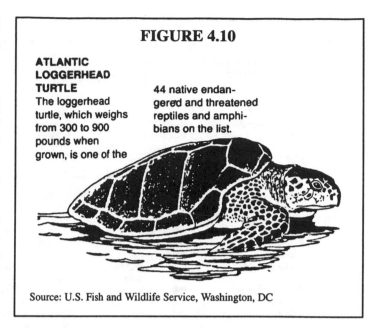

FIGURE 4.10

ATLANTIC LOGGERHEAD TURTLE
The loggerhead turtle, which weighs from 300 to 900 pounds when grown, is one of the 44 native endangered and threatened reptiles and amphibians on the list.

Source: U.S. Fish and Wildlife Service, Washington, DC

and seals are highly sociable creatures, congregating together on the rocky beaches when they are not fishing for food. In the summer they breed and raise their young pups on secluded beaches called rookeries.

Sea lion and seal populations have declined greatly over the past 30 years. Although it is illegal, commercial fishermen often kill them. Nonetheless, scientists believe that food shortages are the greatest danger to sea lions and seals, with many fish species declining because of environmental changes and overfishing.

In 1995, salmon populations in the Northwest were dwindling so dramatically that some people recommended killing sea lions, which were blamed for eating the salmon. Others rejected the suggestion because they believed that salmon populations were dwindling even in areas where there were no sea lions. They blamed the loss of salmon on habitat loss and overfishing, not sea lions. Similarly, baby seals have been found slaughtered in Maine, a federal offense, presumably by fisherman or others who blame them for the loss of lobsters. Scientists found no lobster remains in the stomachs of the harbor seals and report that during the first half of the century, after bounties were placed on seals and their numbers were decimated, the fish stocks were unaffected.

TABLE 4.2

Family and species	Common name	Status*
Chelonidae	Sea turtles	
Caretta caretta	Loggerhead	Threatened
Chelonia mydas	Green sea turtle	Endangered or threatened according to population or geographic area
Eretmochelys imbricata	Hawksbill	Endangered
Lepidochelys kempii	Kemp's ridley	Endangered
L. olivacea	Olive ridley	Endangered or threatened according to population or geographic area
Chelydridae	Snapping turtles	
Macroclemys temminckii	Alligator snapping turtle	Unknown but vulnerable; C² candidate
Dermochelyidae	Leatherback sea turtles	
Dermochelys coriacea	Leatherback	Endangered
Emydidae	Semi-aquatic pond turtles	
Clemmys insculpta	Wood turtle	May become threatened if trade not brought under control
C. marmorata	Western pond turtle	Declining; C² candidate
C. muhlenbergi	Bog turtle	Unknown; are or may be threatened by international trade; C² candidate
Emydoidea blandingii	Blanding's turtle	Declining; C² candidate
Graptemys barbouri	Barbour's map turtle	Unknown; C² candidate
G. caglei	Cagle's map turtle	Unknown
G. flavimaculata	Yellow-blotched map turtle	Threatened, but insufficiently known; may be threatened by international trade
G. oculifera	Ringed map turtle	Threatened; restricted distribution
Malaclemys terrapin	Diamondback terrapin	Some populations unknown, others declining; C² candidate; listing applies to population or geographic area
Pseudemys alabamensis	Alabama red-bellied turtle	Endangered; restricted distribution
P. rubriventris	Red-bellied turtle	Endangered, according to population or geographic area
Kinosternidae	Mud and musk turtles	
Kinosternon flavescens	Yellow mud turtle	Unknown; C² candidate; listing applies to population or geographic area
K. hirtipes	Mexican rough-footed mud turtle	Unknown; C² candidate; listing applies to population or geographic area
Sternotherus depressus	Flattened musk turtle	Threatened
Testudinidae	Tortoises	
Gopherus agassizii	Desert tortoise	Some populations threatened, others are C² candidates; may become threatened if trade not brought under control. Status of Sonoran Desert population unknown
G. berlandieri	Texas tortoise	May become threatened if trade not brought under control. Receiving some conservation action
G. polyphemus	Gopher tortoise	Declining. Some populations threatened, others are C² candidates; may become threatened if trade not controlled. Receiving some conservation action
Trionychidae	Softshell turtles	
Apalone spinifera	Spiny softshell turtle	Are or may be affected by international trade

*C² — Possibly qualifying for threatened or endangered status, but more information is needed for determination.

Source: *Our Living Resources*, U.S. Department of the Interior/National Biological Service, Washington, DC, 1995

Large-scale commercial sealing is still a legitimate industry in the poor country of Namibia, where jobs are scarce, and sealing generates about $500,000 a year. Animal rights groups have protested the slaughter of baby seal pups. They are killed for their penises, which are sold as aphrodisiacs in the Far East, and for their skins, used for shoes, wallets, and accessories.

Fish

In 1991, the Nature Conservancy, a private organization dedicated to protecting endangered plants and animals, issued an "endangerment alert" for the nation's aquatic species. The Conservancy reported that fish and other marine animals that live in North American waterways were disappearing at a much faster rate than land-based animals.

In 1996, the *IUCN's Red List* study found that one-third of the continent's fish are now threatened with extinction.

While this section focuses on endangered fish, it is important to remember that pollution is killing many thousands of fish that are not yet endangered or threatened. Figure 4.12 shows the cyclical relationship of marine life, land, and the economy.

Similarly, more and more coastal waters of the United States have become too polluted for shellfish, such as oysters, clams, and lobsters. Since crustaceans take in water and filter it directly through their bodies, they absorb much of the pollution into their bodies.

Eating fish or shellfish that have lived in contaminated waters can be dangerous, even fatal. Increasingly, many states have posted warnings to recreational fishermen not to eat the fish caught in polluted areas (see above), and restaurant owners must be careful that their seafood comes from safe areas. Fish contamination is a greater risk to pregnant women, to children, and to people who eat higher than normal amounts of fish, such as Native American Indians and people who rely heavily on the fish they catch for food.

Fishermen can fish for shellfish in only about 58 percent of the nation's coastal waters. In the remaining 42 percent, the polluted waters make shellfish dangerous to eat. The situation is especially serious in the Gulf of Mexico and along the Pacific Coast. Almost no harvesting of shellfish is permitted in California, and only 35 percent of the fishing waters off Oregon are approved. In the Gulf of Mexico, only 20 percent of the waters off Alabama may be fished, and fishermen may harvest shellfish in only 32 percent of Florida and Mississippi waters. In 1996, many people on the East Coast became ill from eating contaminated crabs and clams. Shellfish were bringing such good prices that poachers were willing to fish in polluted waters, and many restaurants were unaware of the source of the harvests. In 1998, scientists warned against eating shellfish and shrimp from the Texas Gulf Coast because it carried disease-causing organisms.

Too Many Boats, Not Enough Fish

*Too much is taken from the sea
and too much is put into it.*
— United Nations marine scientist, 1998

FIGURE 4.12

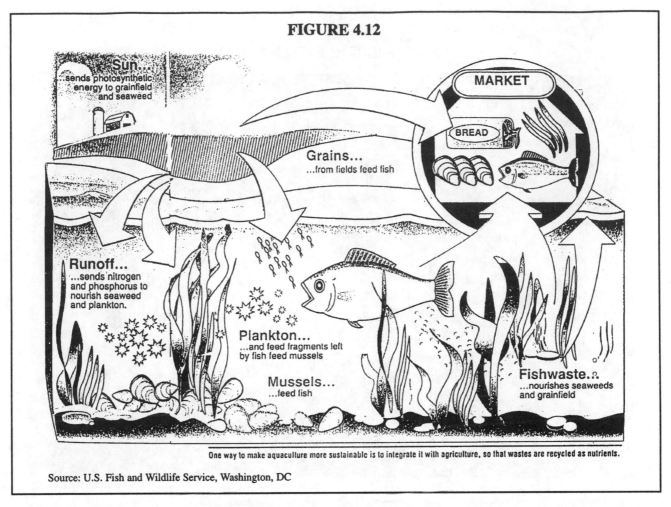

One way to make aquaculture more sustainable is to integrate it with agriculture, so that wastes are recycled as nutrients.

Source: U.S. Fish and Wildlife Service, Washington, DC

Worldwide, humans get 16 percent of their animal protein from fish, although people in developing countries generally rely on fish for a much larger share of their animal protein than people in industrial countries do. People in some countries count on fish for one-half of their animal protein need. As the human population has exploded, the fishing industry has tried to keep up with the demand, growing more than 50 percent in one generation.

The oceans, however, may have reached the limit of what they can produce. A leading cause of overfishing is the fact that world fishing fleets are too large for the available resources. Generally, the harder fishers try, the more fish they will catch — to a certain point. Beyond that, they reach what is known as the maximum sustainable yield. Anything over that is considered overfishing.

U.S. officials thought they could avoid becoming part of a global trend of overfishing when they passed the Magnuson Act in 1976 (PL 94-265), which expanded the coastal economic zone claimed by the United States from 3 miles offshore to 200 miles, chasing away large foreign fishing fleets.

With foreign fishermen gone, however, American fishermen built up their fleets, buying huge, well-equipped vessels using low-interest loans backed by the federal government. Although, for several years, fishermen had record catches, today, catches have declined in most species of fish. "The problem of foreign overfishing has been replaced by an even more serious overfishing by the American fishing industry," claimed Valerie Christy, spokeswoman for the Marine Conservation Network, a coalition of environmental groups.

Government officials report that most of the major commercial fishing areas in this country outside Alaska are in trouble. According to the National Marine Fisheries Service (NMFS), about 40 percent of the nation's saltwater species have been overfished, meaning more fish have been taken than there are young fish to replace them.

Many experts blame the fishermen in New England, the Mid-Atlantic, and the Gulf of Mexico for taking more than the sea could give back. Technology has made fishing so sophisticated that major marine areas can be depleted in a short time. In addition, commercial fishing is regulated by eight regional councils dominated by the fishing industry, which have been unable or unwilling to set limits for themselves. As a result, most fishing areas became free-for-alls with no concern for the future of the industry. Canada has shut down fishing, and in New England, the fishing industry is dying, with fishermen losing their boats and becoming unemployed.

International Overfishing

In 1994, the United Nations focused on the need for developing a comprehensive (multi-national) accord to conserve endangered fish species. "The most daunting challenge," declared Satya Nandan, conference chairman, "will be to persuade rival fishing countries to accept the notion that measures to conserve species like haddock, cod, swordfish, pollack, and tuna must be applied not only on the high seas but also in coastal waters where nations have the right to regulate fishing within 200 miles of their shores." However, in 1997, the United Nations Food and Agriculture Organization (FAO) reported that 11 of the world's 15 most important fishing areas and 60 percent of the major fish species were in decline.

World fish catches increased from 21 million tons to about 93 million tons from 1950 to 1996, although it has leveled off at a plateau of about 90 million. Most experts believe the catch will not rise any further and has reached its maximum sustainable level. Aquaculture is expected to increase to satisfy the demand for fish (see below).

Many of the 70 coastal countries at the talks claimed that the long-range fleets of Japan, Korea, Poland, and China abused their freedom to fish in international waters using methods that hauled in excessive numbers of fish.

Although many of the world's commercial fish supplies are approaching a population collapse, a 1995 study at the Dalhousie University in Halifax, Nova Scotia, reported that fish can recover under the right circumstances. The blue pike in Lake Erie became extinct, and the study predicted that extinction could occur with cod, herring, turbot, sturgeon, haddock, and salmon. Dr. Jeffrey Hutchings, co-author of the study, reported that 125 of the commercial species could bounce back if catches were reduced and the fish were given the chance to reproduce. Dr. Hutchings found that cod populations plummeted because of overfishing off Norway in the 1980s. The country put strict limits on the catches, and now cod has recovered enough to support a reduced level of harvesting.

A Caviar Crisis

With the collapse of the Soviet Union and a loss of state control over sturgeon quotas in the Caspian Sea, illegal fishing has caused the sturgeon population to plunge from 200 million to fewer than 60 million. The result is a crisis in the caviar industry and a booming black market for caviar. Poachers often bypass pasteurization, producing a lower quality, less safe product for an exorbitant price.

In addition to indiscriminate fishing, pollution from petrochemical plants and oil and raw sewage have depleted stocks. Another concern has been a rise in the level of the Caspian Sea — three feet in the last decade, which has submerged sturgeon hatcheries. Silt now almost blocks the sturgeon from reaching their spawning grounds. The construction of hydroelectric dams has also damaged breeding grounds on Russia's Volga River.

Cichlids

All that remains of some species of cichlids, an ancient species of fish, are in the Boston New England Aquarium. Cichlids were a huge family of fish that developed over a period of 750,000 years. Some of them are known as colorful aquarium fish found in pet stores, such as the Jack Dempsey, the oscar, or the discus. Some believe that one species, known as Saint Peter's fish, was the fish that Jesus fed to the multitudes. While some of the species are common, many of their less well-known cousins are facing extinction.

The loss of cichlids is an example of how human interference with nature can destroy entire species. In the 1960s, human beings introduced Nile perch, another type of fish, into African lakes because it grew larger than the fish native to the lakes and could be more easily caught with nets. The aggressive, larger perch ate the cichlid young and competed with them for food. When the algae-eating cichlids were gone, algae grew out of control, rotting and using up oxygen in the lakes. The remaining fish suffocated, and the lakes began to "die."

In 1997, scientists discovered another human-induced ecological change that was affecting cichlids. In murky water found in many polluted lakes, female cichlids are unable to distinguish between the colors of males and breed indiscriminately with males of different species. The result is that the fish are losing their bright colors and becoming one of several drab shades.

Salmon

Ironically, as we work to save the salmon, it may well turn out that the salmon save us.
— Paul Schell, Mayor of Seattle, Washington, 1998

Declining populations of certain salmon species, especially on the Columbia and Snake Rivers in the northwestern United States, led the National Marine Fisheries Service (NMFS) to list some species of salmon as endangered and others as threatened. Nine out of 10 major species of salmon, including coho, sockeye, chinook, and steelhead, are at risk of extinction.

The normal salmon life cycle includes hatching at an upstream location within a river basin, migrating to the sea, and eventually returning as adults to the hatching location to spawn and die. Salmon are of significant economic and social importance to the Pacific Northwest region for commercial food harvest and for sport fishing. The salmon are also important to various Native American tribes of the region for sustenance and for economic, religious, and cultural reasons.

During the 1800s, the annual salmon runs were estimated to be 10 to 16 million salmon. Since that time, total salmon runs have declined to an estimated 2.5 million annually. While experts believe that the decline before 1930 was due to overfishing, since that time the loss is thought to be due to construction of dams in the Columbia River Basin and to water pollution. As of 1992, the NMFS began designating habitat critical to the species and developing recovery plans. In 1994, in an effort to increase the numbers of salmon, the Pacific Fisheries Management Council issued its strictest regulations limiting catches of salmon both commercially and for sport.

In 1998, federal officials announced that Pacific salmon are nearly extinct and declared its runs endangered or threatened under the Endangered Species Act. The listing came after nearly 10 years of studying the signature fish of the Pacific Northwest. It marked the first time that vast urban areas could have land and water use restricted under the Endangered Species Act. Never before has so much land or so many people been given notice that they will have to alter their lives to restore a wild species. Unlike 10 years ago, however, when the listing of the Northern spotted owl threw the timber industry into revolt, this time industries said they will largely go along with efforts to save the salmon.

Officials have known for years that salmon stocks were in precarious shape. In Sacramento, California, winter chinook fell from an average of 86,500 fish a year in the 1960s to 830 in 1998. In the Puget Sound area, 22 of the 25 known chinook salmon runs are in rapid decline. The proposal gave California, Oregon, and Washington about a year until the fish are formally protected in order to consider their options, at which point the federal government could take any steps necessary to protect rivers where salmon spawn. The states and counties have already begun to prepare conservation plans to present to the government. State and federal money would be used to buy out property critical for salmon.

From Driftnets to Long-Lines

Until recently, large-scale driftnets, the world's largest fishing nets, were used on the high seas. This fishing technology, developed in the late 1970s, used nets up to 30 miles long. Floating like curtains on the surface of an open ocean, they were termed "walls of death" by conservationists because they indiscriminately caught and killed almost all creatures snared in their mesh. Over 100 wildlife species — whales, sea turtles, dolphins, seabirds, salmon, shark, and numerous other fish species — were killed in driftnets.

Driftnets have been banned because of their destructiveness to marine life, and, in their place, some fishers now use "long-lines." Long-line fishing lays out a fishing line from the stern of a boat. Attached to the main line are many shorter branch lines terminating in hooks baited with chunks of fish or squid. To catch wide-ranging oceanic species like tuna, swordfish, and sharks, the main line is suspended from a series of floats. A single boat can immerse thousands of hooks from lines stretching 20 to 80 miles. When the target is bottom species, such as cod and halibut, the end of the main line is anchored to the ocean bottom.

Long-line fishing kills fewer marine mammals than driftnets do, but captures more surface-feeding sea birds, especially the rare wandering albatross. Long-lining is an old practice, but modern technology has vastly increased its efficiency and ecological impact, causing decline in the numbers of fish. Experts report that the long-line fleet is growing and now numbers several thousand vessels. Australian scientists estimate that more than 40,000 albatrosses are killed by long-line fishing each year.

Deep Sea Harvesting

After centuries of steady growth, the total worldwide catch of wild fish has leveled off. Fishers are so efficient that they can wipe out entire populations of fish and then move on to different species or to a fishing area in some other part of the world. Typically, after depleting the larger fish, fishers will then haul in species at a younger age and smaller size. Targeting young fish undermines future breeding populations and guarantees a smaller biological return in the coming years. Swordfish, for example, are seriously depleted. So many swordfish are being caught now that many do not grow to full size. In the early part of the century, the average weight of a swordfish when caught was around 300 pounds. By 1960, it was 266 pounds, and today it is 90 pounds.

Furthermore, as a result of the declining catches of fish in shallow fisheries, trawlers are now scouring the deep seas for other varieties of fish, such as the 9-inch long royal red shrimp, rattails, skates, squid, red crabs, orange roughy, oreos, hoki, blue ling, southern blue whiting, and spiny dogfish.

Although limited commercial fishing of the deep has been practiced for decades, new sciences and technologies are making it more practical and efficient. As stocks of better-known fish shrink and international quotas tighten, experts say the deep ocean waters will increasingly be targeted as a source of seafood. Scientists worry the rush for deep-sea food will upset the ecology of the ocean.

Coral Reef Damage from Cyanide Fishing

Coral reefs are the largest living structures on Earth. Biologically, their richness compares with that of the tropical rain forests. It has long been a popular Chinese custom to keep fish alive until moments before cooking, a custom spurred recently by increasing numbers of newly rich in Southeast

Asia and elsewhere. To supply such demands, fishing for live fish in coral reefs has increased.

Fishermen catch such fish by squirting them with sodium cyanide, which stuns and incapacitates the fish. This allows fishermen to select individual fish and to take more fish in a shorter time. Cyanide, the same poison used to execute criminals, is believed not to be toxic in the dose commonly used for fishing. However, scientists have determined that the dose is more than enough to kill sensitive coral reefs, and scientists report that fishing with cyanide has become so widespread that it is destroying broad expanses of reef ecosystems.

Fishing for live reef fish now encompasses an area almost equivalent to a quarter of Earth's circumference — from the Maldives in the Indian Ocean to the Solomon Islands and Australia in the Pacific — containing the biologically richest one-third of the world's coral reefs. Killing coral reefs has the same effect on fish populations as clear-cutting forests has on forest animals — it destroys their habitat, and they disappear. Loss of coral reefs is greatest in Indonesia and the Philippines. Although it is generally illegal to use poison to fish, many governments have been unable or unwilling to enforce the laws.

The Growth of Aquaculture — The Blue Revolution

As levels of wild catches of fish have leveled off, aquaculture (fish farming) has more than tripled from 7 million tons in 1984 (the first year statistics were compiled by the United Nations Food and Agriculture Organization (FAO) to 26 million tons in 1996. This accounts for one-fifth of fish supplies worldwide although the proportion is growing. For some species, farming already accounts for a larger share of the supply. For example, nearly 40 percent of salmon are farm-grown.

Freshwater Mussels

The United States has the greatest diversity of freshwater mussels in the world; the Southeast

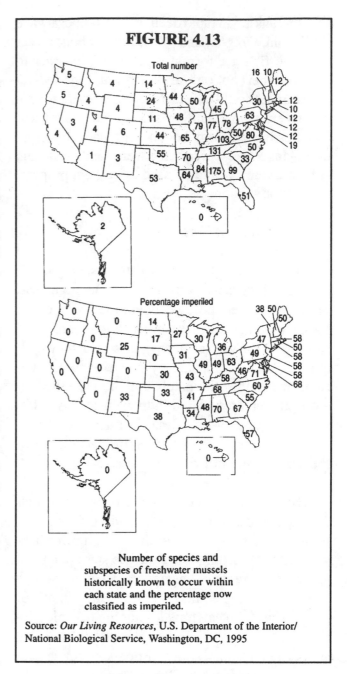

FIGURE 4.13

Number of species and subspecies of freshwater mussels historically known to occur within each state and the percentage now classified as imperiled.

Source: *Our Living Resources*, U.S. Department of the Interior/ National Biological Service, Washington, DC, 1995

alone is unmatched by any other area in the world. Mussels were an important natural resource for the Native Americans, who used them for food, tools, and jewelry. Until the advent of plastic buttons in 1940s, mussel shells were used to manufacture pearl buttons. Today the commercial harvest of mussel shells is exported to Asia for the production of spherical beads that are inserted into oysters and other shellfish to produce pearls. Japanese demand for the high-quality U.S. mussel shells has increasingly pushed prices and exports up.

TABLE 4.3

Estimates of Total Incidental Dolphin Mortality for U.S. and Foreign Purse Seine Vessels in the Eastern Tropical Pacific Ocean, 1971-1995

Year	U.S. Vessels[1]	U.S. Kill[2]	Foreign Vessels[1]	Foreign Kill[3]	Total Kill[4]
1971	124	246,213	48	15,715	261,928
1972	127	368,600	58	55,078	423,678
1973	133	206,697	68	58,276	264,973
1974	135	147,437	77	27,245	174,682
1975	142	166,645	82	27,812	194,457
1976	155	108,740	94	19,482	128,222
1977	142	25,452	104	25,901	51,353
1978	101	19,366	121	11,147	30,513
1979	93	17,938	121	3,488	21,426
1980	89	15,305	132	16,665	31,970
1981	94	7,890	118	7,199	35,089
1982	89	23,267	97	5,837	29,104
1983	60	8,513	99	4,980	13,493
1984	34	17,732	91	22,980	40,712
1985	36	19,205	105	39,642	58,847
1986	34	20,692	101	112,482	133,174
1987	34	13,992	126	85,195	99,187
1988	37	19,712	95	59,215	78,927
1989	29	12,643	93	84,336	96,979
1990	29	5,083	94	47,448	52,531
1991	13	1,004	90	26,288	27,292
1992	7	431	90	15,108	15,539
1993	7	115	89	3,486	3,601
1994	7	106	75	3,989	4,095
1995	5	0	99	3,274	3,274
1996	6	0	88	2,547	2,547

[1]Data from Inter-American Tropical Tuna Commission (IATTC).
[2]Data from National Marine Fisheries Service (NMFS).
[3]Derived by subtracting U.S. data from IATTC total mortality estimates of sets made on dolphin during the period.
[4]Data for 1971-78 from NMFS; data after 1978 from IATTC using MPS method.

Source: *Marine Mammal Protection Act of 1972, Annual Report*, U.S. Department of Commerce, Washington, 1997

Scientists believe that mussels are in the midst of a mass extinction. More species of the family of freshwater mollusks are being considered for protection under the Endangered Species Act than any other taxonomic family. The decline of freshwater mussels, which began as far back as the 1800s, has resulted from various habitat disturbances, especially the modification and destruction of aquatic habitats by dams and pollution. Dams, which alter the flow of rivers and reservoirs, have caused the loss of 30 to 60 percent of native mussels in U.S. rivers. Of the 297 native mussel species in the United States, 71.7 percent are endangered, threatened, or of special concern, including 21 species that are presumed extinct. Figure 4.13 shows the numbers of species of freshwater mussels and the percentage now classified as imperiled.

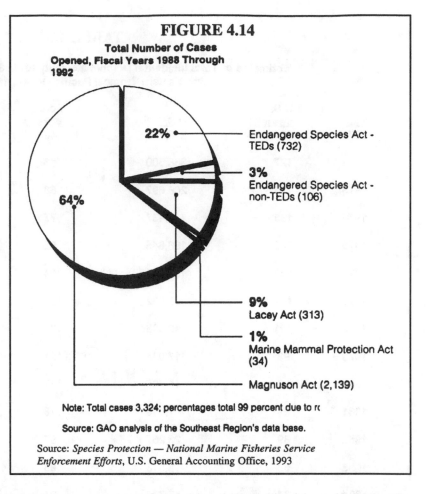

FIGURE 4.14

Total Number of Cases Opened, Fiscal Years 1988 Through 1992

- 22% — Endangered Species Act - TEDs (732)
- 3% Endangered Species Act - non-TEDs (106)
- 64%
- 9% Lacey Act (313)
- 1% Marine Mammal Protection Act (34)
- Magnuson Act (2,139)

Note: Total cases 3,324; percentages total 99 percent due to r...

Source: GAO analysis of the Southeast Region's data base.

Source: *Species Protection — National Marine Fisheries Service Enforcement Efforts*, U.S. General Accounting Office, 1993

Scientists believe that the demise in both species and numbers of mussels is also likely occurring in other freshwater mollusks, especially snails, and aquatic organisms, but too few studies have been conducted to record such trends. The waning of the mussels, scientists fear, is a sign of serious problems in the whole freshwater aquatic ecosystem of the region.

Dolphins, Sharks, Alligators, and Whales

Dolphins, sharks, alligators, and whales are endangered not only because of a loss of habitat and chemical poisoning, but primarily because of their economic value to humans for medicinal, religious, fashion, and dietary uses. (See Chapter VII, Trade in Wild Animals.)

Furthermore, species depleted over centuries of commercial whaling are now threatened by entanglement in fishing gear and other marine debris, collisions with ships, and inbreeding with others of the small population. Table 4.3 shows esti-

mates of dolphins killed "incidentally" (in the course of fishing for other species, commercial fishermen that interact with marine mammals must report the circumstances of those interactions to NMFS within 48 hours if the interaction resulted in an injury or mortality) from 1971 to 1995 in the Eastern tropical Pacific Ocean. The sharp decline in the number of animals killed is accountable to the introduction of fishing methods protecting the dolphin.

The world population of Blue whales is probably fewer than 10,000. There are probably no more than 3,000 Right whales. DNA (deoxyribonucleic acid) analysis of Northern right whales have shown little genetic variation within the species. Mating between genetically similar individuals may result in fewer viable offspring.

Despite measures to protect it, the North Atlantic Right whale, once the "right" whale to hunt for blubber and the first whale species to be commercially hunted, has failed to thrive. In the last

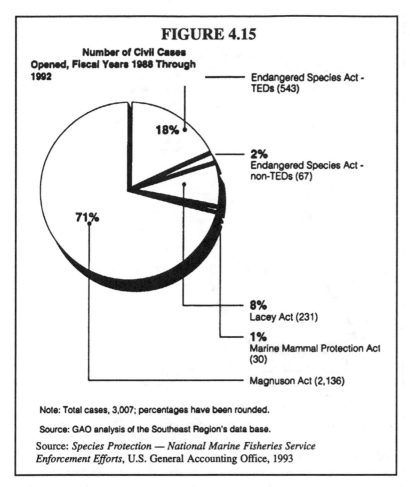

FIGURE 4.15

Number of Civil Cases Opened, Fiscal Years 1988 Through 1992

- Endangered Species Act - TEDs (543) — 18%
- Endangered Species Act - non-TEDs (67) — 2%
- Lacey Act (231) — 8%
- Marine Mammal Protection Act (30) — 1%
- Magnuson Act (2,136) — 71%

Note: Total cases, 3,007; percentages have been rounded.

Source: GAO analysis of the Southeast Region's data base.

Source: *Species Protection — National Marine Fisheries Service Enforcement Efforts*, U.S. General Accounting Office, 1993

Harbor seals, once plentiful along the Connecticut coast and throughout New England until the 1940s, virtually disappeared because of aggressive hunting. The seals, however, rebounded under the Marine Mammal Protection Act of 1972 (PL 92-522). In 1993, an aerial survey of the Gulf of Maine spotted about 28,000 harbor seals, compared with about 4,600 in 1973.

Many sea animals are killed in ways few people would normally consider. For example, in 1997, 42 dolphins, three whales, and schools of sardines died in the Gulf of California as a result of a chemical dropped by drug traffickers. A cyanide-based chemical, NK-19, was used by traffickers to mark drop-off sites.

ENFORCEMENT OF LAWS PROTECTING AQUATIC SPECIES

The Lacey Act

The Lacey Act (31 Stat 187, as amended by PL 97-79, PL 98-327, and PL 100-653) makes it illegal to import, possess, or transport fish and wildlife taken or exported in violation of state, federal, Indian, or foreign laws. Examples of violations include the interstate transportation of shellfish illegally harvested from closed areas or the interstate shipment of lobster in unmarked containers. (See also Chapter VII, Trade in Wild Animals.)

The Magnuson Act

The Magnuson Fishery Conservation and Management Act of 1976 (PL 94-265) established a system for designating and administering fishery management plans to regulate fisheries within U.S. waters. Examples of violations include fishing without a permit, possessing out-of-season fish, or retaining undersized fish.

couple of years there has been a record number of deaths. Scientists speculate the causes of the deaths are ship collisions, entanglement in fishing gear, and habitat decline in feeding areas. Ships from large commercial ports in Georgia and Florida, in addition to Navy installations at Mayport, Florida, and Kings' Bay in Georgia, criss-cross the whales' calving ground.

Only 320 of the giant whales, the most endangered of the great whales, are known to live in the North Atlantic. The National Marine Fisheries Service declared an area off the Georgia and north Florida coast as a critical Right-whale habitat (see Chapter IX). Preliminary research shows that the whale's huge storehouse of fat stores an array of toxic substances, possibly affecting the whales' health. "This is the only whale species we might lose in our lifetimes," reported Dr. Scott Kraus, chief scientist at the New England Aquarium in Boston.

The Marine Mammal Protection Act

The Marine Mammal Protection Act (MMPA; PL 92-522), passed in 1972, recognized the need to protect all marine mammal species, many of which were in danger of extinction or depletion as a result of human activities. Under the MMPA, the National Marine Fisheries Service (NMFS) manages all cetaceans (whales and dolphins) and all pinnipeds (marine carnivores with flippers, such as sea lions) except walruses. The NMFS relies on the U.S. Coast Guard and other federal and state agencies to assist in detecting and documenting alleged violations. The U.S. Fish and Wildlife Service (FWS) manages polar bears, walruses, sea otters, manatees, and dugongs.

The MMPA's primary power is to prohibit the taking (hunting, killing, capturing, and harassing) of marine mammals. The act also bars the importation of most marine mammals or their products. Exceptions are occasionally granted for scientific research, public display in aquariums, subsistence (food for Alaskan natives), and some incidental takings during commercial fishing operations. The goal of the MMPA is to maintain marine populations at or above "optimum sustainable population."

A Congressional Study of Violators

A 1993 Congressional study of federal enforcement efforts and penalties being assessed to enforce federal legislation focused on the four primary laws dealing with water species — the Endangered Species Act (ESA) turtle-extruder device (TED; see also Chapter VII) regulations, the Magnuson Act, the Lacey Act, and the Marine Mammal Protection Act (MMPA). The study found that 64 percent of the cases arose from the Magnuson Act, 22 percent from the ESA's TED

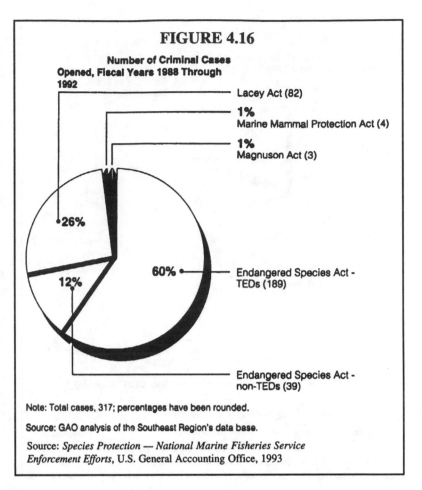

FIGURE 4.16

Number of Criminal Cases Opened, Fiscal Years 1988 Through 1992

Lacey Act (82)

1% Marine Mammal Protection Act (4)

1% Magnuson Act (3)

26%

60% Endangered Species Act - TEDs (189)

12%

Endangered Species Act - non-TEDs (39)

Note: Total cases, 317; percentages have been rounded.

Source: GAO analysis of the Southeast Region's data base.

Source: *Species Protection — National Marine Fisheries Service Enforcement Efforts*, U.S. General Accounting Office, 1993

regulations, 9 percent from the Lacey Act, and 1 percent from the MMPA (Figure 4.14). (Another 3 percent resulted from other provisions of the ESA; see Chapter IX.)

Both civil and criminal charges were assessed against violators of the four laws. Penalties included written warnings, fines, and, in some cases, jail time. The average fine was $2,560. The highest fines were those incurred for Lacey Act violations. Of the civil violations (90 percent of total cases), 71 percent involved Magnuson violations, 18 percent were for ESA TED violations, 8 percent involved Lacey crimes, and the remaining 3 percent involved MMPA and other ESA violations (Figure 4.15). Of the total criminal cases, 60 percent were for failure to use a TED; 26 percent were for Lacey violations, such as the illegal transport of fish across state lines for resale; 12 percent were for other ESA regulations; and 1 percent each were for MMPA and Magnuson violations (Figure 4.16).

CHAPTER V

THE STATUS OF BIRD SPECIES

The coast is a damp sort of place where all sorts of birds fly about uncooked.
— A London sportsman

Sometimes a person hears the phrase "dead as a dodo" because the dodo bird vanished from Earth many years ago. Other times the phrase is "dumb as a dodo" because the bird, which could not fly, appeared to be a comical-looking creature about the size of a turkey. It was apparently ill-suited for walking; old writings describe how it would waddle about, appearing to stumble at times. Extinct since about 1690, the dodo thrived by the many thousands on the islands of Mauritius and Reunion in the Indian Ocean. Zoologists (scientists who study animal life) believe that the settlers to the islands brought in their foreign animals, specifically hogs, that ate the eggs and young of the dodos which nested on the ground. (See Figure 5.1.)

A distant cousin of the dodo, the passenger pigeon was once considered an endless resource in North America. Flocks of passenger pigeons, which nested in huge colonies, once filled the skies by the millions, blocking out the sun. Mercilessly hunted in the nineteenth century, by the turn of the century, the flocks were gone. The last of the species, a bird hatched in captivity, died in the Cincinnati, Ohio, zoo in 1914. (See Figure 5.2.)

Birds were the first animals comprehensively surveyed for their status. BirdLife International, a Cambridge, England-based organization, charts avian habitat and species loss. In 1996, the organization reported that, of the nearly 10,000 species of birds, two out of every three species are in decline worldwide. About 11 percent of all birds are threatened with extinction, and 4 percent — some

FIGURE 5.1

Dodo. *A sketch from Lewis Carroll's Alice in Wonderland.*

Source: Animal Welfare Institute, Washington, DC

403 species — are endangered or critically endangered.

The endangered birds include the California condor, the Bald eagle, the Peregrine falcon, the whooping crane, some woodpeckers, the bobwhite quail, the wood stork, and a few varieties of songbirds.

Since 1600, some 121 bird species have become extinct. The rate of extinctions increases with almost every 50-year period. (See Figure 5.3 for the increasing number of birds that are becoming extinct.) Island species are more vulnerable than mainland species because they occupy limited habitats and because many are, or were, flightless, making it difficult to flee from hunters or adapt to changes in their environment. Until recently, about 75 percent of bird extinctions occurred on islands.

In the nineteenth century, egrets, herons, spoonbills, and songbirds were slaughtered by the thousands to supply feathered plumes for women's hats. The sale of most native bird feathers for fashion went out of vogue until the late 1970s when craft articles adorned with bird feathers began to appear in stores. Other birds are shot for sale to gourmet restaurants. Some hunters kill protected birds in one state and carry them across state lines for sale in another state. There is a growing gourmet market for pheasant, quail, and other game birds.

People's fondness for exotic pets is emptying the skies and trees of some of Earth's most colorful and musical creatures. (See Chapter VII, Trade in Wild Animals.) Hunting for food and for sport accounts for the loss of many other birds. Diseases and ingestion of pesticides and chemicals claim yet others. Nonetheless, the majority of birds are dying because changes in climate and environment have destroyed many of their natural habitats. The phenomenon of disappearing birds is alarming beyond the direct losses of those species — they are indicators of the health of other species and whole ecosystems.

Salton Sea Deaths

The Salton Sea, located 150 miles southeast of Los Angeles, has for the past few years been the scene of successive epidemics and unknown ail-

FIGURE 5.2

The *Passenger Pigeon.*

Drawing from *The Doomsday Book of Animals*

ments among birds and fish. The Salton Sea is second only to the Texas coastline in the number of bird species sighted, 380 at last count. In recent years, shortly after the annual migrations began, birds have been washing ashore, dying from epidemics of avian botulism, Newcastle disease, avian cholera, and poisoning by toxic algae.

Although scientists are uncertain about the link between water quality and bird deaths, they suspect several contaminants are involved, both natural and man-made. Of primary concern is that the Salton Sea is getting increasingly salty. Evaporation and agricultural runoff have made the sea's formerly fresh water 25 percent saltier than the Pacific Ocean. Experts believe that too much salt makes fish susceptible to diseases which pass on to birds that feed on them. Agricultural runoff from the Imperial Valley, one of the most productive farmlands in the country, helps fuel algae blooms that are deadly to fish. The California State legislature is currently considering legislation intended to restore the Salton Sea's health.

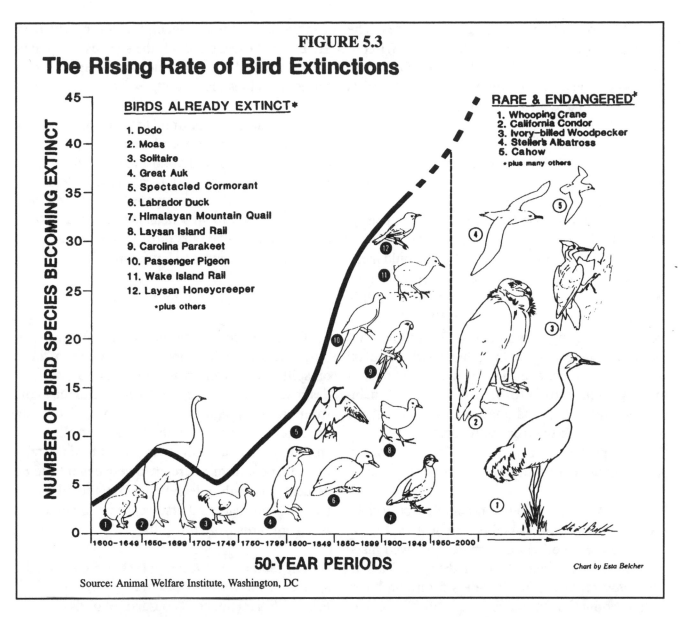

FIGURE 5.3
The Rising Rate of Bird Extinctions

BIRDS ALREADY EXTINCT*

1. Dodo
2. Moas
3. Solitaire
4. Great Auk
5. Spectacled Cormorant
6. Labrador Duck
7. Himalayan Mountain Quail
8. Laysan Island Rail
9. Carolina Parakeet
10. Passenger Pigeon
11. Wake Island Rail
12. Laysan Honeycreeper

*plus others

RARE & ENDANGERED*

1. Whooping Crane
2. California Condor
3. Ivory-billed Woodpecker
4. Steller's Albatross
5. Cahow

* plus many others

NUMBER OF BIRD SPECIES BECOMING EXTINCT

1600-1649 | 1650-1699 | 1700-1749 | 1750-1799 | 1800-1849 | 1850-1899 | 1900-1949 | 1950-2000

50-YEAR PERIODS

Chart by Esta Belcher

Source: Animal Welfare Institute, Washington, DC

WHAT ARE THE MAJOR THREATS TO BIRDS?

Lead Shot

Lead shot is a serious problem for wildlife, including birds. Lead is the preferred ammunition of bird hunters. Spent lead from missed shots at waterfowl remains on marsh and river bottoms. Ducks and other birds inadvertently consume this spent lead shot. While a single #6 lead shot pellet can kill a duck, many waterfowl are killed gradually by lead accumulations. Other species, including humans, may also suffer from lead in waterways.

Wildlife managers have been aware of the lead shot problem since the 1940s. However, it was not until 1976 that the Department of the Interior mandated steel shot in many areas, and by 1993, lead shot was banned throughout the nation for hunting waterfowl. Nonetheless, the use of lead shot for other forms of hunting continues to kill animals that feed on carcasses, such as the California Condors (see below).

Cats As Predators

Studies in the United States and Britain confirm that house cats kill millions of small birds and mammals every year, a death toll that may be contributing to declines in some rare species. The University of Wisconsin reported that in Wisconsin alone, cats killed 19 million songbirds and 140,000 game birds in a single year. The scientists believe cats have also contributed to the declines in grassland birds.

Researchers think that domestic cats do so much damage because there are so many of them — more than 35,000 are born every day. Americans keep an estimated 60 million cats as pets. If each cat kills only one bird a year, and experts believe they kill far more than that, that would mean they kill over 60 million birds each year — more than any oil spill. In fact, U.S. Fish and Wildlife Service studies show cats kill hundreds of millions of migratory songbirds annually. This problem has wildlife managers scratching their heads. "Federal and state wildlife agencies spend a great deal of money on incentives for farmers to provide habitat for wildlife, but that may be a waste of money if the habitat is overrun with cats," said Stanley Temple, professor of wildlife ecology and conservation at the University of Wisconsin, Madison.

The Wisconsin study, and another performed in Britain, found that whether a cat was well-fed at home, wore a bell collar, or was declawed made no difference in whether it hunted or not. The British study reported that Britain's 5 million house cats account for an annual prey toll of some 70 million animals, 20 million of which are birds. The study found that cats were responsible for a third to a half of all the sparrow deaths in England.

Accidental Poisoning of Birds

Over the past 40 years, pesticides and other toxic chemicals have become a major cause of avian mortality. While the Environmental Protection Agency (EPA) regulates the manufacture and use of toxic chemicals, under the Federal Insecticide, Fungicide, and Rodenticide Act (Amended 1988; PL 100-532), the Fish and Wildlife Service is responsible for the prevention of and punishment for the misuse of chemicals against wildlife. Instances in which birds are killed by toxic substances are enforced under the Migratory Bird Treaty Act (40 Stat. 755). If the species are endangered and listed under the Endangered Species Act, further penalties may result.

Many chemicals harmful to birds, such as DDT and toxaphene, have been banned. Other chemicals, such as endrin, the most toxic of the chlorinated hydrocarbon pesticides, are still legal for some uses. Endrin was responsible for the disappearance of the Brown pelican in Louisiana — once a population of 50,000 birds. Many other legal substances are known to harm wildlife.

Oil Spills

Oil spills constitute another major threat to birds. In addition, detergents used to clean up those oil spills are now known to be deadly, as well, by destroying their feathers and causing them to die from chills or trauma. New methods of treating oiled birds and new methods of controlling oil spills have increased the numbers of birds surviving treatment from 5 percent to between 60 and 80 percent. Under the Clean Water Act, the oil industry pays a tax that reimburses any expense involved in saving birds from oil spills.

On March 24, 1989, the tanker *Exxon Valdez* spilled 11 million tons of crude oil into Alaska's Prince William Sound. Thousands of birds died and sank immediately. Exxon personnel burned untold piles of birds, and many others were saved in cold storage under orders of the Fish and Wildlife Service. Thousands of birds were never counted. Wildlife Service biologists estimate that between 250,000 and 400,000 sea birds were killed. Effects on populations of birds will take years to determine, but it is known that the entire population of common murres, estimated at 91,000, was eliminated, and the yellow-billed loons are seriously depleted.

The U.S. national symbol, the Bald eagle, was also hard hit by the oil spill. Many eagles fed on carcasses of dead birds and were poisoned; others were unable to reproduce when eggs in nests became oiled. Biologists estimate that half the sound's eagles — 1,500 birds — died.

Research shows that birds returned to nature after an oil spill, despite careful rehabilitation, typically die in a matter of months. In 1996, Dr. Daniel Anderson, a biologist at the University of California at Davis, found that only 12 to 15 percent of rehabilitated pelicans survived for two years, compared to 80 to 90 percent of pelicans that were not exposed to oil. To some ornithologists (scientists who study birds), such dismal results raise the question whether such avian rescue efforts are worthwhile. Could the money spent on rehabilitation be better used for spill prevention and habitat restoration instead? As Oregon ornithologist Dr. Brian Sharp concluded, "We're doing this cleaning, which is supposed to be a fix of some kind and allows the public and politicians to ease their conscience. But the birds aren't benefiting."

Oil Spills and Penguins

Oil spills have forced some penguins to hunt so far away from their rookeries (breeding places) that their chicks starve to death before the parents can swim back with food. Studies performed with radio satellites have tracked penguin adults 147 miles from their rookeries, trips that can take them more than three weeks. Oil pollution, which can also kill the parents, apparently can cause them to wander aimlessly.

Habitat Loss

Habitat loss takes away appropriate breeding and wintering grounds. The birds hardest hit by habitat loss are those with small ranges. Birds that have very specific and, often remote, locales are more susceptible to disturbances. No birds have been more decimated than those in Hawaii. Virtually all of Hawaii's original 90 bird species were found nowhere else in the world. Barely one-third remains today, and two-thirds of those are threatened with extinction. The degree of habitat destruction in Hawaii is so great that all Hawaiian low-

**FIGURE 5.4
BALD EAGLE**

Source: U.S. Fish and Wildlife Service, Emanna Verano

land songbirds are now nonnative species introduced by humans.

THE BALD EAGLE

Almost everyone recognizes the Bald eagle. Symbol of honor, courage, nobility, and independence (eagles do not fly in flocks), the Bald eagle is found only in North America. Its image is engraved on the official seal of the United States of America. (See Figure 5.4.)

The large bird, with dark body, smooth, white head, and huge, white-tipped wingspread, nests over most of the United States and Canada. The Bald eagle builds its nest in mature conifer forests (trees that make cones such as pine and other evergreens) or on the top of rocks or cliffs overlooking lakes or streams well stocked with fish. It builds nests so big that only large rocks or huge trees can hold them. It uses the same nest year after year, adding to it each nesting season until it may be the size of a small car. It is believed that eagles mate for life.

Enacted in 1940, the Bald Eagle Protection Act was intended to save the national symbol from extinction and made it a federal offense to kill Bald eagles. Many killings are deliberate or accidental shootings by private citizens flouting the law or ignorant of the identity of their targets. There is a black market for Bald eagle feathers. Native Americans are exempt from restrictions only for religious reasons, although that exception is sometimes abused. Many eagle feathers and trinkets are sold in European countries as well as in the United States, mostly for crafts and jewelry.

The Bald eagle came dangerously close to extinction from eating fish that had been poisoned with the pesticide DDT. The birds that did not die immediately after eating the fish either could not reproduce, or the shells of the eggs they laid were so thin they could not protect the eggs long enough for the babies to hatch. A generation ago, Bald eagles had almost disappeared from many states, and, 12 years ago, they were put on the endangered list.

Many people have become more aware of how important it is to keep water supplies for animals as clean as their own. In addition, they have learned how important it is to save tall trees near clean lakes and rivers for eagle nesting. Increased knowledge about certain pesticides and fertilizers has led to decisions to stop using some of the poisons that were polluting the lakes and streams and killing the fish. As a result, several species of eagles have recovered. In 1994, the Bald eagle was moved from endangered to threatened status. By 1997, Bald eagle populations — 500 breeding pairs — in the lower 48 states were 10 times higher than their lowest point in 1963, and Secretary of the Interior Bruce Babbitt proposed the removal of the Bald eagle from the Endangered Species List over the next two years.

GOOD NEWS ABOUT SONGBIRDS

There was a strange stillness. The birds, for example — where had they gone? Many people spoke of them, puzzled and disturbed. The feeding stations in the backyards were deserted. The few birds seen anywhere were moribund; they trembled violently and could not fly. It was a spring without voices.
— Rachel Carson, *Silent Spring*, 1962

Rachel Carson's book *Silent Spring* warned Americans that the use of pesticides threatened the existence of songbirds. During the 1980s, scientists observed a decline in the number of migratory birds. Many suburban homeowners and city-dwellers noticed that fewer and fewer birds were singing in their yards. Since the late 1970s, the number of flycatchers, orioles, tanagers, vireos, warblers, and other songbirds seemed to have declined. From 1978 to 1987, the National Academy of Sciences studied 56 songbird species and found noticeable decreases in 70 percent of the birds. Many people began to fear that Rachel Carson's prediction might be fulfilled.

Every year, more than 120 songbird species migrate between North America and the warm, tropical climates of Central and South America. Some of these songbirds are dying out because their homes in both places are being destroyed. In North America, real estate development is using up the forests in which songbirds once built their nests. People need homes and stores, and developers cannot worry about songbirds. To the south, in Central and South America, where the birds migrate during the cold winters of North America, farmers and ranchers burn and clear away tropical forests to plant crops and grow pasture land for livestock. People of developing countries argue that they are too poor to feed their own people and cannot worry about protecting migrating songbirds.

While birds that migrate, like the songbirds, can adjust to habitat changes better than birds that stay in the same home the year round, the rate of deforestation has proceeded much too fast for some of them to adapt or find new habitats. The U.S. Forest Service reports that in some areas, such as those around Washington, DC, half the forests have been destroyed over the past 30 years. (For more information on deforestation, see Chapter III.)

As mentioned earlier, pesticides are a great danger to songbirds. Many birds have died from the effects of the deadly chemical DDT, and many more chemicals are used in fertilizers and pesticides that poison the birds.

Songbirds are important to human beings not only for their pleasant bird calls and their decorative colors, but also because they eat insects and help control those populations. Scientists predict that the decline of these birds could threaten the productivity of forests throughout their range. For example, during spring migration in the Ozarks, some 40 to 50 bird species arrive to eat the insects on oak leaves.

Tom Hinckley, professor of forestry at the University of Washington, said, "These birds enrich our environment, whether it's urban or rural, but it's sometimes difficult to put a value on them other than enrichment. Now here's a case where their value can perhaps be translated to a clear economic value." At a time when pesticides are often being found harmful to the environment, these creatures serve as an ecologically safe form of pest management. Some countries, such as Belize, Costa Rica, Guatemala, and Mexico, have set up safe habitats for songbirds, but improved forest management is needed to save them.

The 1997 *North American Breeding Bird Survey* — Surprising Results

For two decades, it has been conventional wisdom that songbirds are declining and headed for trouble. Now a new analysis of 30 years of data from the *North American Breeding Bird Survey* has found that, on the whole, the numbers of birds remain stable. The study, a continent-wide survey begun in 1966, has been maintained by the Biological Resource Division (BRD) of the United States Geological Service.

The study found that grassland birds are in serious decline. One species, the bobolink, has suffered a catastrophic decline of 90 percent. Many of the grasslands have been converted to croplands.

On the other hand, the numbers of forest songbirds are stable or growing. The large chunks of North American forest serve as sufficient breeding habitat.

The researchers believe the impression that the number of songbirds has been declining has occurred because most people are looking locally. The scientists reported that although catastrophic regional declines have been reported, nationwide, the population is generally stable. The birds have left developed areas for less developed areas. The scientists contend, therefore, that a major priority must be to preserve large-tract forests to make up for small-tract losses. Another priority is to maintain stop-over areas between North America and the tropics.

Similarly, since 1992, the Sutton Avian Research Center, in Bartlesville, Oklahoma, has been conducting a study, the nation's largest, on migratory grassland songbird species. The study includes observations of 5,000 nests and 4,500 banded birds, and the results are expected to be released in late 1998. Based on early results, Mark Howery, of the Oklahoma Department of Wildlife Conservation, concludes, "I don't believe all birds are going to become rare in the future. A good percentage of birds, maybe 30 percent, have a good potential of becoming rare within our children's lifetimes if current trends continue."

Songbirds on the Plates of Epicures

In France, the ortolan, a tiny songbird, is one of France's greatest delicacies. It has also been illegal to hunt, sell, or eat since 1979. The only exception to the law is in the Landes region, where the culinary tradition of eating ortolans is centuries old. The bird weighs just over an ounce and is caught and held in captivity 12 to 28 days before it is eaten — whole and in a single bite. Eating ortolans includes a ritual of covering the head and face with a napkin to intensify the aroma. Regardless of the law, thousands of Frenchmen, and even some Americans in the United States, eat ortolans privately.

The Golden-Cheeked Warbler and the Black-Capped Vireo

The tiny Golden-Cheeked Warbler and the Black-Capped Vireo, which nest in central Texas and winter in Mexico and Central America, are among the songbirds that are threatened. The major cause for the decline of both species has been the loss of habitat caused by clearing of land for development. The vireo went on the endangered species list in 1987, the warbler in 1990.

The Hill Country of central Texas forms a passageway between the temperate environments of the United States and Canada and the tropical environments of Mexico and Central America. It is characterized by diverse habitats that host a high concentration of rare bird species. Because their habitats lie near the Edwards Aquifer, protecting the species' environment also protects the watershed that feeds the underground water systems in the region. The Edwards Aquifer, located in south-central Texas, is also the source of many springs in the area. As the aquifer water level has dropped 30 feet due to increased use by metropolitan areas and the recent drought, bird species have suffered. The U.S. Fish and Wildlife Service estimates that this bird habitat has shrunk by at least 15 to 45 percent in the past decade.

The vireo is a summer resident of the brushy canyon of Big Bend National Park in Texas. It was first listed as endangered in 1987. Black-capped vireos also nest at scattered locations in central Oklahoma, central and western Texas, and northern Mexico.

Songbirds have many predators, species that capture, kill, and eat them or their eggs and young. Other predators destroy or take over their nests. For example, in certain areas, more than half the nests, especially of the vireos, are taken over by cowbirds during nesting season. The larger cowbirds lay their own eggs in the nests of the vireos and leave. Although the vireos will "baby sit" the cowbird young, soon the cowbird babies are larger

FIGURE 5.5

NORTHERN SPOTTED OWL

and more competitive than the vireos and kill or harm the baby vireos.

In an effort to balance development with wildlife preservation, the city of Austin, Texas, invited the Nature Conservancy to develop a plan to protect the environment while enabling building. The result is the Balcones Canyonlands Conservation Plan, a 75,000-acre preserve in the Texas Hill Country, which has been home to a number of endangered species.

The California Gnatcatcher

The California gnatcatcher is a small, gray and black songbird known for its "kitten-like" mewing call. Gnatcatchers are non-migratory, permanent residents of California coastal sage scrub, a plant community considered by many experts to be one of the most threatened vegetation types in the nation. Estimates of coastal scrub loss in the United States range from 70 to 90 percent of historic levels.

Fewer than 2,000 pairs of the birds are estimated to remain in the United States. The coastal California gnatcatcher has come to symbolize concern over protection of coastal sage scrub. Many environmentalists believe that protection of gnatcatchers would be an important major step toward conserving all components of this ecosystem.

Grassland Birds — The Shrikes

In 1993, scientists from 20 countries met at the first International Shrike Symposium in Boise, Idaho, to consider the plight of many grassland species, especially the shrike, a robin-sized predatory species, technically classified as a raptor (bird of prey). The once-common Loggerhead shrike was listed as extinct in Maine and Pennsylvania, endangered in 11 states, and threatened in two others. They are representative of many other birds that inhabit the grasslands from Canada south into Mexico.

The serious situation is similar for members of the 70 species in the shrike family around the world. As grasslands are being converted into urban areas, birds are losing their habitat. Some researchers believe fire ants, which kill insects and small animals, have depleted food supplies for the birds. Pesticides may also have killed off much of the insect base. Because shrikes are carnivorous, they may ingest poisons from their prey. Scientists have found that by adding fence posts for use as hunting perches, many more shrikes can survive.

THE NORTHERN SPOTTED OWL

The Northern spotted owl lives primarily in mature forests (200 years old or more). In the United States, this large, brown forest owl, with a wingspan of 43 inches, is most often found in California, Washington, and Oregon. One of the most nonthreatening creatures, the owl does not generally seem afraid of humans and appears curious about humans and human activity. (See Figure 5.5.)

Unlike most species protected by the Endangered Species Act, the owl covers a much larger

FIGURE 5.6

Drawing courtesy of Texas Parks and Wildlife Department

Red-cockaded Woodpeckers *have become endangered. Discovering the causes and evaluating the efforts to help them make a challenging project.*

Source: Animal Welfare Institute, Washington, DC

geographic range, from northern California to Washington State. Most of the private lands in this region have been heavily logged, leaving the Northern spotted owl with only public lands, such as national forests and parks, in which to survive. Logging was also permitted on some of those public lands, leaving the spotted owl fewer and fewer places to live.

In 1990, the U.S. Fish and Wildlife Service placed the Northern spotted owl on the list of threatened species and, in 1992, set aside 7 million protected acres — both private and public — as "critical habitat" for the bird. That kind of protection meant that some logging would have to be stopped, and that action caused considerable disagreement among politicians, environmentalists, loggers, and businessmen.

Loggers feared that many people would lose jobs and businessmen thought that their businesses would lose money if they could not harvest as many trees as they wished. Supporters of the ban on logging claimed that most logging jobs were already lost and that continued logging would preserve only existing jobs for a short time. This battle between economic development and species preservation on federal land in the Pacific Northwest resulted in lawsuits and an eventual compromise whereby logging is limited to trees under a certain size, leaving the mature growth for the owls' habitat. By early 1993, almost all old-growth logging on federal lands had been stopped by court action.

**FIGURE 5.7
PEREGRINE FALCON**

photo by William G. Mattox/Greenland Peregrine Falcon Survey

Source: U.S. Fish and Wildlife Service

RED-COCKADED WOODPECKER

The Red-cockaded woodpecker is a small bird named for the red patches (cockades) of feathers on the heads of the males. It is found in old pine forests in the southeastern United States, nesting in hollows that it digs within the pine trees. These cavities are the single most important resource for the species, serving both as nesting sites and as protection from predators. The woodpeckers rarely use trees less than 80 years old. (See Figure 5.6.)

Heavy logging of the forests has destroyed homes for the woodpeckers, and in 1970, they were put on the endangered list. These birds are "indicator species," which means that their decreased numbers are evidence that the forests they depend on are also in trouble. Like the Northern Spotted owl, the fate of these woodpeckers has led to debate between environmentalists, who want to preserve the forests and wildlife, and the logging industry, which wants to use "clear-cutting" logging techniques. The "clear-cutting" method of logging cuts down all the trees in an area. Some environmentalists prefer selective cutting of younger, smaller trees or "thinning" forests.

THE PEREGRINE FALCON

Falcons, the swiftest of all birds of prey, have been used in the sport of "falconry" for hunting and sport since medieval times. Like other birds of prey, they have often been shot, both because they were large targets and because they were suspected of killing chickens or livestock. Many naturalists argue that the Peregrine falcon is the most exciting of the raptors, with tremendous dives of more than 200 miles per hour. It is the preferred bird of falconers in Europe, North America, and other parts of the world. (See Figure 5.7.)

Peregrines have never been very abundant. Studies in the 1930s and 1940s estimated about 325 nesting pairs of falcons in the eastern United States. Beginning in the 1940s, the Peregrine falcon, like the Bald eagle, fell victim to the dangers of the pesticide DDT, which had seeped into waters and food chains, and was brought to the brink of extinction by that poison. The Peregrine falcon was one of the first species to be listed as endangered. In 1972, the federal government banned the use of DDT, and since that time, the falcon has begun to recover.

FIGURE 5.8

photo by W. Kubichek

WHOOPING CRANES

Source: U.S. Fish and Wildlife Service, Washington, DC

To strengthen their comeback, Peregrine falcon breeding centers have been established on several continents. By the end of the 1980s, 4,000 Peregrines had been released into the wild in 28 states, many of which survived. Although the Peregrine is found on every continent except Antarctica, its population has increased only in North America. South Texas' Big Bend National Park has been successful in restoring its falcon population by protecting nesting areas from disturbance during the breeding season.

In 1996, the U.S. Fish and Wildlife Service declared the Peregrine falcon "officially recovered" and began the process to remove the bird from the endangered species list. There are now about 1,200 breeding pairs of Peregrines in the lower 48 states, some nesting on skyscrapers rather than cliffs. New York City alone has 15 pairs.

87

Falconry

Falconry, the training of birds of prey to hunt on command, has been gaining popularity in recent years. The two species most coveted by falconers are the Peregrine falcon and the Gyrfalcon. Both are listed in Appendix I of CITES. CITES regulations do not prohibit capture but pertain only to international trade. The Peregrine is also on the U.S. Endangered Species List (ESL), although a request has been made to remove it.

In 1983, after years of pressure from falconers, the Endangered Species Act (ESA) was amended to allow purchase, barter, and sale of captive-bred raptors and, in 1989, trade in native raptors was reopened. The birds must be banded with U.S. Fish and Wildlife Service seamless bands distributed by permit from the government. Peregrine falcons can cost as much as $50,000 per bird.

When Birds and Humans Collide

The Federal Aviation Administration has estimated that the bill for damage to civilian and military aircraft from collisions with birds is more than $400 million a year in the United States alone. Aviation officials report that the Israeli Air Force has lost more planes to birds than to enemy fire. Worldwide, the problem is increasing as conservation efforts are helping to expand bird populations while commercial flights are also increasing.

A handful of airports around the world are today using falcons to reduce the chances of geese, gulls, and other birds colliding with planes. The presence of the raptors generally frightens other birds away. So far the falconry program seems to be working. At Kennedy International Airport, site of the largest falconry program, in 1996, the first year of the program, the number of birds striking aircraft while falcon flights were underway declined 61 percent. The Kennedy program includes six falconers and 13 birds of prey in rotating shifts. The Port Authority approved a $228,000 annual contract for the falconers.

FIGURE 5.9
CALIFORNIA CONDOR

Source: U.S. Fish and Wildlife Service, Washington, DC

THE GREAT WHITE WHOOPING CRANE

North America's tallest birds, whooping cranes are the rarest and most endangered of Earth's 15 crane species and are probably the best-known of the endangered species in the United States. They were once heavily hunted, and by the 1940s, only 15 birds were left. Today, because of concentrated conservation efforts, 369 survive, with 114 in captivity. They occupy wetland areas, returning to the same nesting site each year with the same mate. Both sexes share in the nurturing of their young. Each year, whooping cranes fly 2,500 miles from their nesting grounds in Canada to South Texas to spend the winter before returning north in March. (See Figure 5.8.)

THE CALIFORNIA CONDOR

California condors, whose wingspans exceed nine feet, are among the continent's most impressive birds (Figure 5.9). Ten thousand years ago, this species soared over most of North America. As large ice-age mammals became extinct, the California condor's major food supply diminished. Eventually the birds were found only along the Pacific coast, where they fed on beached whales and seals. Shooting, poisoning, and loss of habitat decimated the condor population, which reached a low point of 22 individuals in 1983.

Today there are 75 condors, 66 in captive breeding flocks and nine that have been released into the wild. The San Diego Zoo in California instituted a pioneer program to raise condors in captivity (Figure 5.10). Over recent years, twenty young California condors have been released into the wild in California and several in Arizona and the Grand Canyon, providing spectacular opportunities to view the largest bird in North America.

SOUTH AMERICAN FLAMINGOS

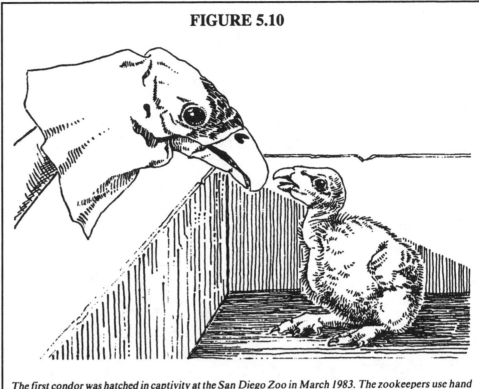

FIGURE 5.10

The first condor was hatched in captivity at the San Diego Zoo in March 1983. The zookeepers use hand puppets that look like adult condors to feed it.

Source: U.S. Fish and Wildlife Service, Washington, DC

In 1997, scientists from four South American countries — Peru, Bolivia, Chile, and Argentina — did a joint study of Andean flamingos. The team counted 47,600 flamingos, close to the 50,000 estimated in the 1970s. However, only eight nesting colonies were found. Because flamingos are long-lived (50 years or more) birds, they can appear to be doing fine, but without producing young, their populations are likely aging and will become seriously depleted when the old birds die.

For information on the commercial trade of birds, see Chapter VII.

CHAPTER VI

VANISHING LAND CREATURES —
MAMMALS, HERPETOFAUNA, INSECTS, AND PRIMATES

Some mammals (animals that produce milk to suckle their young) and insects are facing extinction from the loss of their habitat (natural homes). Endangered mammals include bears, deer, caribou, the Gray bat, the Black-footed ferret, and the Red and Gray wolf. (Other mammals, such as elephants and wild cats, which are threatened primarily because they are valuable to human beings for trade, are discussed in Chapter VII.)

FIGURE 6.1

photo by William S. Keller

grizzly bear

Vanishing insects include beetles and many varieties of butterflies. Some amphibians, animals that live equally well in water and on land, such as salamanders, frogs, and toads, are in trouble as their homes disappear, and they apparently seem unable to adapt to changes in the water and air.

LEVELS OF ENDANGERMENT

In 1996, the International Union for Conservation of Nature and Natural Resources (IUCN), based upon a review of mammal species (*1996 IUCN Red List of Threatened Animals*, Gland, Switzerland), reported that of 4,355 species surveyed, about 25 percent are likely to disappear if no intervention occurs. This means that mammals are substantially more threatened than birds (11 percent), according to IUCN criteria. An additional 14 percent of mammal species also come close to qualifying as threatened. Among major mammalian groups, primates (lemurs, monkeys, and apes) are most endangered, with nearly half of all primates threatened with extinction. Also under severe pressure are hoofed animals (deer, antelope, horses, rhinos, camels, and pigs), with 37 percent threatened.

Thirty-six percent of insectivores (shrews, hedgehogs, and moles) are threatened, as are 33 percent of marsupials (opossums, wallabies, and wombats). In slightly better shape are bats and carnivores (dogs, cats, weasels, bears, raccoons, and hyenas) at 26 percent each. At 17 percent, rodents are the least threatened mammalian group, but also the most diverse.

Reptiles and amphibians, known collectively by scientists as *herpetofauna,* are less well-known and studied less than many other species. Scientists have assessed only one-fifth of reptiles and barely one-eighth of amphibians. Among reptiles, turtles and crocodiles have been extensively studied, but most snakes and lizards remain unassessed, as do the two main orders of amphibians, frogs, and salamanders.

The herpetofauna that have been surveyed reveal a level of endangerment similar to that of mammals. Twenty percent of surveyed reptiles rank as endangered or vulnerable, while 25 percent of amphibians are endangered. Australia (62 species) has the highest number of documented threatened herpetofauna, followed by the United States with 52 species. These countries are not the most species-rich countries for these creatures. (Brazil leads in amphibians, and Mexico has the most reptiles.) Australia and the United States have, however, been more thoroughly surveyed.

The biggest cause of loss of mammals in the twentieth century is the same as for birds — habitat loss and degradation. As humans convert old-growth forests, grasslands, riverways, and wetlands for human uses, they relegate many species to precarious existences in fragmented, small habitat patches.*

The main reason primates are so threatened is that they are dependent on large expanses of tropical forests, a habitat under siege around the globe. In regions where tropical forest degradation and conversion have been most intense, such as South and East Asia, Madagascar, and Brazil, on average, 70 percent of the endemic primate species face extinction.

FIGURE 6.2

GREATER PANDA

WHO CARES ABOUT BEARS?

According to the U.S. Fish and Wildlife Service, bears have been eliminated from about 50 to 75 percent of their natural range, the areas where they roam freely. Of the seven species of bear, five are in decline — the Sun bear, the Sloth bear, the Spectacled bear, the Asiatic Black bear, and the brown or "Grizzly" bear, named after the grizzled appearance of its coat hairs (Figure 6.1). The American Black bear and the Polar bear are the only species not currently threatened.

---

*The intrusion of modern civilization has become a serious problem for wildlife photographers. This is particularly true for mammals. Many people who watch wildlife shows want to believe that lions and elephants are roaming about virgin forests or savannahs. This is often no longer the case. Therefore, many wildlife filmmakers are careful to film in such a way that telephone lines, homes and factories, or roads do not appear in their presentations. Others carefully edit their film to cut out any shots that reveal how much civilization now encroaches on the world's wildlife habitats.

What is happening to the bears? First, some people believe that bears, like the rhinoceros, have healing qualities. In Asia, many people believe that they can take on the characteristics and qualities of the animals they eat, and that certain animals and specific body parts of animals are necessary for healing specific ailments and illnesses. Some people believe that by eating certain parts of animals, they can delay the effects of natural aging. As a result, many bears are killed for the money that poachers (illegal hunters) can make from selling the bears' body parts. (For more information on animals endangered by trade, see Chapter VII.)

Bears were once hunted because they were considered predators, while other bears were hunted for sport. Some bears are being squeezed out of their habitat by human beings using the land for agriculture, highways, homes, railroads, and cities. As human civilization expands, less and less area is left for the bears. Such development forces bears into less suitable habitats where, in order to survive, they often become crop raiders and scavengers of garbage. When bears enter human territory for food, they are often killed as pests. When human beings and bears compete for the same area, food, and survival, the bears lose.

Bear habitat has been fragmented significantly in the past 200 years. Populations living in small habitat fragments are more vulnerable than those in undisturbed, intact ecosystems.

Female bears produce very few young in their lifetimes, and they protect their cubs fiercely. Because of their low reproductive rate, bears cannot reproduce fast enough to replace the numbers being destroyed by civilization. Without enough food, they cannot mate and reproduce. Many cubs die when their mothers are killed, and others are never born because the adults do not have enough space to live in and gather food, and therefore, cannot reproduce.

FIGURE 6.3

RED WOLF

THE GIANT PANDA — LOVED TO DEATH?

Few creatures have engendered more human affection than the Giant panda, with its roly-poly size, small black ears, and eye patches on its snow-white face (Figure 6.2). Although pandas look like bears, they actually are related to the raccoon family. Pandas have become stars among exhibit animals at zoos. Loans of the animals from China, their natural habitat, were commonplace in the 1980s. The birth of a panda in captivity has become a national event.

**FIGURE 6.4
GRAY WOLF**

Fish and Wildlife Service photo

However, the practice of lending pandas set off controversy, with experts fearing that the public's love of the creature could be contributing to its demise in the wild. In 1993, the American Association of Zoological Parks and Aquariums instituted a policy to restrict panda loans. The program requires that monies received are reinvested in panda research and preservation and that animal breeding is given priority over loans for exhibition. Although some progress has been made, fewer than 1,000 pandas survive in the wild, and fewer than 100 live in captivity.

THE WOLF

The wolf has an almost mythical heritage. Stories about the wolf, giving it a mysterious and mystical nature, have been told throughout history as far back as Romulus and Remus, the mythical founders of Rome, being raised by wolves. Western culture has demonized the species. Others have developed romantic impressions of the wolf from fiction, such as Jack London's novel *The Call of the Wild*. Superstition about men turning into wolves has been favorite material for television and movies.

Popular ideas about the wolf are usually based on fiction rather than fact. Some ranchers dislike the wolf because the wolf sometimes preys on cattle, sheep, and other livestock, although it prefers wild animals. However, no one has ever documented a fatal attack by a nonrabid wolf on a human in North America. The creatures are afraid of humans and flee them. Wolves do not howl at the moon. A wolf pack is a highly structured hierarchy with a dominant male and female, the alpha pair, at the top and close social bonding among the other members.

Wolves were once among the most widely distributed mammals on Earth. Prior to European

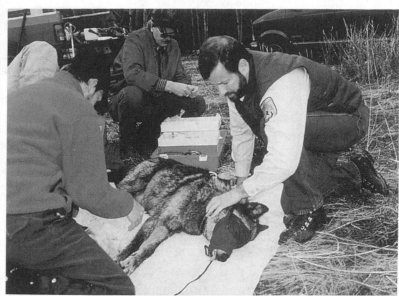

FIGURE 6.5

A wolf gets a radio collar and health check before being released.
USFWS

Source: *The Road Back — Endangered Species Recovery*, U.S. Fish and Wildlife Service, Washington, DC, no date

settlement, wolves ranged over most of North America, from central Mexico to the Arctic Ocean. Because so many people feared the wolf and believed that it preyed on people as well as valuable livestock, human beings hunted wolves until very few survive today. Wolves were not just shot, trapped, and poisoned but burned alive, dragged behind horses, and mutilated. Other people hunted them for their luxurious, warm coats.

In 1914, Congress authorized funding for the removal of all large predators, including wolves, from federal lands. In fact, the wolf became so valuable at one time that bounties were paid to hunters. By the 1940s, wolves had been eliminated from most of the contiguous United States. Two species of wolves exist in North America: the Gray wolf and the Red wolf. Both species are threatened with extinction. (See Figures 6.3 and 6.4.)

By the 1970s, almost all the wolves had been killed in some parts of the United States. In 1973, the Endangered Species Act (ESA; PL 93-205) was signed into law. Since the wolf had all but disappeared, it became the first animal listed as endangered under the ESA. The wolf could not be hunted in those areas where it was endangered, which included every state except Alaska and Minnesota.

The Wolf Reintroduction Program

In 1991, Congress passed PL 102-154, which instructed the U.S. Fish and Wildlife (FWS) to prepare an environmental impact statement that studied alternatives for reintroducing wolves to Yellowstone Park and central Idaho. The FWS approved a recovery plan for the Gray wolf in the northern Rocky Mountains. (The Red wolf was bred in captivity in national refuges, and, in 1993, there were more than 100 Red wolves in 22 captive breeding facilities and more than 20 in the wild.)

Plans to protect the Gray wolf did not meet everyone's approval. In fact, legislators continue to debate how to protect the wolf, other animals, and ranchers' and hunters' interests. In 1995, biologists introduced 14 Canadian wolves into Yellowstone Park. A similar program began in Idaho. To date, the FWS has reintroduced a total of 41 wolves into Yellowstone and 35 wolves into central Idaho.

Of the wolves brought into Yellowstone, four are known to have died, two from "foul play." Some ranchers who oppose wolves have said openly that they will shoot them. A number of lawsuits are pending, seeking damages for lost livestock and asking to stop the reintroduction program. The ranchers are concerned not only that the wolves will attack their livestock and cause economic losses but also that their land may come under government restrictions as a result of the wolves' presence.

Under the terms of the reintroduction program, the government has agreed that any wolves proved to have killed livestock can be killed, and ranchers are to be reimbursed for any documented losses to wolves from a $100,000 compensation fund maintained by the Defenders of Wildlife, a con-

FIGURE 6.6

FLORIDA "PANTHER" COUGAR

servation group in Washington. As of 1997, the fund had paid out $29,456 to 34 ranchers, covering 57 cattle and 51 sheep killed by wolves in the Rocky Mountains. Defenders of Wildlife also established the Wolf Habitat Fund in 1992 to award $5,000 to landowners who allow wolves to raise pups to adulthood on their land. By 1997, the fund had made payment to two landowners.

The success of the recovery program exceeded FWS expectations and, in 1997, Secretary Bruce Babbitt announced that further reintroductions would not be necessary. Wolf packs in both Yellowstone and Idaho have produced several successful litters since their release. The Yellowstone population now approaches 100 wolves, and the Idaho population has grown to about 70 wolves. In northwestern Montana, the FWS estimates there are 100-120 wolves.

The wolf population in Minnesota, Michigan, and Wisconsin is estimated at about 2,500. Experts predict that the species could be moved from endangered to threatened status on the Endangered Species list in 1999 because of the success of the recovery program. (Figure 6.5 shows a wolf being examined and fit with a radio tracking device.)

Biologists have found that, in the Yellowstone area, a recovered wolf population only slightly reduces populations of cattle, sheep, elk, moose, bison, and deer. Some observers believe this is as nature intended — the wolves weed out sick and weak animals, which improves the overall health of other species, takes some pressure off vegetation, and produces carrion for an array of scavengers, such as eagles, ravens, cougars, and foxes. In addition, the presence of wolves increases visitor attendance to the area and generates an estimated $7-10 million in additional net economic benefits each year.

Other Wolf Populations

Three small populations of Red wolves have been released on small coastal islands off South Carolina, Mississippi, and Florida. Wild populations there have grown to about 60. Remaining Red wolves are maintained in 31 captive breeding facilities across the United States, with populations totaling 180 animals. In the 1998 Interior Appropriations Act (H.R. 2107), the House of Representatives earmarked $300,000 to reintroduce Gray wolves into Olympic National Park, Washington.

In 1998, the FWS began introducing rare Mexican Gray wolves, the smallest of North America's Gray wolf species, into federal lands in the Southwest. The animals were hunted to near extinction in the United States by the government on behalf of the livestock industry; by 1960, only seven survived in captivity. The animals that have been released are being tracked with radio collars. Subsequent releases are expected to create a viable population of 100 by 2005 at a cost of $7.2 million. If the reintroduction program is successful, the wolf could be removed from the endangered species list in eight to 10 years.

The FWS has designated New York State's Adirondacks and Maine's larger North Woods as primary areas where wolves might be reestablished. Based on the habitat criteria set by the FWS on road and population densities in the areas, the researchers have concluded that the Adirondacks should be able to support roughly 150 wolves and Maine even more than that.

FIGURE 6.7
SIBERIAN TIGER

Controversy has already begun. Farmers contend the wolves would endanger livestock, especially dairy cows. Advocates of the plan say livestock losses would be small, as was the case at Yellowstone. They also claim the wolves would become a tourist attraction wherever they exist and that the dollars they would generate in the economically depressed Adirondacks would outweigh livestock losses. Proponents also contend that the wolf would restore wholeness and balance to an out-of-kilter ecosystem, for instance, by reducing a runaway beaver population.

Wolves in Alaska

Gray wolves in Alaska have never been endangered or threatened. There are more than 7,000 wolves in Alaska. In Canada, Gray wolves number in the thousands and are hunted legally. Because other species of animals, especially caribou and moose, are fewer in number and are sometimes killed and eaten by wolves, some people think hunting wolves will protect the caribou and moose.

Until 1991, Alaskans were allowed to hunt wolves for sport; some hunters even shot them from airplanes. Aerial wolf killing was a simple and effective procedure in which state workers trapped individual wolves in the summer, fit them with radio-collars, and released them. In the winter when the wolves packed together, hunters in aircraft found them with radio tracking devices, and wildlife agents shot the non-collared wolves from the air, leaving the collared wolves alive to go find another pack.

In 1992, some tourists to Alaska protested the shooting of wolves, threatening to boycott the state if the wolf kills continued. Additional threats of boycott from conservationists led the State of Alaska to stop killing wolves from the air. Eventually, a modified plan was adopted that allowed hunters to locate wolves from the air and then land and shoot the animals if they were at least 100 yards away. Hunters were also allowed to snare wolves in traps.

In 1995, Alaska's Governor Tony Knowles cancelled the wolf-killing program after finding that not only had 134 wolves been killed, but also many moose, caribou, eagles, and red foxes had died in the snares. Snares had proven to be a cruel means of hunting — many animals had been killed or injured indiscriminately.

Public Opinion About Wolf Management — A Polarization of Views

Efforts to reintroduce wolves or to allow or disallow hunting of wolves, as in Alaska, have increasingly polarized public opinion. A majority of people interviewed, many urban or not living in affected areas, want the immediate reintroduction and full protection of wolves. Many others, primarily rural residents in or near central Idaho, Yellowstone, or Alaska, indicate they do not want wolves to be recovered. Many in the ranching and hunting industries strongly oppose the return of wolves, while environmentalists have nearly unanimously supported recovery efforts.

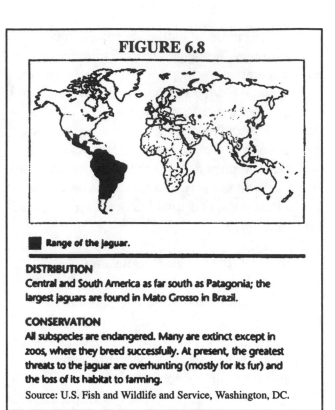

FIGURE 6.8

■ Range of the jaguar.

DISTRIBUTION
Central and South America as far south as Patagonia; the largest jaguars are found in Mato Grosso in Brazil.

CONSERVATION
All subspecies are endangered. Many are extinct except in zoos, where they breed successfully. At present, the greatest threats to the jaguar are overhunting (mostly for its fur) and the loss of its habitat to farming.

Source: U.S. Fish and Wildlife and Service, Washington, DC.

THE BIG CATS

As undeveloped land becomes harder to find all over the world, the large cats, such as lions, panthers, mountain lions, tigers, jaguars, and cheetahs, are left with less and less natural habitat in which to live. In addition, some cats have been hunted for their colorful coats, while other species have been hunted by farmers who fear the cats will prey on their livestock herds. As a result of the increased sharing of land by animals and humans, the number of some species has declined dramatically.

In California, humans and mountain lions, or cougars, are running into one another so often that game wardens are now trained in the ways of the big cats. Scientists attribute the increased encounters to more venturing into the wilds by humans, more cougars (an estimated 6,000), and a ban on hunting cougars since the 1960s. Some people are demanding that the hunting ban be lifted to reduce the number of cougars. In the eastern United States, cougars are so rare that no one can say for sure whether they exist any more. The Eastern cougar, sometimes called a ghost cat, has been presumed extinct. In 1997, however, several sightings were reported in the Appalachian Mountains, although wildlife experts still have not verified the accuracy of the reports.

The Florida Panther

The Florida panther is one of 27 subspecies of a widespread cat of the Western Hemisphere. In Florida, it is called a panther; elsewhere in North America it commonly called a puma, cougar, or mountain lion. The seven-foot long, 100-pound cats prey on large animals, mostly deer. Therefore, they require large home ranges for securing food. By 1900, the big cat had largely died out, or been killed out, in North America. The Florida panther has been considered endangered since 1967.

Only 30 to 50 Florida panthers survive worldwide. The species was named after the state of Florida where it once lived. (See Figure 6.6.) The cats have died from genetic disorders, loss of habitat, water contamination, and being killed by traffic on highways. Ninety percent of male Florida panthers suffer from sperm abnormality, sterility, congenital heart defects, and possible immune deficiencies because of long-term inbreeding. As a result, experts fear the species may die out in less than 20 years.

Consequently, in 1994 and 1995, scientists and wildlife managers introduced Texas cougars, their closest relatives, into the panthers' habitat in hopes that breeding with the panthers would strengthen their genetic pool. "This is a very drastic measure and not one we ordinarily undertake...," reported Dr. John Fay of the U.S. Department of the Interior. Dr. Fay observed that the technique saved woodland caribou in Idaho and Washington in the 1980s, when the species bred with Canadian caribou. Florida panthers and Texas cougars once ranged freely throughout the Southeast and bred with each other until the two populations were separated by human civilization more than a hundred years ago. Breeding the two cats is not considered hybridization since the two are subspecies of the same species.

FIGURE 6.9 JAGUAR

Source: U.S. Fish and Wildlife and Service, Washington, DC.

Other efforts are also underway to maintain the existing gene pool. Seven panthers that were not inbred are living in a 550-acre preserve to save their strong genetic stock for the future. Some scientists believe that the habitat destruction that threatened the panther has lessened. The main problem today is to provide large enough expanses of territory, since male panthers are territorial and do not overlap their ranges with other males.

As a result of the panther's plight and Americans' affection for the animal, the state of Florida made the panther the state animal. Wayne Huizenga, the owner of the new National Hockey League (NHL) team, named the team the Florida Panthers and pledged many thousands of dollars to panther recovery efforts.

The demise of Florida's panthers, as well as bears and coyotes, has led to an overgrowth of wild hogs. The hogs, which arrived with Spanish conquistadors more than 450 years ago, now number over one million. They are rooting up farm fields, spreading disease, causing traffic accidents, and consuming food for endangered animals. A special team of workers stands by to scare the hogs off the Kennedy Space Center shuttle runway.

The Siberian Tiger

All species of tigers are listed as endangered. Experts believe there may be as few as 5,000 tigers left in the wild, two-thirds of them in India and another 2,000 in captivity. The Siberian tiger is the largest tiger in the world and one of the world's most endangered species. (See Figure 6.7.)

FIGURE 6.10

Black-footed ferrets produce four or five young once each year. Born in May or June, the young do not come above ground until they are six weeks old.

Source: U.S. Fish and Wildlife and Service, Washington, DC.

The Siberian tiger, also known as the Amur tiger, lives primarily in Russia. It is dying out because of habitat loss and being captured or killed for trade. The Siberian tiger is sought for its skin, bones, eyes, whiskers, teeth, internal organs, and genitals for everything from skin cures to tooth medicine. In Russia, where unemployment is high, poachers have flooded nearby Asian markets with animal parts sought by hundreds of millions of Chinese, Japanese, and Koreans for use in medicines. In 1995 alone, poachers killed more than 65 Siberian tigers — a quarter of those believed to be alive. The unstable and financially strapped Russian government can devote neither money nor time to saving the tigers.

Moreover, like the Florida panther, the species has been weakened by inbreeding, which happens when very few animals remain in a colony, and they must mate with biologically-related animals — their own offspring, parents, brothers, and sisters. This inbreeding increases the chances of passing along undesirable traits or diseases, and, as a result, birth defects often occur in the offspring. The Siberian tiger, the panther, and the cheetah (see below) are species that have been damaged or weakened by inbreeding.

Cheetahs

The cheetah is the fastest cat, able to sprint at speeds up to 70 miles-per-hour. The cheetah lives in Africa, especially in Namibia, but is now almost extinct. Farmers shoot them as predators, and the cats have not been able to reproduce quickly enough to replace themselves. In addition, most are badly inbred. Studies of the cheetah chromosomes (bundles of genes that determine inherited characteristics) show that they are almost all similar.

As a result of this inbreeding, many of the specimens are infertile and unable to produce offspring. In addition, cheetahs are not as aggressive as other big cats and, when forced to share habitats with bigger or more aggressive cats, are unable to defend their food kills and protect their young. Environmentalists have determined that in order for the cheetah to survive, it will need both human assistance to protect it from other animals and healthier breeding conditions so that continued inbreeding and weakening of the species can be stopped.

98

Jaguars

Jaguars once ranged from Arizona to Argentina, but are now quite rare in the United States. (Figure 6.8 shows the distribution of the jaguar.) They live in a wide variety of habitats, from dense jungle and scrub land to reed thickets, forests, and even open country. The jaguar is the subject of many myths and hunters' tales that originated with the Aztecs and other pre-Columbian people, many of whom considered the jaguar holy. Fewer than 200 wild jaguars are left in all of Argentina. Because they are so rare, most knowledge about them comes from zoo populations. (See Figure 6.9.)

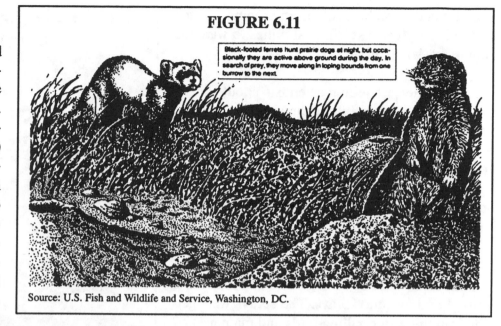

FIGURE 6.11

Black-footed ferrets hunt prairie dogs at night, but occasionally they are active above ground during the day. In search of prey, they move along in loping bounds from one burrow to the next.

Source: U.S. Fish and Wildlife and Service, Washington, DC.

THE BLACK-FOOTED FERRET

The Black-footed ferret is a small furrow-digging mammal and member of the weasel family (Figure 6.10). Nocturnal creatures, ferrets are very good at controlling reptile populations, such as snakes, and rodents, like prairie dogs. Ferrets are endangered primarily because of mass poisonings of prairie dog "towns" by human beings (Figure 6.11).

Farmers and livestock owners destroy prairie dogs because they dig tunnels in ranch land. These holes and tunnels, which are usually shallow and lie just beneath the surface of the ground, can cause serious injury to a horse or other large animal when the earth gives way under its step. Some municipalities poison prairie dogs in city parks, where borrow holes can trip and injure humans. The poison kills some ferrets, and those that survive have lost a major food supply.

The Black-footed ferret has never been very abundant. Even after the burrowing creatures were put on the Endangered Species List in 1973, the poisonings continued until 1979, and, as a result, the Black-footed ferret was thought to have been destroyed. However, a ferret was sighted in Wyoming, and rewards were offered for finding them. In 1981, a few Black-footed ferrets were found living closely with prairie dogs in sagebrush-grass areas. Environmentalists hope that prairie dog "towns" will continue to be protected from trapping, poisoning, and shooting so ferrets will also survive.

In 1985, the Fish and Wildlife Service captured six ferrets to start a captive breeding facility. By the summer of 1991, this number had increased to over 300 and, by 1995, to 1,400. The FWS reintroduced ferrets in several states, but many of the animals have not survived, primarily because their primary food, prairie dogs, continue to be killed off or die from disease. In fact, many of the ferrets are believed to have succumbed to a viral plague common to prairie dogs.

BUTTERFLIES AND MOTHS

Scientists and conservationists around the world are watching the 20,000 known species of butterflies very carefully. (See Figure 6.12.) Like frogs, butterflies are what scientists call "indicator species," meaning that they warn human beings about the condition of the environment, much as the canary was used in coal mines to warn the miners of deadly gases.

Butterflies are telling scientists about climate change and other habitat changes. They require exact temperatures, rains, and foods to survive. Thriving butterfly populations mean that the environment is in good balance. When any one of those things is upset or disrupted, the butterflies die, and scientists are warning that changes are happening in the environment.

In southern Florida, the decline of Swallowtail butterflies alerted biologists to the harm being caused by mosquito sprays. The sprays were getting into the water, killing birds and mammals.

Butterflies also help conservationists decide where to locate parks and nature refuges around the world. Healthy butterfly populations tend to occur in areas with healthy ecosystems in which there is the proper balance of nature between plants, animals, and environment, so that all creatures in the system can thrive and live well. Generally, the more varieties of butterflies existing in an area, the more species of other animals and plants live there. Unfortunately, the butterfly population is disappearing around the world, an example, many scientists believe, of the heavy toll human civilization takes on wildlife.

In 1996, scientists in Michigan and in England reported, in the *Journal of Heredity* (September/October 1996), that during the 1960s, on both continents, the dark-colored form of moth began to predominate over light, white- and- black flecked moths in polluted areas. In both countries, clean air laws were passed with resulting decreases in pollution. Now, in both countries, lighter forms of moths are predominant.

Scientists believe that with cleaner the air, the darker forms lost their evolutionary advantage. They claim that other species also act as living indicators of air quality. Dr. Douglas Futuyma, biologist at the State University of New York at Stony

**FIGURE 6.12
BUTTERFLY**

Source: U.S. Fish and Wildlife and Service, Washington, DC.

Brook, reported that other insect species have shown increases in the proportion of darkened individuals in industrialized areas, a phenomenon called industrial melanism. In those species, as well, the proportion of dark specimens drops as air quality improves.

AMPHIBIANS

This may be the crisis biologists have been warning of.
— Alex Chadwick, Reporter, National Public Radio

One of the most troubling losses of wildlife to scientists is that of the many species of frogs and toads. These species are also considered "indicator species" — their sensitivity to environmental conditions makes them indicative of the state of the environment. A 1995 Worldwatch Institute report noted frog decreases in at least 17 countries, citing habitat loss, chemical pollution, the pet trade, and the human taste for frog meat.

In 1991, the marked decline of the amphibian species — frogs, newts, toads, and salamanders — around the world prompted biologists to form

FIGURE 6.13

BOYS AND LEMURS, MADAGASCAR

Photo by R.A. Mittermeier

Source: *Conserving the World's Biological Diversity*, prepared and published by the International Union for Conservation of Nature and Natural Resources, World Resources Institute, Conservation International, World Wildlife Fund-U.S. and the World Bank, no date

the Declining Amphibian Populations Task Force. Mike Sredl, a scientist with the Arizona Game and Fish Department, remarked, "Organisms that were previously common were getting harder and harder to find." Other factors blamed for the loss are damming and diversion of waterways, acid rain, and ultraviolet radiation, levels of which have increased because of the loss of much of the protective ozone layer in the atmosphere.

The "Texas Horned lizard," or horny toad, once abundant in the state and designated the state reptile in 1992, is now listed as a threatened species. It is now illegal to collect, possess, or remove Texas Horned lizards from their habitats. Wildlife scientists blame pesticides, fire ants, and habitat loss for the decline of this lizard.

In 1998, U.S. Secretary of the Interior Bruce Babbitt summoned several top government offi-

cials to discuss findings of research biologist Dave Wake of the University of California-Berkeley. "For the first time," Mr. Wake reported, "I think we have a major group of organisms — a group of vertebrates — that's experiencing a substantial number of extinctions over a short period of time." In addition to species, especially frogs, disappearing, others were failing to reproduce, and some were born with gross deformities, such as extra limbs. Dr. Wade revealed that frogs are dying out even in places he would not expect — protected national parks in the West. Secretary Babbitt added,

Those frogs and amphibians have been in an evolutionary relationship with our landscape for millions of years, and when all of a sudden they start to just, in the blink of an eye, disappear, there's clearly some external cause that's probably related to something that we are doing across the broader landscape. The deformities are particularly ominous because of the potential human implications as well.

PRIMATES

The International Union for Conservation of Nature and Natural Resources (IUCN), in its *1996 Red List of Threatened Animals* (Gland, Switzerland), reported that collectively, the 233 known species of primates (excluding humans) are in danger of extinction. The IUCN estimates that nearly half of all apes, monkeys, and lemurs are in trouble. That is a higher proportion than for any other major group of mammals and even higher than for birds. An additional 18 percent of primate species are in decline and may soon reach threatened status. (Human beings are a glaring exception among primates; human populations continue to rise.)

Brazil is home to the largest number of primate species — 77 at present — followed by Indonesia (33 species), Zaire (33), and Madagascar (30). Habitat loss, especially the fragmentation and conversion of tropical forests for road building and agriculture, contributes to the decline of nearly 90 percent of the threatened primate species. Thirty-six percent of threatened species face pressures from excessive hunting.

As Africa's population increases, in some nations as rapidly as 3 percent per year, more forests are being cleared, forcing apes — gorillas, orangutans, and chimpanzees — out of their habitat. Their numbers are also being decimated by hunters and poachers and by using the apes for entertainment in zoos, circuses, and street acts, as pets, and for scientific experimentation (Figure 6.13).

FIGURE 6.14

WILD HORSES

Source: *Managing the Nation's Public Lands: Annual Report of the Department of the Interior's Bureau of Land Management, Fiscal Year 1992*, U.S. Bureau of Land Management, Washington, DC, 1992

In Indonesia and Borneo, home to virtually all the world's 20,000 to 30,000 orangutans, loss of forests has shrunk the orangutan habitat by 90 percent. Logging and extensive fires have caused many of the apes to flee the forests for the villages, where they have been killed by villagers or captured. Some people train them to do simple tasks like servants, and many others keep them in cages. (See Chapter VII — Trade in Wild Animals — for a discussion of the condition of ape species.)

Not all relationships between primates and humans are exploitative. People in some regions protect primates from harm by according them sacred status or by making it taboo to hunt or eat them. One of the rarest African monkeys, the Sclater's guenon, survives in three areas of Nigeria in part because the residents treat the animal as a sacred species.

SYMBOLS OF THE AMERICAN WEST

Three animals — the wild horse, the buffalo, and the bighorn sheep — are icons of the American West. The buffalo was imprinted on the five-cent coin, "the Buffalo nickel," beginning in 1913, when it was believed that the buffalo had become extinct. But unlike many of the symbols of a bygone era, the wild horse and the buffalo are success stories. Recent efforts aim to return bighorn sheep to the West as well.

The Wild Horses of North America

The wild horse was once threatened with extinction (Figure 6.14). In 1900, approximately two million horses and burros roamed North America, primarily in the public lands of the Western states. In 1971, the Bureau of Land Management (BLM) reported that number had dwindled to fewer than 20,000 and, as a result, Congress enacted the Wild, Free-Roaming

FIGURE 6.15

Buffalo Herd in Snow

Horses and Burros Act (PL 92-195). Ironically, today many people feel that the rangelands are overgrazed and that the number of wild horses needs to be reduced.

In 1992, the BLM implemented a plan to reduce the number of wild horses and burros. The program provided three methods of controlling the number horses: (1) relocation to other areas of public lands; (2) removal from the range and placement in the care of qualified individuals or agencies; and (3) destruction in a humane manner. The program uses "selective removal" to remove animals less than nine years old to reduce herd size.

The program makes thousands of horses available each year through an Adopt-A-Horse Program, which sells horses to individuals for $125 a head. Each year, the bureau culls thousands of horses from federal rangelands in the West for adoption. The effort is costly, however, and new foals quickly replace the horses removed. In 1996, the BLM began vaccinating mares with a long-lasting con-

traceptive to reduce the birth rate, in hopes that the West's 42,000 wild horses and burros could live out their lives in the wild.

The American Horse Protection Association and the Colorado Horse Rescue organization believe that estimates of horse populations are inflated and that herds cannot withstand population control measures. In addition, adopted animals often end up in the wrong hands, suffering abuse or sale to meat packing plants for horsemeat. Profits for selling wild horses vary widely, depending on the size and condition of a horse and on meat prices.

In the West, Idaho is the home of one of the largest herds of wild horses, with more than 200 in the herd. The BLM wants to protect the herd, known as the Owyhee herd, by reducing cattle grazing on public lands where the horses roam. The plan would devote one-third of the pastureland to wild horses. The action has become fiercely controversial. Ranchers claim their cattle can tolerate neither the planned one-third reduction in grazing area nor removal of their herds during certain months of the year, as other have suggested.

The Bison

Oh, give me a home where the buffalo roam...
— "Home on the Range," American song

Although once near extinction, buffalo (more accurately known as bison in the United States) are coming back. Although bison once existed as far east as the Appalachians, today the Great Plains from Mexico to Canada are bison country. Bison have inhabited the region for ten thousand years, since the last ice age, having crossed the Bering Strait land bridge from Eurasia. The European bison, a taller but lighter species, is almost extinct; only a few survive in parks and zoos. Many books refer nostalgically to the day when 60 million buffalo roamed the grasslands of America. Although Native Americans hunted bison, their numbers became depleted when Whites came with firearms. Many shot the animals for fun, while others sold the hides, eventually reducing their numbers to fewer than 1,000. (See Figure 6.15.)

The bison is the largest terrestrial animal in North America. It is characterized by a hump over the front shoulders and short, pointed horns. The head, neck, and front parts of the body have a thick, dark coat of long, curly hair; the rear part of the animal has shorter, lighter hair. The adult males can weigh as much as 1,800 to 2,400 pounds; the female is smaller. The adult male has a black beard about a foot long.

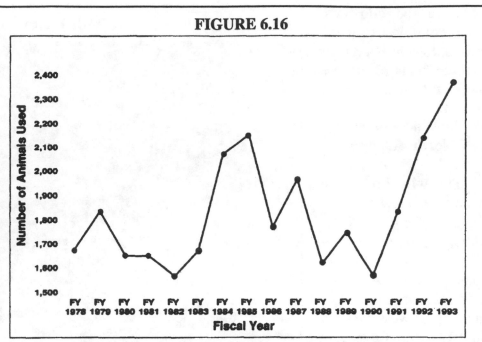

FIGURE 6.16

Animal use in laboratories regulated under the Animal Welfare Act from 1978 to 1993. APHIS started to keep records of the number of farm and wild animals used in laboratories in 1991.

Source: Animal Welfare Institute, Washington, DC

Bison travel in herds, except for old, solitary bulls. Considering their size and weight, buffalo are remarkably light on their hooves. Unlike cattle, they love to run and are surprisingly fast. Their stampedes literally make the earth tremble. Bison were central to the existence of the plains people, who used them for food, hides, and bone implements; even the dried dung, called buffalo chips, was used for fuel. Historical accounts describe herds stretching as far as the eye could see.

In 1994, there were 140,000 buffalo in the United States, most on the estimated 2,000 bison ranches in the United States, with conservative predictions of 175,000 by 2000 (and another 120,000 in Canada). Herds exist in all 50 states, and herds in Yellowstone National Park and other public parks have multiplied greatly.

Much of the explanation for the return of the bison is economic. Today bison are managed more like livestock than as wildlife because they have become a food source for humans. Some bison ranches are for tourists; many are commercial breeding or food production ventures. Bison are a source of high-protein, low fat, low cholesterol meat, which makes them attractive to ranchers, restaurateurs, and people watching their diets. "Whatever the role of economic considerations, it is likely that many Americans will want to eat bison instead of beef if they become convinced of its relative healthfulness," reports researcher and writer Ernest Callenbach.

In most places, with the exception of Colorado, Texas, and California, buffalo meat is still hard to find. Buffalo meat, however, may be mail-ordered. The National Bison Association estimates that 150,000 bison are slaughtered each year, producing 7.5 million pounds of meat. Bison meat is not expected to replace beef, but some people think it might become an alternative red meat source. As Callenbach reports, in *Bring Back the Buffalo!* 1996),

Because bison are more productively adapted to grasslands than are cattle, they will gradually gain partisans for both ecological and economic reasons. And because they naturally fit the land without requiring human management, we need to learn again to treat bison as wild but usable animals, just as the Native American peoples of the Plains did until little more than a century ago.

Exporting bison has become a sideline for many American ranches, and there are also small bison ranchers in other countries, including Quebec in Canada, Southern France, Switzerland, Belgium, and other parts of Europe.

In Montana, some cattle ranchers and state agents began slaughtering bison in recent years because they feared the animals could contaminate cattle with brucellosis, a disease that causes pregnant cows to abort their young). Although there is no evidence that transmission has occurred, in the winter of 1997 alone, more than 1,000 bison that had wandered out of Yellowstone were killed.

The Bighorn Sheep

To see these rams on a bluff with their horns accentuated by the blue sky behind them — they're a magnificent animal. If you can't get excited about that, there's something wrong with you.
— Van Horn, Texas, rancher

A hundred years ago, desert bighorn sheep were commonly seen climbing in the mountains of the West. The three-foot-tall sheep have heavy, curled horns. Overhunting and disease decimated their population. By 1903, the number of bighorn sheep in Texas fell to an estimated 500, and the state of Texas banned bighorn hunting. In 1945, the state set aside 11,625 acres for sheep habitat in the Sierra Diablo Wildlife Management Area near Sierra Blanca in the Big Bend area of Texas. Twelve years later, Texas imported desert bighorns from other states for captive breeding on state property. Despite these efforts, the last native sheep in Texas is believed to have died in the 1960s. (Populations of bighorns existed in other desert and Rocky Mountain States.)

In the 1980s, Texas focused on breeding in captivity, but diseases and mountain lions took a toll. In 1997, captive breeding was abandoned. In the 1980s, however, wildlife officials tried a new tactic — asking private landowners to help. Unlike other Western states, Texas has little public land for the sheep to roam. Only 3 percent of Texas land is owned by the government, compared with, for example, Nevada, where more than 82 percent of the state is government land. For the sheep to flourish, private landowners had to host them on their farms and ranches.

Many landowners welcomed the sheep, some donating thousands of acres of mountainous terrain for breeding grounds for the bighorns. Unlike some predators involved in restoration efforts, such as wolves, bighorn pose no threats to ranchers. They do not prey on other animals, and they graze in remote areas, not taking grazing from livestock. In 1998, experts estimate the population of bighorn sheep in Texas at 320 and nationwide, almost 30,000. The Parks and Wildlife Department hopes to raise the number of bighorns in Texas to 600 by 2002. The State of New Mexico is also considering similar reintroduction programs.

The sheep offer landowners potential income through the sale of hunting permits. When biologists determine the sheep population has surplus rams, the state allows limited hunting. The permits are rare — only 15 have been issued in 11 years. Permits are very expensive — five-figure prices — and are issued only to landowners participating in the restoration effort. The first Texas permit sold for $61,000. All the money raised from permits is plowed back into sheep restoration. Because of their scarcity, bighorns are highly prized trophy animals — in 1993, a hunter paid more than $300,000 at auction for an Arizona permit.

WHEN HUMANS AND
WILDLIFE COLLIDE

In industrialized areas with spreading human populations, wildlife are increasingly being displaced from their habitats. The inevitable result is confrontation between humans and animals.

In Yosemite National Park in California, Black bears have increasingly confronted park visitors. Although there has not yet been a human fatality or serious mauling, there have been many minor injuries and much damage. In 1997 alone, there were 600 car break-ins by bears, causing over $500,000 in damage, up from $300,000 in 1996. Biologists attribute the incidents not to aggressive bears but to careless park visitors.

In India, wolves are believed to have caused many human deaths. Experts attribute the attacks to hunger as India's fast-growing population competes with wild animals for land and resources.

Australia is overrun with house cats whose ancestors were brought by settlers to the island continent 200 years ago. Stray domestic cats have multiplied in the deserts, forests, and alleys, driving some indigenous species, including bandicoots, bettongs, numbats, wallabies, and a dozen birds and marsupials found nowhere else on Earth, to extinction. Richard Evans, a member of the Australian Parliament, claims the cats are responsible for the extinctions of 39 species in Australia. He has called for total eradication of cats from the island by 2020 by neutering pets and spreading feline diseases in the wild. The Australian National Parks and Wildlife Service reports that domestic cats each kill some 25 native animals each year, and wild cats kill as many as 1,000 per year.

Changing Philosophies

As people move further and further from their rural heritages, they sometimes begin to question previously held postures involving wildlife. In Michigan, where Black bears are plentiful, rural hunters with hounds traditionally pursue Black bears into trees or draw the bears with bait. The hunters then shoot the bears. However, a coalition of wealthy, retired landowners and animal-rights activists have proposed a statewide referendum to ban this traditional method of bear hunting. Experts believe that more and more affluent men and women, moving into rural areas to retire or work by telecommuting, have brought with them an aversion to traditional pastimes like hunting, shooting, and trapping. Some of them are upset about bear hunters who trespass on their property, and many have a philosophical or ethical distaste for the activities.

Some critics of traditional hunting have formed Citizens United for Bears, an anti-hunting group, maintaining that bears can be hunted without hounds or bait, methods that account for 95 percent of the estimated 1,500 bears shot in Michigan each year. Colorado, Pennsylvania, and New York ban the killing of bears with hounds or bait.

In November 1997, the British Parliament proposed the banning of the traditional British sport of fox hunting. Polls showed that three-quarters of the British public supported the ban. Although some British residents believe that witnessing or participating in a hunt is a cherished part of English history and claim that fox hunting is necessary to rural areas, critics oppose the practice on grounds that the hunt is cruel to the foxes. The proposal will not be acted upon until some time in late 1998.

ANIMALS USED FOR RESEARCH

Animal research has played an important part in medicine and science. A number of species, such as dogs, cats, rabbits, primates (apes), hamsters, guinea pigs, rats, and mice, are used for scientific research. In addition, an estimated 14 million animals a year, or 20 percent of the animals used in experiments in the United States, are used to test the safety of cosmetics and household products. Most biomedical research involving primates takes place in industrial nations; the United States, United Kingdom, and Japan are the top primate-importing countries.

Controversy has developed between universities and laboratories, which use the animals as subjects for study and research, and animal rights groups, which seek to protect animal populations and eliminate their suffering. Both sides agree that the U.S. Department of Agriculture should do a better job of keeping track of how many animals are used in research and whether they suffer as a result.

Not until 1985, in a section of the U.S. Farm Bill (PL 99-198), did the United States enact legislation protecting laboratory animals comparable to that already in effect in 14 western European countries.

Differing Estimates

A 1994 Tufts University study found that animal use and suffering was underestimated by researchers who used animal subjects and exaggerated by animal rights groups. The study showed that since 1968, the number of animals used in re-

search has dropped by approximately half from 2.3 million per year to about 1.2 million in 1992.

Researchers J.R. Held and T.L. Wolfe, in "Imports: Current Trends and Usage" (*American Journal of Primatology*, 34, 1994), reported that approximately 40,000 primates are required each year for biomedical research worldwide. Since the 1970s, however, most countries with wild primate populations have restricted their export, and the demand for primates in research labs is increasingly being met through captive breeding. In 1994, Indonesia and the Philippines adopted export bans on wild primates. In previous years, those countries had supplied 50 to 80 percent of all internationally traded primates.

Many authorities believe, however, that the numbers of rats and mice used are difficult to document and that the amount of pain suffered by research animals is impossible to estimate. Europe, where records are more accurate, has also reported sharp reductions in the number animal subjects.

The Tufts study recommended that an official board be established to monitor animal use. The study suggested that opposing sides modify their views, encouraging scientific groups to relieve or lessen animal suffering and animal rights groups to recognize that animal research must play a part in medicine and science. Some companies, for example, cosmetic manufacturers, are advertising the fact that they no longer use animals in their product research of formulation to promote their products.

On the other hand, the U.S. Department of Agriculture's Animal and Plant Health Inspection Service (APHIS) has reported a recent, sharp increase after 1990 in the number of animals used in laboratories. In 1990, approximately 16,000 animals were used for research; by 1993, almost 24,000 were used. (Figure 6.16 shows the use of animals since 1978.) The APHIS reports that, since 1990, the use of primates, dogs, cats, guinea pigs, hamsters, and rabbits has remained approximately the same.

107

On the other hand, the use of farm animals and wild animals, which began to be recorded in 1991, has increased dramatically. Federal law does not require that the numbers of mice, rats, and birds be reported to any government agency. Undoubtedly, some of the disparity in conclusions comes from the different methods of tallying experimental subjects.

Animal Dissection in Schools

Killing animals for classroom dissection is a commonplace occurrence. No reliable numbers exist for the number of animals used for dissection in U.S. schools since biological supply companies do not divulge complete information. The Humane Society of the United States estimates that about six million vertebrates (and probably an equal number of invertebrates) are dissected yearly in U.S. high schools alone, with many more used in colleges, universities, and middle and elementary schools.

The most commonly dissected vertebrates are frogs, fetal pigs, and cats. Others include sharks, perch, rats, pigeons, salamanders, turtles, snakes. mink, foxes, and bats. Invertebrates include crayfish, grasshoppers, earthworms, clams, sea stars, squid, sea urchins, and cockroaches. One U.S. biological supply company sells more than 170 different species of preserved animals. Some dissection exercises involve animal parts rather than whole animal bodies. Animal parts — cow's eyes, hearts, lungs, and sheep brains — are sometimes obtained from slaughterhouses. Frogs make up half the vertebrates used in dissection.

Animals bound for dissection are acquired from a variety of sources. Some species are caught in the wild, in wetlands, or in nets of fishermen. Dogs and cats are often procured from animal shelters, breeders, or from private individuals. Many animals are bought from biological supply companies.

Available Alternatives

Alternatives to dissection are available. CD-ROMs have been added to an arsenal of computer programs. Hundreds of videotapes show detailed dissections of various animals. Three-D models exist for a wide variety of animals, as well as highly sophisticated models and simulations of the human body. Although biology teachers often defend dissection, some studies show that the academic performance of students using alternatives to dissection is at least as good as students who dissect animals.

Legislation

As of June 1997, four states had dissection-choice laws: Florida (enacted 1985), California (1988), Pennsylvania (1992), and New York (1994). These laws give students the option of not dissecting animals. The student can choose another exercise not involving dissection. Some school boards around the country have voluntarily embraced such choice policies. The majority of schools, however, have no dissection-choice policies.

Internationally, Argentina and the Slovak Republic have banned dissection in schools. In Italy and India, students may refuse to perform dissections.

Breeding Animals for Science and Reseach

The discovery of acquired immuno-deficiency syndrome (AIDS) made primates, especially chimpanzees even more valuable to the medical research industry. Researchers initially thought that, due to their biological similarity to humans, chimpanzees would be a good model for AIDS research. Chimpanzees had been listed as "threatened" on the Endangered Species list since 1976, but the additional trade pressure for research prompted primatologists to petition the FWS to upgrade wild "chimps" to "endangered" status. Fearing opposition from the medical community, FWS made a compromise decision. Chimpanzees outside the United States would be classified as "endangered," while captive populations would retain their "threatened" status. In 1990, wild chimps were formally reclassified as "endangered."

In 1992, scientists thought they had discovered a viable substitute to chimpanzees, pig-tailed macaques. The macaques were also abundant and cheap. A buying spree ensued, but scientists soon found the macaques were not a comparable substitute. Sales of the monkeys flattened.

In 1994, both Indonesia and the Philippines stopped exporting wild-caught monkeys. Although that action helped the native population of wild monkeys, it also contributed to the growth in the captive-bred primate trade, essentially viewing primates as renewable resources. Since 1988, China has been a major source of captive-bred rhesus monkeys for the United States and Europe. Barbados has the largest monkey colony in the Northern Hemisphere, with a population of 8,000 monkeys supplying a steady flow for research purposes.

Both Indonesia and the Philippines supply U.S. importers with crab-eating macaques that are claimed to be captive bred. However, numerous sources believe that many breeding farms simply camouflage the fact that a large number of monkeys are still being removed from the wild. Vietnam has become the newest export center for captive-bred primates. Some officials claim that primates shipped from there are actually wild-caught.

In the United States, many of the nation's 1,800 chimpanzees used for research are owned by Dr. Frederick Coulston, of the Coulston Foundation in Alamogordo, New Mexico. His organization's 650-chimpanzee colony is the largest in the world. The foundation has drawn fire from animal rights groups and some scientists, who question the wisdom of allowing one man to control so many of the captive chimps used for research. Dr. Coulston, citing the fact that chimpanzees are more than 98 percent genetically identical to humans and exhibit many of the same symptoms as humans, contends they are excellent subjects for research.

That genetic similarity to humans makes some critics particularly uncomfortable. Dr. Coulston has asked for millions of dollars in federal funding to use chimpanzees to study aging and diseases of aging, such as arthritis, Alzheimer's disease, diabetes, senility, and Parkinson's disease.

CHAPTER VII

COMMERCIAL TRADE OF WILDLIFE

Commerce in wild animals and plants and products made from them has been a part of human civilization since prehistoric times. Animal skins provided basic warmth. Clothes made from rare animals have often been a symbol of wealth and success. Flashy feathers taken from South American birds were a tribute to Inca chiefs from their subjects. East Asians have long used condiments, powders, and ointments prepared from animal parts as medicines and aphrodisiacs (substances that increase sexual desire). Coonskin caps crowned American explorers, while nineteenth century women wore ostrich feathers in their hats, and men donned beaver hats.

The excessive hunting or capturing of wildlife species for commercial gain is the second most common cause of animal extinction after loss of habitat. Once a nondomesticated animal species becomes a commodity in demand by human beings, its existence is likely threatened.

Some of the animals disappearing for this reason are whales, valued for their oil and blubber, and exotic birds, captured because many collectors find them beautiful. Rhinoceros are wanted because their horns allegedly have magic and medicinal properties, and minks are killed so their pelts can be turned into fur coats, which many people use to display their wealth. Elephants are slaughtered for their ivory tusks to make jewelry and sculptures. Figure 7.1 shows the argali, a wild sheep whose existence is threatened because trophy hunters seek its massive horns. In each case, these animals are valued by human beings for some physical trait or as pets. Figure 7.2 shows some of the products that are derived from wildlife.

**FIGURE 7.1
ARGALI**

Source: Fish and Wildlife Service, U.S. Department of the Interior, Washington, DC

THE GREAT WHALES

Whales are the largest animals on Earth. Many of these giant mammals (animals that suckle their young) are even bigger than many of the dinosaurs were. There are many species of whales — Blue whales, Humpback whales, Sperm whales, and many others — scattered throughout the world's oceans. (See Figure 7.3.) They spend the summer feeding in cold polar waters and then swim to the

FIGURE 7.2

Source: CITES — *Enforcement Not Extinction*, Environmental Investigation Agency, Washington, DC, no date

tropics to breed during the winter. Studies of the complicated whale "songs" show that whales are highly intelligent animals that communicate with each other.

As early as the eighth century, whales were hunted for meat and whalebone. Human beings also slaughtered whales for whale oil, once used for lighting lamps. Today, whales are still hunted and slaughtered by human beings for whale oil to use in cosmetics and industrial lubricants. These oils, however, can be replaced by other substances.

The International Whaling Commission (IWC)

In 1946, the International Whaling Commission (IWC) was established to regulate the business of whaling. The IWC, whose membership now stands at 38 nations, set quotas on whale kills. The commission declared a moratorium on whaling, effective in 1986. Aboriginal subsistence whaling (catches for food, generally by the Alaskan Indian population) is still allowed by the IWC, although quotas were established. The quotas include 51

Bowhead whales for the United States, 140 Gray whales for Russia, 19 Fin whales and 165 Minke whales for Greenland, and 2 Humpback whales each for St. Vincent and the Grenadines (islands in the Caribbean). The California gray whale was removed from the Endangered Species list in 1994.

Whaling for research purposes is, in theory, allowed by the 1946 convention. However, controversy continues over so-called research whaling by Japan and Iceland. The IWC has condemned the proposals for research whaling by these nations as being a thinly veiled ruse for continued commercial whaling. Figure 7.4 shows a whaling ship towing its catch.

Despite international pressure to obey the moratorium, some nations, such as Japan, Norway, and Russia, continue to practice commercial whaling. The IWC is powerless to enforce its resolutions and depends on international pressure and the enforcement policies of individual nations.

If a country does not wish to comply with restrictions imposed by an agreement, it can refuse

FIGURE 7.3

Even the enormous Brontosaurus was smaller than the Blue Whale, largest animal ever to have lived on earth.

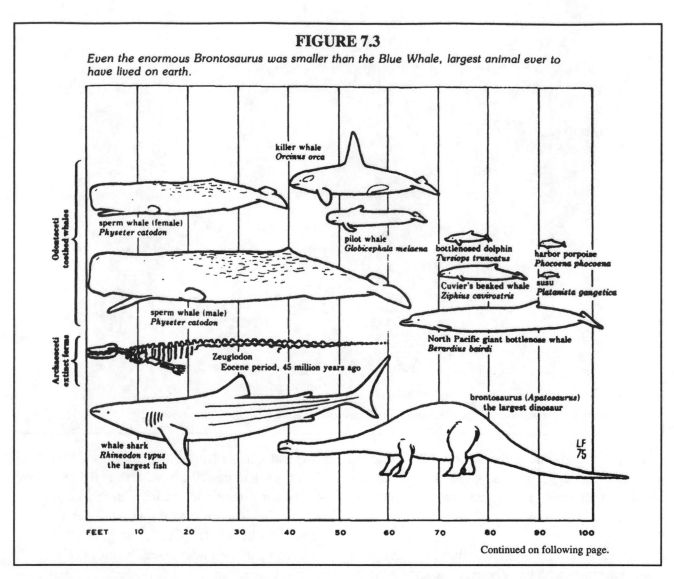

Continued on following page.

to participate, as Norway did with the whaling moratorium, or it can simply quit the IWC, as Iceland did. Conservationists sought a permanent ban on whale hunting, but in 1993, President Bill Clinton delayed sanctions against Norway, preferring to rely on "good faith efforts" to persuade Norway to comply.

Japan continues to try to gain approval for whaling; the Japanese have a fondness for whale meat. In addition to the "legal" whaling practiced by the Japanese, ostensibly for scientific purposes, Japanese and Taiwanese companies have been caught smuggling huge amounts of whale meat.

In 1994, the IWC banned whaling in the 11 million square miles around Antarctica, called the Antarctic Sanctuary. The plan would create a sanctuary for more than 90 percent of the world's whales, which feed in large numbers in those waters. The sanctuary will be in effect for 10 years and must be reauthorized at 10-year intervals. The campaign to save whales has made greater progress than any other international attempt to protect endangered animals.

In 1997, the IWC gave permission to members of the several Indian tribes — the Makah of Washington State, the Inuits of Alaska (formerly known as Eskimos), and the Chukchi of Siberia — to resume whale hunts. The groups claimed that the whale is necessary to their subsistence and is a significant part of their tradition and lore. Critics of the exemptions claim the tribes no longer depend on whaling for food. Furthermore, Indians used to kill with spears and so could not kill as many whales as they do today with harpoon guns.

FIGURE 7.3 (Continued)

Sizes of Whales—Compared with Other Animals

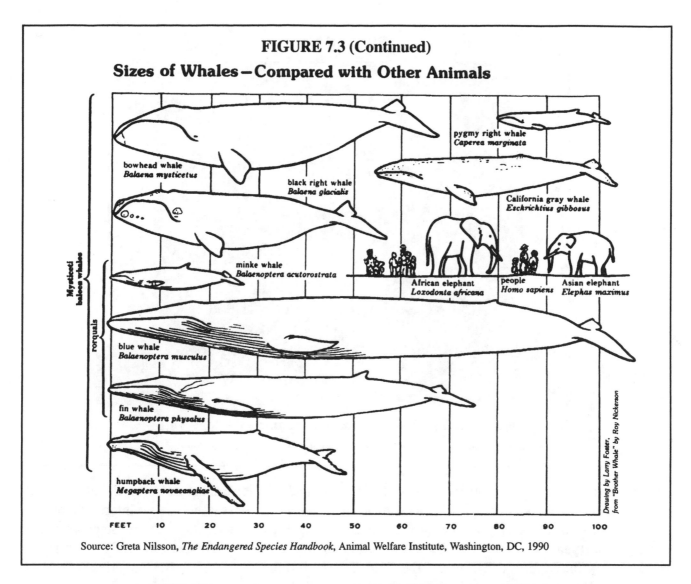

Source: Greta Nilsson, *The Endangered Species Handbook*, Animal Welfare Institute, Washington, DC, 1990

SHARKS

Sharks have been predators of the seas for nearly 400 million years. More than 350 species exist today, ranging in size from the tiny Pygmy shark to the giant Whale shark. Sharks are frightening creatures to many people. Television, films, and the popular press, recognizing that sharks engender fear in many people, have related horrifying stories of shark attacks on swimmers and boaters at ocean beaches in order to sell tickets or boost ratings.

Shark meat, once a delicacy, can now be found in the food section of some local supermarkets. As a result, shark populations are being decimated because of the growing market for shark meat and shark fins. Fins and tails sell for as much as $100 a pound. Fishermen are killing sharks so fast that scientists fear for the survival of entire populations because sharks reproduce slowly and are not replacing the numbers now being killed. Most of the sharks caught in the United States are sent to Asia, where shark-fin soup is a very popular delicacy.

Health Fads

Sharks are being killed at an alarming rate for another reason — some people believe that shark cartilage can prevent or cure disease, especially cancer. Proponents claim that since sharks do not develop cancer, there must be something in them that inhibits the growth of cancer. As a result, entrepreneurs are hauling thousands of sharks from the sea, stripping out the cartilage that makes up their skulls and spines, drying and pulverizing it,

FIGURE 7.4

A Whale Being Towed Aboard a Japanese Factory Ship

Source: *Whales vs. Whalers*, Animal Welfare Institute, Washington, DC, no date

and slipping it into gelatin capsules for over-the-counter sale as "food supplements." An estimated 111,000 large coastal sharks are being made into powder each year. The annual U.S. commercial shark fishery quota for the Caribbean, the Gulf of Mexico, and the Atlantic coast is not much more — only about 150,000 large coastal sharks — and many people consider that number too high to be sustainable.

The sale of shark cartilage is an estimated $50-million-a-year industry — between 25,000 and 100,000 people are now using one of dozens of brands of cartilage sold in health food stores, by infomercials, and over the Internet. Medical researchers are studying the health benefits of shark tissue.

In the United States, some shark populations have already declined 70 to 80 percent in the last two decades because of overfishing. Shark fin harvesting, which has more than doubled since 1980,

has had a major impact on shark fisheries worldwide. Nonetheless, there are no international treaties and few national laws that protect sharks. In the United States, however, shark fishing is monitored by the National Marine Fisheries Service. In 1997, the National Marine Fisheries Service cut by half the quotas on commercial harvests of some sharks and banned harvest of the most vulnerable species — Whale sharks, White sharks, Basking sharks, Sand tiger sharks, and Bigeye sand tiger sharks.

Fishermen in Costa Rica, where some major cartilage manufacturers operate, claim that the real problem is the big foreign fishing fleet from China, Japan, and elsewhere that trolls the waters. In 1994, environmentalists persuaded CITES (see below) to call for new study on the biological and trade status of sharks. Eventually, the members of CITES could decide to ban or restrict trade in some of these products as they have done with rhinoceros horns and elephant ivory.

DOLPHINS

The dolphin is one of the most intelligent sea mammals. In addition to the loss of many dolphins to viruses linked to water pollution and to loss of habitat, tuna fishing nets, which trap and drown dolphins, are decimating dolphin populations. (See Figure 7.5.)

Dolphins tend to swim with schools of tuna in the Pacific Ocean. In fact, tuna fishermen often locate tuna by spotting the dolphins. As a result, the nets used by commercial fisheries to catch tuna also entrap dolphins. Since netting began in 1958, millions of dolphins have been killed.

In 1972, a year when more than 360,000 dolphins were killed by U.S. tuna fishermen, Congress passed the Marine Mammal Protection Act (PL 92-522) to reduce the loss of dolphins in tuna catches. The law was amended in 1982 and 1985 to stop the United States from buying tuna from countries that use fishing methods that endanger dolphins. The law was often ignored, but as the public was made aware of how dolphins were being killed in tuna harvests, many more people became concerned. A 1988 reauthorization of the law (PL 100-711) required observers on all tuna boats. Nevertheless, slaughter of untold numbers of dolphins continued.

In 1990, StarKist, the biggest tuna canner in the world, declared that it would no longer purchase tuna caught in association with dolphins. Within hours of the press conference, the next two largest tuna canners followed suit. Canners of tuna caught by methods that do not catch or harm dolphins now label their canned tuna as "Dolphin Safe."

In 1992, the Bush Administration signed into law the International Dolphin Conservation Act (PL 102-523) that reduces the number of dolphins allowed to be accidentally caught. The law also made the United States a dolphin-safe zone as of 1994, when it became illegal for anyone to sell, buy, or ship tuna products that are not dolphin-safe.

FIGURE 7.5
DOLPHINS

Source: Greta Nilsson, *The Endangered Species Handbook*, Animal Welfare Institute, Washington, DC, 1990

THE RHINOCEROS

The last unicorn is dying. He is not the unicorn of ancient legend; this unicorn is real. He resembles a creature part prehistoric, part modern. He is the African rhinoceros, the huge, gentle, social white, and his smaller cousin, the more aggressive, solitary black. When the last in the wild dies, we will have witnessed the unthinkable, the loss of a species during this era of modern conservation and environmental sensitivity — David K. Wills, "The Last Unicorn"

Rhinoceros are powerful. The largest of the species can grow larger than any land mammal, except the elephant, and can weigh up to 8,000 pounds, as much as 50 average-sized men. Rhinoceros are grazers and vegetarians that move slowly about the plains looking for and eating only grasses and other vegetation. The name *rhinoceros* is made up of two Greek words meaning "nose" and "horn," an appropriate name because rhinoceros are the only animals on earth having horns on their noses (a horn made of hardened hair); other animals have horns on the tops of their heads. (See Figure 7.6.)

Unfortunately, the horns that make rhinoceros unique are also the reason they are endangered. In certain places, such as Taiwan (Republic of China), rhinoceros horn is twice as valuable as gold. Although no scientific tests have ever proven that rhinoceros horn has medicinal powers, in some parts of the world, especially in Asia, the rhinoceros horn is valued because some people believe it has magical and healing powers. Most of the horns come from animals illegally killed in Africa and Asia by poachers who break the law and kill the animal for the money they can make.

Rhinoceros have existed on Earth for more than 40 million years. But in less than a century, man, its only predator, has reduced the number of rhinoceros to fewer than 10,500 animals. Experts predict that the current rate of poaching could destroy the five known species of rhinoceros by the year 2000. The World Wildlife Fund estimated that, in 1994, the population of black rhinoceros had fallen to fewer than 2,000. Figures 7.7 and 7.8 show the decline in the numbers of rhinoceros and the number of rhinoceros remaining.

The rhinoceros has been a protected species since 1976, when it was listed by the Convention on International Trade in Endangered Species (CITES; see below), which banned commercial trade in rhinoceros. In 1992, CITES began to require destruction of the horn caches when captured

FIGURE 7.6

Every week, three black rhinos are poached in Zimbabwe.

Jonathan Scott/Planet Earth Pictures

Source of all three figures: *The Animal Welfare Institute Quarterly*, Washington, DC, Fall 1992

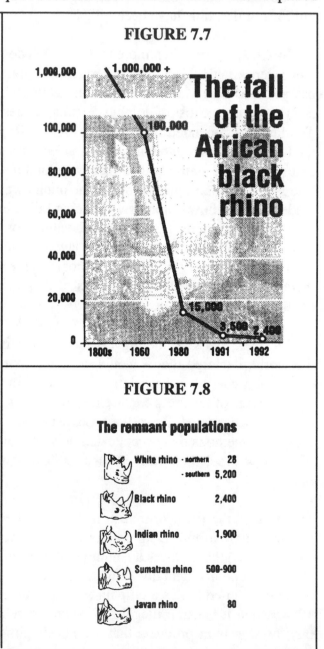

FIGURE 7.7

1,000,000 + **The fall of the African black rhino**

FIGURE 7.8

The remnant populations

White rhino - northern	28
- southern	5,200
Black rhino	2,400
Indian rhino	1,900
Sumatran rhino	500-900
Javan rhino	80

in order to eliminate the supply, but people continue to buy and consume the horn. There is huge profit to be made, and many poachers are willing to risk even death to earn money from selling rhinoceros horn. In 1996, British authorities broke up a criminal ring selling rhinoceros horn that allegedly accounted for 10 percent of the White rhinoceros population in the world.

REPTILES

Many reptiles are suffering from loss of habitat as rivers and seas become polluted with chemicals, pesticides, and acid rain. Dredging of waterways and fishnets also claim many species. In addition, some reptiles are hunted by human beings for their skins, shells, and meat. As a result, many species of reptiles, including rattlesnakes, the desert tortoise, and the green sea turtle, are becoming extinct.

Green turtles are struggling to survive massive killings for their meat, shells, and oil. Snakes, alligators, and lizards are highly prized for their colorful skins, which can be used for making shoes, purses, belts, luggage, and other clothing accessories.

Crocodiles and alligators play an important role in the balance of nature. They eat certain kinds of fish and keep those populations under control. They also dig water holes in the swamps and jungles, which can save the lives of many other animals in times of drought. The disappearance of alligators and crocodiles would likely result in imbalances in the growth of plants and other animals. (Figure 7.9 shows the geographic range of the alligator.) In the United States, the alligator, once a threatened species, has recovered enough that the state of Louisiana permits limited, controlled shooting of some alligators. (See Figure 7.10.)

EXOTIC BIRDS

Wild birds are classified as either psittacines or passerines. *Psittacines* are all members of the parrot family (333 species). The most commonly

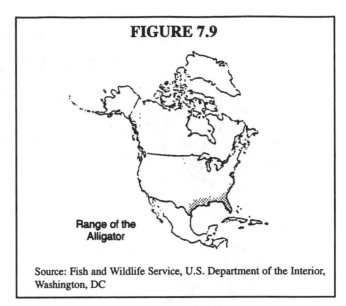

FIGURE 7.9

Range of the Alligator

Source: Fish and Wildlife Service, U.S. Department of the Interior, Washington, DC

traded psittacines are macaws, Amazons, cockatoos, lovebirds, lories, and parakeets. They are generally considered high-value birds, birds that can be sold for a lot of money. *Passerines* are any of the 4,770 species of perching birds. The most commonly traded passerines include warblers, buntings, weavers, finches, starlings, flycatchers, and sparrows. They are usually considered low-value birds.

Birds are among the most popular pets in American homes today. In addition to their vivid colors and pleasant songs, the ability of some to copy human sounds or "talk" is another source of enjoyment for humans. Between 6 and 10 percent of American households now own pet birds. Some of these homes have the common finches, canaries, and parakeets, which are raised in captivity in the United States. About 15 percent of the pet bird market are exotic birds: parrots (Figure 7.11), macaws, and cockatoos, which have been imported from other countries. Within the past 25 years, bird dealers have created a new demand for an ever-increasing variety of birds, including diverse species of parrots, macaws, cockatoos, parakeets, mynahs, toucans, tanagers, and other tropical species.

Each year, millions of birds are captured in the rain forests and savannas (grassy plains in hot regions with few trees) of Latin America, Africa, and Asia to supply the international trade in wild birds.

FIGURE 7.10
AMERICAN CROCODILE

Reprinted with permission from *Conserving the World's Biological Diversity* published by World Resources Institute, World Conservation Union, Conservation International, World Wildlife Fund, and the World Bank, Washington, DC, 1990

The United States, the largest importer of birds, legally brings half a million exotic birds into the country each year. An estimated 100,000 more may be smuggled into the country, with as many as 60 percent of the birds dying from the terrible shipping conditions.

Approximately 75 percent of the exotic birds sold as pets in the United States are caught in the wild rather than bred and raised in captivity. Demand for the rare birds results in very high prices, sometimes as much as $10,000 for one prized bird. One thousand of the world's 9,000 bird species are threatened with extinction, not only from habitat loss, but also from the pet trade. Tropical parrots are especially at risk.

In 1992, the Wild Bird Conservation Act (PL 102-440) banned the import of 10 species of threatened birds. Conservationists believe the ban should be extended to many more wild bird species. Breeding certain birds in captivity to supply the pet market is still legal.

Bird smuggling is a big problem along the Texas-Mexico border. In 1994, in a 20-count indictment, federal officials uncovered what they believed to be one of the nation's largest parrot-smuggling operations. Agents seized smuggled birds with a retail value of $70,000 from a Mexican gang in what is thought to be just a tiny part of a major smuggling market responsible for the illegal importation of between 25,000 and 150,000 birds each year.

In 1998, customs officials announced another arrest, of more than 40 people, for smuggling hundreds of rare parrots and other wildlife across the Mexican border. The animals seized were believed worth hundreds of thousands of dollars, although some were considered priceless because of their rarity in the wild. "It is the second most lucrative type of smuggling on the border after dope," reported James Broadus, a Rio Grande Valley parrot breeder who has assisted federal agents in smuggling investigations. "It's as difficult to stop as drug smuggling, and I don't think they [law enforcement officials] get 5 percent of what comes across."

The 1992 law that halted importation of parrots is, ironically, believed to have increased smuggling. Laws in Mexico, Guatemala, and Honduras ban trade in parrots, and U.S. law bars importation of birds taken illegally from other countries. Peasants, however, can earn a month's salary for snatching even a single fledgling from a nest.

The profit margin for exotic birds, especially parrots, can be enormous. In the United States, a single parrot can command $800 to $1,200. Although no accurate figures are available, researchers estimate that only 1 in 10 smuggled birds survives to reach the United States. (The death rate of smuggled birds is higher than the rate for legally imported birds because conditions are poorer.) Table 7.1 shows the potential profit to be made in various countries for certain species.

New York Zoological Society bird curator Don Bruning believes that some birds, such as the scarlet macaw, "are essentially gone throughout Central America. They've been eliminated largely because of the bird trade." Over the past 20 years, smuggling has reduced red crown parrot populations by 80 percent and yellow-headed parrots by 90 percent in Mexico.

Exporting Countries

Those who benefit from the traffic of birds . . . are the international traffickers and not the citizens of the country of origin. Far from benefiting our countries, this traffic is the cause of extinction of neotropical avifauna.
— Jose Luis Mateo, President, Sociedad Conservacionista Audubon de Venezuela

The five major exporters of wild birds for the international market are Senegal, Tanzania, Argen-

FIGURE 7.11

Photo by Helen Snyder Fish and Wildlife Service

Capture for the pet trade played a role in endangering the **Puerto Rican Parrot**. There are less than 30 birds left in the wild.
Source: Animal Welfare Institute

tina, Guyana, and Indonesia. Although quotas are set, they are routinely ignored, and notoriously hard to verify.

Senegal

Senegal exports between 1 and 10 million birds each year, mainly passerines (songbirds), although psittacines realize the greatest value. About 65 percent of the value of bird exports comes from a single species, the African grey parrot. This species does not occur naturally in Senegal, so these birds are imported from other African countries to be traded with other countries.

Tanzania

Tanzania supplies the international market with a variety of songbirds, including the popular Fischer's lovebird, an endemic Tanzania species whose numbers have been drastically reduced. Tanzania exports from 200,000 to 3 million birds per year. Despite government attempts to control trade, species banned from capture are routinely exported.

Argentina

Argentina is the largest supplier of wild psittacines, between 63,000 and 183,000 each year, al-

TABLE 7.1

Country and Species	Price for Trapper (4)	Exporter Declared Value (5)	Exporter Price List (6)	Retail Value in Importing Country (7)
Senegal				
Quelea	$ 0.09	N/A	0.50	22
Senegal parrot	$ 1.82	4	2.70	115
Tanzania				
Meyer's parrot	$ 2.10	7 (3)	17.25	105
Guyana				
Blue and Gold macaw	$ 5.00	175	325	750
Orange-winged Amazon	$2-3.00	25	32	298
Argentina				
Blue-fronted Amazon	$1.20-3.50	23	70-130	340
Indonesia				
Red lory	$2.52	18	15-20 (8)	230 (9)
White cockatoo	$6.50	85	100 (8)	800-900 (9)

Source: *Flight to Extinction — The Wild-Caught Bird Trade*, Animal Welfare Institute and Environmental Investigation Agency, Washington, DC, and London, United Kingdon, no date

though the extent of illegal traffic is difficult to determine. The blue-fronted Amazon parrot accounts for 27 percent of the trade. This species is threatened with extinction due to exploitation, with tree-felling for the collection of young birds from nests causing extensive habitat destruction.

Guyana

Guyana officially exports between 15,000 and 19,000 birds each year, including some valuable larger macaws. National legislation allows for the capture of any species, regardless of its endangered status, and inspectors have documented the trade of dozens of rare scarlet macaws.

Indonesia

Indonesia legally exports between 58,000 and 91,000 birds each year, mainly cockatoos, lories, and other psittacines. There is so little trade control in Indonesia that the European Community has banned imports of threatened birds from that country. Failure to control trade is complicated by the large number of islands (more than 13,600) that make up Indonesia. Approximately 126 avian species are threatened due to trade or habitat destruction. Bird exporters are believed responsible for the serious decline in Moluccan cockatoos, the red lory, and many other species.

The Capture of Wild Birds

Trapping methods vary from country to country. Most methods are indiscriminate, regularly catching untargeted species. "Liming" is a common method for trapping birds — a "teaser" bird lures the birds to trees where they become stuck on "limes" or glued sticks. Liming causes great stress to birds. Limes are sometimes set and left; birds often break legs or wings while struggling to get loose, and predators sometimes take them.

Nylon loops are sometimes used to capture birds; the loops are strung around perches so that birds become entangled. As with liming, limbs are sometimes broken, and capture is indiscriminate. It is reported that, in Indonesia, 10 to 30 percent of the cockatoos caught this way are rendered "noncommercial" due to injuries to the legs and feet.

Wing shooting is another common method of bird capture. Pellets aimed at flocks of birds render some unable to fly and, thus, they can be captured. More birds are killed than are captured in the process, and many others die later from lead poisoning.

Taking young or baby birds from their nests is another method for capturing wild birds, especially parrots. Pet dealers prefer the young birds because they can more easily be trained to "talk" than adults. In order to obtain baby birds, the nesting tree is often cut down or hacked apart, rendering it useless as habitat in the following years, making this one of the most destructive methods of capture. Mortality is high among young birds captured this way, and many deaths occur within a few days from shock, overcrowding, and inadequate care.

Nets of various types are the major tools for capturing most wild birds in Latin America and Africa. Decoy birds attract wild birds, which are trapped by spring or "mist" nets. Night capture is used in some parts of the world. With this method, sociable birds such as cockatoos are immobilized by shining a torch at them.

Transport from Forest to Living Rooms

Air transport plays a large role in moving delicate species of birds that could not survive the rigors of slow and difficult journeys by sea or over land. Because much of the importation of birds is done illegally, accurate figures are not available on how many birds die during transport. Experts estimate that half, and possibly more, of the birds transported into the United States die en route from shock, crowding, inadequate or improper feeding, choking from forced feeding, suffocation, decompression in aircraft holds, cold, crushing, drowning when crushed into water containers, or disease.

When birds arrive legally in the importing country, they will usually be quarantined as a protection against disease, especially Newcastle disease, salmonellosis, and psittacosis, which not only kill birds, but also can be transmitted to humans. Many birds die in quarantine and even in the months following their release from quarantine.

Illegal Bird Trade

Exporting or importing countries rarely enforce regulations and laws designed to control the wild bird trade. Lack of financial resources is often cited, despite the fact that the trade is worth millions of dollars in retail value. Even the U.S. Fish and Wildlife Service is grossly underfunded when it comes to wild bird trade enforcement. The European Community has no enforcement agency.

Consequently, and not surprisingly, the bird trade is out of control. The illegal bird trade is common throughout the world. The illegal trade often uses the legal trade as a cover. Some of the most common methods of smuggling work in tandem with the legal trade, relying on falsification of documents, under-declaration of numbers of birds, concealment of illegal birds in "legal" shipments, capture in excess of quotas, and misdeclaration of species.

The American Market for Wild Birds

The American market has decreased dramatically over the past few years due to the introduction of humane transport regulations and increased reliance on birds grown in captivity. Between 1986 and 1990, the number of birds imported tumbled from 800,000 to 220,000 birds. The most alarming aspect of U.S. trade is its preference for the large psittacines, such as Amazon parrots, African Grey parrots, and Indonesian cockatoos, precisely those species most endangered. The Moluccan cockatoo has been devastated by the U.S. pet trade.

Trade in the American Bald Eagle

In 1996, the U.S. Fish and Wildlife Service (FWS), after a two-year investigation into the black market in eagle parts, arrested eight men and cited eight tourist shops in the Four Corners region of Arizona, Colorado, New Mexico, and Utah. Carcasses of the Bald eagle were being sold for $1,000. The FWS reported that more than 60 Bald and golden eagles were shot or trapped that winter to feed the clandestine traffic in feathers, wings, tails, and talons. Many other tourist centers were fined for selling the feathers of the protected birds, which are on the threatened list (see Chapter V).

For information on declines of domestic birds, see Chapter V.

ELEPHANTS

Elephants are the largest land animals on Earth. The largest elephants, the African, sometimes weigh as much as six tons (Figure 7.12). (Figure 7.13 shows the geographic range of the African elephant.) Asian elephants are smaller. The African variety is now threatened.

Elephants are the "architects" of the savannas where they live. They help maintain other plant and animal life by digging water holes, keeping forest growth in check, and opening up grasslands that support other species, including the livestock of African herders. They are highly intelligent and emotional animals, with complex social networks within the herds.

The elephant has tusks, called ivory, which, like the rhinoceros horn, are valuable and are used for making fine jewelry and figurines. In the past, piano keys were made almost exclusively of ivory; however, that practice has stopped. While elephant hunting is banned, poaching for ivory is still widespread. The price of elephant ivory has reached approximately $90 a pound, and an elephant with tusks weighing 100 pounds each can provide large profits for the people who can deliver them.

This desire for ivory has had tragic consequences for elephants. In the African country of Kenya alone, the numbers of elephants have been reduced from 150,000 to 30,000 in just the past 10 years. In 1990, the Convention on International Trade in Endangered Species (CITES) (see below), a United Nations-administered body that oversees trade, banned the worldwide commerce in ivory and other elephant products.

In 1997, however, Zimbabwe hosted the tenth conference of CITES (see below) and asked that

FIGURE 7.12

AFRICAN BULL ELEPHANT

the African elephant be downlisted from Appendix II to Appendix I under CITES in three African nations, thereby allowing limited trade in elephant products from those nations. The African nations believe that by permitting limited trade in ivory, they can more easily control poachers and better protect the elephants. They also feel that they have a right to profit from the harvest of animals that they believe are no longer as threatened as many people think.

Although the United States opposed the change, the proposal passed, allowing the three countries to sell one large batch of ivory a year to Japan, which has promised not to export any of it. Critics of the proposal believe the resumption of the ivory trade will lead to poaching in other countries as well. They fear a return to declining populations of elephants as poachers take advantage of the legal market to disguise the illegal origin of their ivory products.

THE FUR TRADE

Some people profit from using the luxurious fur pelts of wild animals, especially for making coats and hats. Animals such as the mink, fox, beaver, seal, chinchilla, otter, and wild cats have nearly been exterminated because they are so desired for their fur. Poachers use cruel traps to capture their prey, while seals are bludgeoned to death on the shores of the Aleutian Islands in the Antarctic.

Not to protect wildlife so much as to satisfy the human desire for fur, ranches for raising wild animals were begun in the nineteenth century. Fur farms were started in Canada on Prince Edward Island in 1887 and spread across the country until there were 10,000 such farms. By 1939, however, higher costs, loss of European markets, and changes in fashion reduced the demand for furs. By the middle of the 20th century, Canadian fur farms numbered less than 2,000, mainly mink farms, with very few on Prince Edward Island.

The fur trade business, finding it too economically risky to leave acquiring pelts to chance and the fluctuations in supply, has turned more and more to domestically raised animals. That policy would seem to lessen the danger to animals living in the wild, although they are still threatened.

In August 1998, animal rights activists in England released thousands of minks from cages on a farm. The minks escaped into the New Forest where they created havoc on the habitat. They also attacked chicken farms. The minks have no natural enemies. The British are trying to trap them, killing many of them to prevent more damage.

PRIMATES — APES, CHIMPANZEES, AND MONKEYS

The primate trade can be traced back thousands of years. Mesopatamians used monkey bones in making drugs, and Egyptians trained baboons to

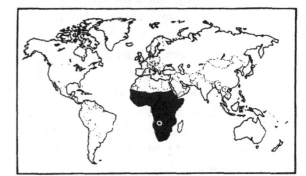

FIGURE 7.13

■ **Range of the African elephant.**

DISTRIBUTION
In most parts of Africa, south of the Sahara.

CONSERVATION
The African elephant is now endangered. Hunting is banned, but poaching for ivory is still widespread. In Kenya alone, numbers have been reduced from 150,000 to 30,000 in the last 10 years. Gamekeepers are almost powerless against the sophisticated machine guns used by poachers.

Source: Fish and Wildlife Service, U.S. Department of the Interior, Washington, DC

harvest figs. In this century, primates have been valued for research and testing.

In the 1950s, more than 1.5 million monkeys were imported into the United States each year for use in developing a polio vaccine. Of all living species, the apes have a genetic make-up most similar to humans. Because of this, apes, especially chimpanzees or rhesus monkeys, are regularly used for medical, chemical and nuclear radiation testing.

While the results from this research are often of great medical value, the chimpanzees are sometimes mistreated. (See Chapter VI for discussion of primates used in laboratory research.) All non-human primates are listed under Appendix I (meaning it cannot be traded) or Appendix II (allowed for trade with reguialtion) of CITES (see below). According to CITES, international trade now numbers 40,000 primates a year for biomedical research.

Chimpanzees are also captured to provide entertainment for tourists, in circuses and zoos, or for sale as pets. Today, almost all countries have banned or strictly regulated the live export trade, but such bans have been hard to enforce.

In Africa, poachers deliberately trap or shoot gorillas, which are killed for their heads, that are sold as trophies for tourists, and for their hands, which are cut off and sold as ashtrays. In Nigeria, more lowland gorillas are being killed each year than are being born. At this rate, they will become extinct in as few as 12 to 15 years.

Monkeys in Vietnam are used to produce brain wine and monkey balm-items used in traditional Chinese medicine. Approximately 50 monkeys are killed every three months for this use. One monkey brain produces about 10 bottles of wine. The skin, organs, and bones are ground up as ingredients for "balm," or powder, which is dissolved in water and taken in liquid form by women who have recently given birth or those who are weak.

Illegal Trade

Primate smuggling has become a booming business. CITES estimated that, in 1990, 40,000 primates were traded illegally every year. The underground world of animal smuggling is a lucrative business, and it has become the second leading cause of species extinction, surpassed only by destruction of habitat. International efforts to halt wildlife trade have not been successful, primarily because inspection of shipments is generally shoddy or non-existent due to lack of funds or manpower.

At present, the worst offender in extinction of wildlife species is Vietnam. As other countries in Southeast Asia have tightened their borders against wildlife smuggling, Vietnam has welcomed the trade with open arms, turning itself into the largest endangered species market in the world. In market stalls in Ho Chi Minh City, a wide variety of wildlife, both dead and alive, spills out into the street. Vietnamese poachers are more than happy to meet the voracious demand for outlawed wildlife by depleting their own forests, Although Vietnam

joined CITES in 1994, without enforcement, little has changed.

WORLD LEADERS IN WILDLIFE TRADE

The United States — A Consuming Giant

In 1994, the U.S. Fish and Wildlife Service (FWS) reported that U.S. trade in wildlife represented a $20 billion market, an estimated $5 billion of that in illegal trade. Claiming to be a leader in protecting plant and animal species, the United States has some of the best legislation in the world to implement CITES and regulate international trade in plants and animal species. Nonetheless, the insatiable demand of the American market place, combined with inadequate resources to enforce laws, has made America a mecca for illegal trade in wildlife.

Traditional Chinese Medicine in the USA

At least one-third of all patented oriental medicine items recorded as available in the United States contained protected species.
— The wildlife organization TRAFFIC USA

TRAFFIC USA, a wildlife advocacy organization, believes the true extent of the trade of Chinese medicines containing endangered species is unknown, although informed opinions estimate its value to be several billion dollars a year. In the United States alone, at least 430 different oriental medicines containing endangered or threatened species have been documented. In 1992, the FWS seized over $500,000 in oriental medicines containing parts of endangered species, including rhino horn, at the Port of Newark (New Jersey). Recent reports reveal smuggling of prohibited products among shipments of electronic equipment from Asia.

Asia — A Black Hole for Endangered Species

The failure of some Asian countries, most particularly China, Hong Kong, Japan, South Korea, and Taiwan, has combined with the economic growth in the Far East to produce a huge demand for many endangered species. Although some effort has recently been made to enforce CITES within Asia, these steps cannot combat the organized crime networks or change ancient cultural habits, such as the use of traditional Chinese medicines that contain endangered species products. Figure 7.14 shows the trade routes into and out of the area.

China

With a population in excess of 1.2 billion, the People's Republic of China has become one of the world's largest consumers of wildlife and endangered species, and threatens to become the largest. The massive growth in consumption of wildlife within China is matched by growth in the export and import of endangered species, their parts, and medicines containing products from endangered species. Despite the threat of sanctions by CITES and the United States, the Chinese government largely turns its back on the growing illegal wildlife trade. The political will to enforce CITES is virtually lacking, and domestic incentives to control the massive wildlife trade are absent. Furthermore, corruption is widespread. A number of investigations have revealed the involvement of Chinese government stores and officials in the sale of restricted products.

Japan — A History of Conspicuous Consumption

With a population over 124 million, Japan has one of the highest per capita levels of wildlife consumption in the world. Japan has fought an aggressive campaign for the uncontrolled consumption of wildlife. Moreover, it has lobbied at CITES and behind the scenes for increased trade, rather than conservation.

Japan's population of Black bears is listed on CITES Appendix I (meaning it cannot be traded) and its Brown bear on Appendix II (allowed for trade with regulation). Nonetheless, domestic trade is both legal and completely unregulated. Up to one-fifth of Japan's Black bear population is killed each year. Figure 7.15 shows the wildlife imported into Japan.

COLLECTORS OF RARE SPECIES

Biologists worry that enthusiastic collectors threaten some rare species of animals and plants, especially butterflies and spiders. Although species on the Endangered Species Act cannot legally be collected, poaching of rare species and the existence of a black-market for specimens has driven prices up for "scientific collectors." Federal biologists worry about revealing the critical habitats of endangered species because poachers have been known to snatch protected specimens from federal lands. Some collectors, however, defend themselves, claiming that federal officials are cracking down on hobbyists and "scientists" when there is no definitive proof that a species can be wiped out by collecting.

THE ECONOMISTS' ARGUMENT

Defenders of the trade in animals argue that countless people are employed in or are supported by wildlife trade industries. Except for poachers, who are obviously breaking laws to make a profit at any cost, most people in the animal trade are ordinary, law-abiding citizens working at the only trades they have ever known. Just as most Americans know that tobacco products cause hundreds of thousands of human deaths each year, there are many, many people making their living producing and selling tobacco products. Free trade advocates argue that a country should not restrict imports of a product solely because it originates in a country whose environmental policies are different. Furthermore, exporting countries should use every possible method of bringing money into their country.

Finally, should people of Third World countries stop farming the lands and cutting down forests to save wild animals while their own babies starve? Wayward elephants trample crops, and lions attack cattle. Certainly, at one time, today's

FIGURE 7.14

Asia: Some Endangered Species Trade Routes

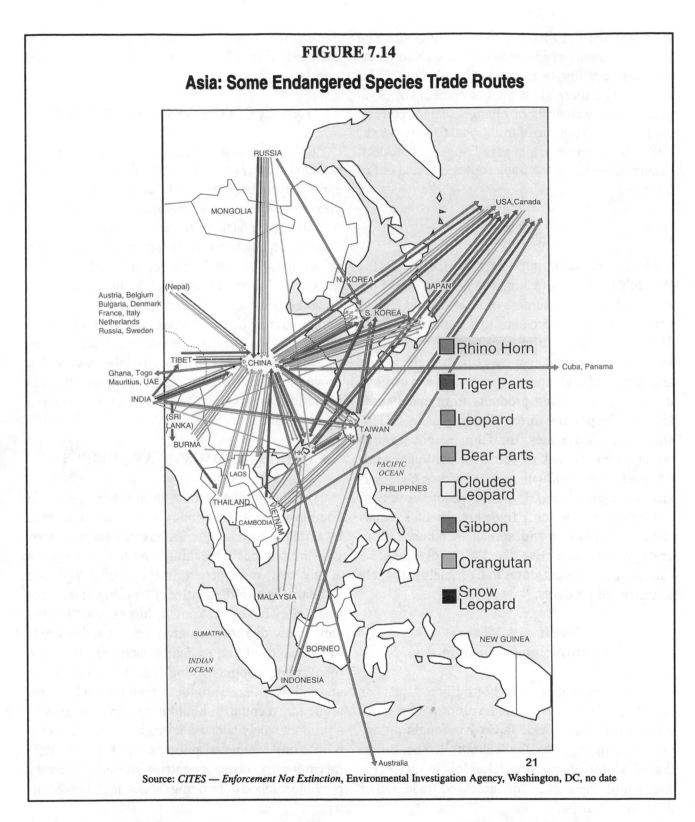

Source: *CITES — Enforcement Not Extinction*, Environmental Investigation Agency, Washington, DC, no date

wealthy industrial nations did the same thing. Where does humankind draw the line between greed and need? These are among the hard questions facing every nation of the world, both now and in the twenty-first century.

THE LACEY ACT

In the United States, the wildlife slaughters of the nineteenth century brought about the extinction of many species, including the Passenger pigeon (see Chapter V), and caused shock and dismay among the American public. To respond to the unregulated killing of wildlife, such as the shooting of thousands of plumed birds for their feathers at the turn of the century, the Lacey Act (31 Stat 187) was enacted in 1900. It prohibited the interstate transport of wildlife killed in violation of a state law and

FIGURE 7.15

J A P A N : Destination Of Endangered Wildlife

Whale meat from Denmark and Norway
Leopard cat skins and tiger and rhino derivatives from China
Whale meat from South Korea
Skins from Italy
Monitor lizard skin smuggling from Bangladesh
Bear gall bladder from India
Improper trade in chimpanzees from Ghana and Sierra Leone
Lowland gorilla smuggling from Cameroon for a Japanese zoo
Contraband African elephant ivory and hippo teeth from Uganda
Illegal musk imports from Hong Kong and China
Illegal Asian arowana imports from SE Asia
Gibbon smugling from Thailand for the pet trade
Illegal ivory from the Philippines

Trade in endangered cacti from North America
Skins of Olive Ridley turtle smuggled from Equador and Panama
Illegal trade in Spectacled caiman skins from Paraguay, Bolivia and Indonesia
Spectacled caiman from Barbados
Whale meat from Chile
Illegal Hawksbill turtle shell imports from Indonesia
Improper trade in Black palm cockatoos from Singapore

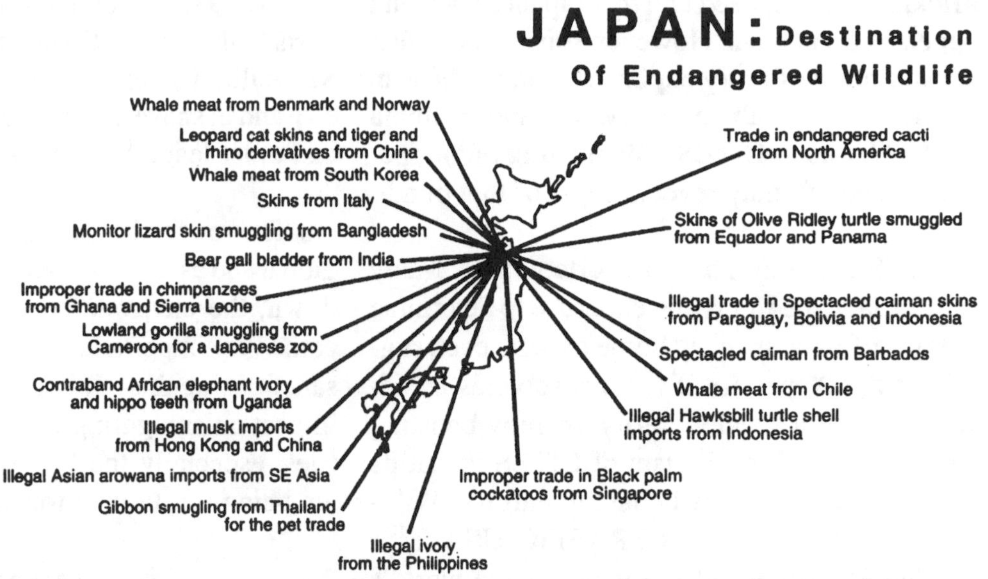

Source: *CITES — Enforcement Not Extinction*, Environmental Investigation Agency, Washington, DC, no date

allowed a state to prohibit import of an animal even if killed lawfully.

Thus, for example, egret plumes taken in a state where the bird was protected could not be shipped to other states. A state could outlaw their entry even if the exporting state did not protect them. In 1908, the law was first applied to wildlife imported from another country which had taken it illegally, thus expanding its scope to cover laws of other countries. The Lacey Act was a major step toward elimination of the meat markets where the last Labrador Ducks were sold, and the plume trade which nearly led to the extinction for the Snowy and Common Egrets and other water birds.

THE CONVENTION ON THE INTERNATIONAL TRADE IN ENDANGERED SPECIES (CITES)

The Convention on the International Trade in Endangered Species (CITES) is the international treaty that regulates commerce in wildlife. First ratified in 1975, the treaty is now observed by 115 countries to block both the import and export of endangered species and regulate the trade in threatened species. Countries involved in the commerce

of a threatened species must first guarantee that trade in that species will not deplete the population of those species. CITES is generally regarded as the most important legislative step taken to regulate trade in declining species.

CITES has three levels of control. Appendix I, the highest, contains the names of those species threatened with extinction — trade in these species is authorized only in special circumstances. Appendix II lists species not presently threatened but in danger of such if trade in them is not regulated. It allows commercial trade under strict monitoring, if the exporting country is satisfied that any trade is not detrimental to the future survival of the species. Appendix III contains species identified by each country as being subject to conservation regulations within its jurisdiction and requiring the cooperation of other parties to make such regulation effective. Countries may list their populations of a species on Appendix III if they wish to monitor international trade in it.

The African elephant, whose population stabilized after having dropped drastically in the preceding two decades, was one of the successes of CITES. Some wildlife experts believed that the market for ivory products in North America and Western Europe evaporated since the ban on ivory trafficking was imposed and that Japanese demand dropped by 50 percent. However, some experts fear the resumption of ivory export from three African countries — Zimbabwe, Botswana, and Namibia — in 1997, due to CITES' downlisting of the species (see above), may reverse some of that trend.

CITES has a number of shortcomings. Many countries lack the funds and expertise to determine the status of their species. Some experts even suggest that the Appendix II listings serve as an advertisement of a species' rarity, thereby boosting its trade. The major criticism of CITES is that its agreements are notoriously hard to enforce. Wildlife organizations, such as TRAFFIC USA, estimate that 30 percent of the value of the world's wildlife trade is made up of illegal goods moving in violation of CITES and national laws. Other problems include the absence of laws to implement CITES, weak penalties for violators, and widespread corruption among public officials.

Many nations are not even parties to the convention, making them potential wildlife bazaars where animals and plants illegally imported or exported from CITES nations can be laundered by having their country of origin changed and re-exported to other nations. Among the biologically wealthy nations that have chosen not to sign the treaty are Cambodia, Vietnam, Laos, Saudi Arabia, South Korea, and Taiwan. A final limitation is that CITES is concerned only with trade across international borders. It does not address the problem of trade within countries, which is a major part of the economy in some areas.

THE UNITED STATES GOVERNMENT GETS INVOLVED

In April 1994, the Clinton Administration imposed trade sanctions on Taiwan for refusing to halt the sale of tiger bones and rhinoceros horns. While the United States has often used trade sanctions as a lever to promote human rights or to lower trade barriers imposed by other countries, this was the first time that Washington had deployed trade sanctions to protect endangered wildlife. The sanctions on Taiwan banned all wildlife-product exports to the United States, which amounts to about $25 million a year in coral and mollusk-shell jewelry and in snake-, lizard-, and crocodile-skin shoes and other leather products.

The move shows that as trade becomes more global and as trade barriers between countries come down, the environmental consequences can become very important. Administration officials hope sanctions against Taiwan will have a significant impact on smuggling in that country. Other countries, especially the People's Republic of China, are being scrutinized for their wildlife practices.

NAFTA and GATT

The North American Free Trade Agreement (NAFTA) is a trade agreement signed in 1993 between the United States, Mexico, and Canada. Its goal was to eliminate trade barriers between the three countries by eliminating most tariffs, investment restrictions, and quotas.

Conservationists believe that the passage of NAFTA could result in the weakening of numerous species protection laws, much as has happened with the GATT (General Agreement on Tariffs and Trade), and the reversal of 30 years of advances in animal protection. Under these agreements, trade barriers have been removed in order to ease commerce between countries. Laws designed to protect animals could be considered "technical barriers to trade." For example, in 1991, Mexico successfully challenged U.S. tuna import restrictions (based on fishing methods that led to the unnecessary deaths of dolphins) under GATT. Under NAFTA, Mexico or Canada could similarly dispute other U.S. environmental laws.

As a result of NAFTA, 22 new border crossings have been proposed, with no additional resources for enforcement appropriated for the Fish and Wildlife Service (FWS). Customs and FWS workers admit they are already unable to do any more than carry out spot checks on the constant flow of traffic through border crossing points. The Environmental Investigation Agency, an environmental watch-group, concluded,

Just as the 1988 U.S.-Canada Free Trade Agreement led to an increase in commercial trade on wildlife products, NAFTA's tariff eliminations can only stimulate the already high demand for, and exploitation of, wildlife products from Mexico, particularly leather goods.... The free-for-all philosophy of trade liberalization will mean improvements in transportation and infrastructure, including increased numbers of border crossings. This can only facilitate the illegal trade and increase the inspection and observation burdens of already over-stretched FWS inspectors and Special Agents.

THE WORLD TRADE ORGANIZATION'S IMPACT ON WILDLIFE TRADE

The World Trade Organization (WTO), a global trade accord, has broad authority to rule on disputes among more than 120 nations. In 1996, the WTO determined that the U.S. Clean Air Act (CAA; PL 91-604) discriminated against foreign oil refiners and ordered the United States to develop a plan to change its rules on imported gasoline or face sanctions. (The dispute arose when a Venezuelan petroleum company wanted to ship gasoline that was below U.S. Clean Air Act standards to its Citgo stations in the Northeast.)

The decision was significant, critics believe, because a degree of American sovereignty was lost by the United States to the WTO, and President Clinton, who backed the trade pact, has placed the fate of the American environment in the hands of other nations. The WTO is fundamentally an economic, not an environmental, agreement. Critics fear that the WTO could demand that the United States back down on laws protecting wildlife trade if those laws restrict the free trade of other countries.

That fear seemed justified when, in April 1998, the WTO ruled that the United States was wrongly prohibiting shrimp imports from countries that fail to protect sea turtles from entrapment in shrimp nets. The United States imports most of the shrimp that Americans consume and has negotiated agreements with several countries to protect turtles from shrimp boats by helping pay for installing turtle extruder devices. More than three dozen countries have been certified by the United States as safe shrimpers, either for having adopted the devices or fishing only in waters where turtles are not usually found.

India, Thailand, Pakistan, and Malaysia had petitioned the WTO, claiming the U.S. law discriminated against them. Conservation groups called on the Clinton Administration to defy the WTO decision, fearing the environment would take a back seat whenever there is a direct conflict with open and free trade. As Daniel Seligman, of the Sierra Club, concluded, "This is the clearest slap at environmental protection to come out of the WTO to date."

CHAPTER VIII

WILDLIFE AS RECREATION

SPORTS INVOLVING WILDLIFE AND NATURAL RESOURCES

America is a country with a rich tradition of enjoying nature. Many Americans find wildlife-associated recreation a source of pleasure. Some of the most popular recreational activities involve wildlife and wild places. For many people, animals and plants play an important role in their lives as sport and recreation; others hunt and fish for food.

The 1997 National Sporting Goods Association survey of recreational preferences found that fishing (7th) and camping (4th) were among the top most popular sports among Americans age 7 and older. Hiking (10th) and hunting with firearms (18th) also ranked among the most enjoyed activities. (See Table 8.1.)

The mission of the U.S. Fish and Wildlife Service (FWS) is to conserve and enhance the nation's fish, wildlife, and habitat. For conservation efforts to be effective, the FWS needs information on how people use fish and wildlife resources. Since 1955, the FWS has conducted the National Survey of Fishing, Hunting, and Wildlife-Associated Recreation. The result is its ninth report, the *1996 National Survey of Fishing, Hunting, and Wildlife-Associated Recreation* (U.S. Department of the Interior, Fish and Wildlife Service, and U.S. Department of Commerce, Washington, DC, 1996). The survey found that approximately 77 million Americans over the age of 16 participated in some form of wildlife-related activity in 1996.

During 1996, 35.2 million people in the United States fished, 14 million hunted, and 62.9 million enjoyed some form of wildlife-watching recreation, including photographing or feeding animals. Among anglers (those who fish), hunters, and nonconsumptive participants, many of those who participated in one activity often enjoyed the other activities as well.

Adventure Vacationing

The Travel Industry Association, in its 1992 to 1997 study, "The Adventure Travel Report, 1997," reported that one-half of American adults (98 million) have taken an adventure vacation in the last five years. About 46 percent took "soft-adventure" vacations. Among soft vacations that involved wildlife or natural resources were bird- or animal-watching, participated in by 12 percent of vacationers; horseback riding, 12 percent; wilderness touring in off-road vehicles, 8 percent; going on safaris to take photographs, 4 percent; and visiting a cattle or dude ranch, 3 percent.

Sixteen percent of American vacationers took "hard adventure" vacations. Among those that involved wildlife or natural resources, 8 percent went whitewater rafting or kayaking; 6 percent, snorkeling or scuba diving; 5 percent, mountain biking; 4 percent, backpacking across wild terrain; 4 percent, mountain climbing; and 3 percent, cave exploring (spelunking). Spouses were the most popular companions for soft adventure, while friends most often accompany hard-adventure vacationers. Hard-adventure vacationers spent an average of $465 per trip, while soft adventure travelers spent $325.

TABLE 8.1

SPORTS PARTICIPATION

Participated more than once (in millions)
Seven (7) years of age and older

SPORT	1997	1996	1995	1994	1993	1992	1991	1990	1989	1988	1987
1. EXERCISE WALKING	76.3	73.3	70.3	70.8	64.4	67.8	69.6	71.4	66.6	62.3	58.1
2. SWIMMING	59.5	60.2	61.5	60.3	61.4	63.1	66.2	67.5	70.5	71.1	66.1
3. EXERCISE w/EQUIPMENT	47.9	47.8	44.3	43.8	34.9	39.4	39.2	35.3	31.5	28.9	34.8
4. CAMPING	46.6	44.7	42.8	42.9	42.7	47.3	47.1	46.2	46.5	42.3	44.2
5. BICYCLE RIDING	45.1	53.3	56.3	49.8	47.9	54.6	54.0	55.3	56.9	53.8	53.2
6. BOWLING	44.8	42.9	41.9	37.4	41.3	42.5	40.4	40.1	40.8	37.9	40.1
7. FISHING	44.7	45.6	44.2	45.7	51.2	47.8	47.0	46.9	46.5	45.7	45.8
8. BILLIARDS/POOL	37.0	34.5	31.1	34.0	29.4	29.3	29.6	28.1	29.6	32.4	29.3
9. BASKETBALL	30.7	31.8	30.1	28.2	29.6	28.2	26.2	26.3	26.2	23.1	25.1
10. HIKING	28.4	26.5	25.0	25.3	19.5	21.6	22.7	22.0	23.6	19.9	17.4
11. BOATING (Motor/Power)	27.2	28.8	26.8	26.4	20.7	22.3	22.4	28.6	29.0	32.5	30.9
12. ROLLER SKATE – INLINE	26.6	25.5	23.9	19.5	12.4	9.7	7.3	3.6	na	na	na
13. AEROBIC EXERCISING	26.3	24.1	23.1	23.2	24.9	27.8	25.9	23.3	25.1	24.2	23.1
14. GOLF	26.2	23.1	24.0	24.6	22.6	24.0	24.7	23.0	23.2	22.7	20.3
15. RUNNING/JOGGING	21.7	22.2	20.6	20.6	20.3	21.9	22.5	23.8	24.8	22.9	24.8
16. DART THROWING	21.4	21.3	19.8	21.2	19.2	18.8	17.0	16.4	17.4	17.8	13.1
17. VOLLEYBALL	17.8	18.5	18.0	17.4	20.5	22.1	22.6	23.2	25.1	22.0	23.6
18. HUNTING w/FIREARMS	17.0	18.3	17.4	16.4	18.5	17.8	17.1	16.5	17.7	na	na
19. SOFTBALL	16.3	19.9	17.6	18.1	17.9	19.2	19.6	20.1	22.1	20.6	21.6
20. MOUNTAIN BIKE (On Road)	16.0	13.3	10.5	9.0	10.5	na	na	na	na	na	na
21. BASEBALL	14.1	14.8	15.7	15.1	16.7	15.1	16.5	15.6	15.4	13.4	15.2
22. SOCCER	13.7	13.9	12.0	12.5	10.3	10.6	10.0	10.9	11.2	8.7	9.8
23. TARGET SHOOTING	13.5	14.7	13.9	12.2	12.8	12.3	11.5	12.8	na	na	na
24. BACKPACKING	12.0	11.5	10.2	9.8	9.2	9.7	10.4	10.8	11.4	9.1	8.9
25. FOOTBALL (Touch)	11.9	11.6	12.1	na	na	na	na	na	na	na	na
26. TENNIS	11.1	11.5	12.6	11.6	14.2	17.3	16.7	18.4	18.8	17.3	16.9
27. CALISTHENICS	11.0	10.1	9.3	8.5	10.8	11.5	12.3	13.2	15.1	13.6	17.1
28. ROLLER SKATING – 2x2	10.9	15.1	14.4	14.0	15.3	16.8	18.6	18.0	21.5	20.5	19.8
29. STEP AEROBICS	9.6	11.3	11.4	11.5	10.6	9.2	6.8	na	na	na	na
30. SKIING (Alpine)	8.9	10.5	9.3	10.6	10.5	10.8	10.4	11.4	11.0	12.4	10.3
31. TABLE TENNIS	8.8	9.5	9.3	7.8	na	9.5	na	11.8	13.7	15.6	14.1
32. FOOTBALL (Tackle)	8.2	9.0	8.3	na	na	na	na	na	na	na	na
33. MOUNTAIN BIKE (Off Road)	8.1	7.3	6.7	5.7	4.6	na	na	na	na	na	na
34. ICE/FIGURE SKATING	7.9	8.4	7.7	7.8	6.9	6.7	7.9	6.5	7.0	7.0	6.4
35. CANOEING	7.1	8.4	8.7	8.5	6.5	7.2	8.7	8.9	9.4	9.7	8.5
36. WATER SKIING	6.5	7.4	6.9	7.4	8.1	7.9	9.0	10.5	10.8	12.8	10.8
37. SKATE BOARDING	6.3	4.7	4.5	4.9	5.6	5.5	8.0	7.5	na	7.4	7.0
38. SNORKELING	6.3	7.1	6.5	5.9	4.9	4.8	5.4	na	na	na	na
39. BADMINTON	5.6	6.1	5.8	5.4	na	7.0	na	9.3	na	12.4	na
40. HUNTING w/Bow & Arrow	5.3	5.5	5.3	na	na	na	na	na	na	na	na
41. MARTIAL ARTS	4.9	4.7	4.5	na	3.6	na	3.2	na	na	2.7	na
42. ARCHERY (Target)	4.7	5.3	4.9	na	na	na	na	na	na	na	na
43. RACQUETBALL	4.5	5.3	5.0	5.3	5.4	6.6	6.3	8.1	8.2	9.3	7.9
44. SAILING	3.4	4.0	3.9	4.1	3.8	3.5	4.1	4.9	4.7	6.7	5.3
45. SNOWMOBILING	3.4	na	na	na	na	4.0	na	na	na	na	na
46. HOCKEY (Roller)	3.0	3.4	3.1	2.2	1.5	na	na	na	na	na	na
47. MUZZLELOADING	2.9	3.2	na	na	na	na	na	na	na	na	na
48. KAYAKING/RAFTING	2.7	3.6	3.5	na	2.1	na	2.0	na	na	na	na
49. SKIING (Cross Country)	2.5	3.4	3.4	3.6	3.7	3.5	4.4	5.1	4.9	5.8	5.0
50. SNOWBOARDING	2.5	3.1	2.8	2.1	1.8	1.2	1.6	1.5	1.6	1.3	na
51. SCUBA (OPEN WATER)	2.3	2.4	2.4	2.2	2.4	2.2	2.0	2.6	2.0	2.7	2.3
52. HOCKEY (Ice)	2.0	2.1	2.2	1.8	1.7	1.6	1.8	1.9	1.5	1.8	1.2
53. BOXING	0.8	na	1.4	na	0.7	na	na	na	na	na	na
54. SNOWSHOEING	0.7	na	0.6	na	na	0.4	na	na	na	na	na
55. WINDSURFING	0.5	0.7	0.7	0.7	0.6	0.8	0.8	0.9	na	na	0.8
56. RUGBY	0.4	na	na	na	na	na	na	na	0.3	na	na
57. FENCING	0.3	na	na	na	na	na	na	na	na	na	na

Source: National Sporting Goods Association, Mt. Prospect, IL, 1997

People who enjoy adventurous vacations were most likely to live in the West (19 percent), while only 14 percent came from the Midwest. Twenty percent of men have taken an adventure trip, compared to 12 percent of women. A person was more likely to participate in hard adventures when young. Twenty-two percent of people aged 18 to 34, and 18 percent of those 35 to 54 took a hard-adventure vacation, compared with only 5 percent of those older than 55.

TRENDS

People are enjoying wildlife-related activities as much as ever. In 1996, the number of anglers (35.2 million) decreased only slightly since the all-time peak of 35.6 million in 1991, still well above the 100 million in 1955, the first year of the study. That represents a 138 percent increase, compared to a 62 percent increase in population. In 1996, the number of hunters (14 million) remained about the same as in 1991, although the number had grown 41 percent since 1955. (See Figure 8.1.) The number of those who took trips away from their homes to observe, feed, or photograph wildlife (23.7 million) decreased by 12 percent from 1980 (the first year it was measured). Those who enjoyed those activities locally (within one mile of their homes) (60.8 million) decreased by 21 percent over that time.

EXPENDITURES

In 1996, Americans spent a total of $101.2 billion on wildlife-related recreation. Fishing accounted for approximately 37 percent of that expense; wildlife-watching activities, 29 percent; and hunting, 20 percent. (Another 13 percent was unspecific.) Sixty percent of the expenditure was for equipment, 30 percent was trip-related, and 11 percent was "other."

WHO PARTICIPATES IN WILDLIFE SPORTS?

The greatest number of wildlife enthusiasts lived in California, Texas, New York, and Florida (Table 8.2). The greatest percentage (24 percent) and the largest number of anglers and hunters were between the ages of 25 and 44. Seventy-three percent of anglers were male, and 27 percent were female. Among hunters, 91 percent were male; 9 percent were female. Of those who watched wildlife, 54 percent were female, and 46 percent were male.

Most hunters (95 percent) were White; 2 percent were Black, and 3 percent were other races. Among anglers, 90 percent were White, 5 percent

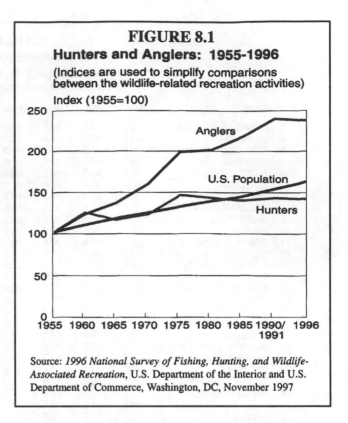

FIGURE 8.1
Hunters and Anglers: 1955-1996
(Indices are used to simplify comparisons between the wildlife-related recreation activities)

Source: *1996 National Survey of Fishing, Hunting, and Wildlife-Associated Recreation*, U.S. Department of the Interior and U.S. Department of Commerce, Washington, DC, November 1997

were Black, and 5 percent were other races. Among those who participated in wildlife-watching activities, 34 percent were White, 10 percent were Black, and 15 percent were other minorities.

Thirty-six percent of anglers had a high school education; 24 percent had one to three years of college, and 27 percent had 4 years of college or more. Only 13 percent had less than 12 years of school. Among hunters, 41 percent had a high school diploma, 22 percent had one to three years of college, 22 percent had 4 years of college or more, and only 15 percent had fewer than 12 years of school. For those who enjoyed wildlife watching activities, 27 percent had a high school diploma, 26 percent had one to three years of college, and 39 percent had 4 or more years of college. Only 7 percent had less than a high school education.

HUNTING

In 1996, 14 million Americans 16 years and older enjoyed hunting a variety of game animals within the United States. In order of preference, hunters sought big game (deer, elk, bear, and wild turkey), small game (squirrels, rabbits, pheasants, quail, and grouse), migratory birds (doves, ducks,

TABLE 8.2

Participants in Wildlife-Related Recreation, by Participant's State of Residence: 1996

(Population 16 years old and older. Numbers in thousands)

Participant's state of residence	Population	Total participants		Sportsmen		Wildlife-watching participants	
		Number	Percent of population	Number	Percent of population	Number	Percent of population
U.S., total	201,472	76,964	38	39,694	20	62,868	31
Alabama	3,306	1,264	38	788	24	988	30
Alaska	432	279	65	187	43	216	50
Arizona	3,234	1,210	37	497	15	999	31
Arkansas	1,914	890	47	596	31	658	34
California	23,777	7,097	30	2,938	12	5,959	25
Colorado	2,929	1,535	52	732	25	1,244	42
Connecticut	2,514	928	37	375	15	774	31
Delaware	560	232	41	118	21	192	34
Florida	11,239	3,642	32	1,988	18	2,840	25
Georgia	5,544	1,960	35	1,093	20	1,622	29
Hawaii	900	201	22	136	15	123	14
Idaho	879	484	55	336	38	355	40
Illinois	8,979	3,740	42	1,761	20	3,137	35
Indiana	4,456	1,876	42	972	22	1,542	35
Iowa	2,174	1,032	47	607	28	828	38
Kansas	1,916	793	41	437	23	607	32
Kentucky	3,001	1,206	40	779	26	951	32
Louisiana	3,227	1,271	39	927	29	861	27
Maine	966	511	53	266	28	443	46
Maryland	3,912	1,537	39	629	16	1,323	34
Massachusetts	4,726	1,835	39	622	13	1,638	35
Michigan	7,267	3,134	43	1,748	24	2,585	36
Minnesota	3,473	1,663	48	1,212	35	1,325	38
Mississippi	2,032	680	33	519	26	458	23
Missouri	4,056	1,888	47	1,081	27	1,623	40
Montana	672	394	59	222	33	315	47
Nebraska	1,232	539	44	289	23	428	35
Nevada	1,214	365	30	223	18	258	21
New Hampshire	887	448	51	181	20	394	44
New Jersey	6,129	1,864	30	821	13	1,574	26
New Mexico	1,276	501	39	281	22	370	29
New York	13,944	3,800	27	1,708	12	3,169	23
North Carolina	5,605	2,364	42	1,217	22	1,984	35
North Dakota	483	190	39	148	31	112	23
Ohio	8,522	3,281	39	1,280	15	2,816	33
Oklahoma	2,484	1,199	48	798	32	860	35
Oregon	2,472	1,260	51	619	25	1,048	42
Pennsylvania	9,298	3,886	42	1,664	18	3,442	37
Rhode Island	759	284	37	111	15	243	32
South Carolina	2,842	1,093	38	718	25	829	29
South Dakota	541	249	46	204	38	165	30
Tennessee	4,120	1,792	44	820	20	1,507	37
Texas	14,186	4,695	33	2,772	20	3,553	25
Utah	1,396	558	40	331	24	415	30
Vermont	455	242	53	116	26	217	48
Virginia	5,168	2,278	44	1,090	21	1,905	37
Washington	4,207	1,908	45	1,018	24	1,621	39
West Virginia	1,467	593	40	374	26	452	31
Wisconsin	3,897	1,961	50	1,151	30	1,651	42
Wyoming	366	192	53	139	38	143	39

Note: Detail does not add to total because of multiple responses. U.S. totals include responses from participants residing in the District of Columbia, as described in the statistical reliability appendix.

Source: *1996 National Survey of Fishing, Hunting, and Wildlife-Associated Recreation*, U.S. Department of the Interior and U.S. Department of Commerce, Washington, DC, November 1997

and geese), and other animals (groundhogs, raccoons, foxes, and coyotes). Hunters spent $20.6 billion on trips and equipment during the year (Table 8.3). Collectively, they hunted 257 million days and took 223 million trips.

People living in the west-north-central states were most likely to hunt (14 percent); residents of the Pacific (4 percent), New England and Middle Atlantic (5 percent each) areas were least likely (Figure 8.2). Most people (51 percent) hunted on private land only; 30 percent, public and private; 17 percent, public only; and 2 percent unspecified.

FISHING

In 1996, more than 35.2 million U.S. residents enjoyed a variety of fishing activities throughout the United States. Collectively, anglers fished 626 million days and took 507 million fishing trips. Eighty-four percent of anglers fished for freshwater species; 26 percent fished for saltwater fish. (There is some overlap due to the anglers who fished for both.) Anglers spent $38 billion on fishing-related expenses during the year. Forty-one percent of that amount was trip-related; 51 percent went for equipment; and 9 percent for other.

WILDLIFE-WATCHING ACTIVITIES

Wildlife-watching activities, including observing, feeding, and photographing wildlife, continue to be popular in the United States. These activities are considered to be either residential (within a mile of one's home) or nonresidential (at least one mile from home). In 1996, 31 percent (62.9 million) of the American population 16 years and older enjoyed watching wildlife. They spent an average of $554 per spender. Fifty-seven percent of the total

TABLE 8.3 Total Hunting Expenditures	
Total hunting expenditures	**$20.6 billion**
Total trip-related	**$ 5.2 billion**
Food and lodging	2.5 billion
Transportation	1.8 billion
Other trip costs	0.9 billion
Total equipment expenditures	**$11.3 billion**
Hunting equipment	5.5 billion
Auxiliary equipment	1.2 billion
Special equipment	4.5 billion
Total other hunting expenditures	**$4.1 billion**
Magazines, books	0.1 billion
Membership dues and contributions	0.2 billion
Land leasing and ownership	3.2 billion
Licenses, stamps, tags, and permits	0.7 billion

Source: *1996 National Survey of Fishing, Hunting, and Wildlife-Associated Recreation*, U.S. Department of the Interior and U.S. Department of Commerce, Washington, DC, November 1997

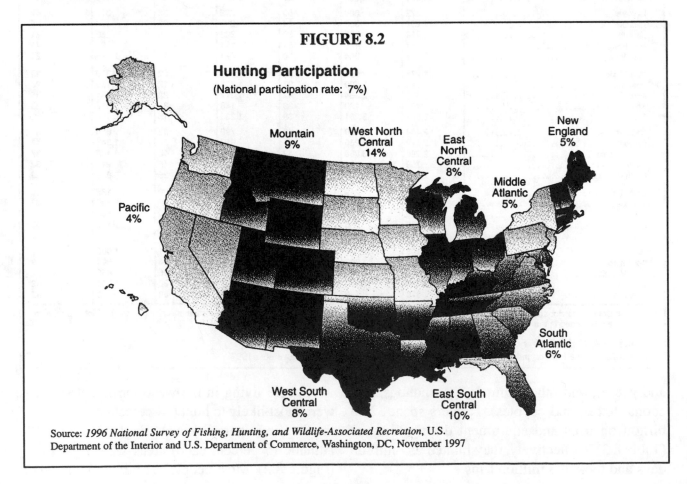

FIGURE 8.2

Hunting Participation
(National participation rate: 7%)

Mountain 9%

West North Central 14%

East North Central 8%

New England 5%

Pacific 4%

Middle Atlantic 5%

South Atlantic 6%

West South Central 8%

East South Central 10%

Source: *1996 National Survey of Fishing, Hunting, and Wildlife-Associated Recreation*, U.S. Department of the Interior and U.S. Department of Commerce, Washington, DC, November 1997

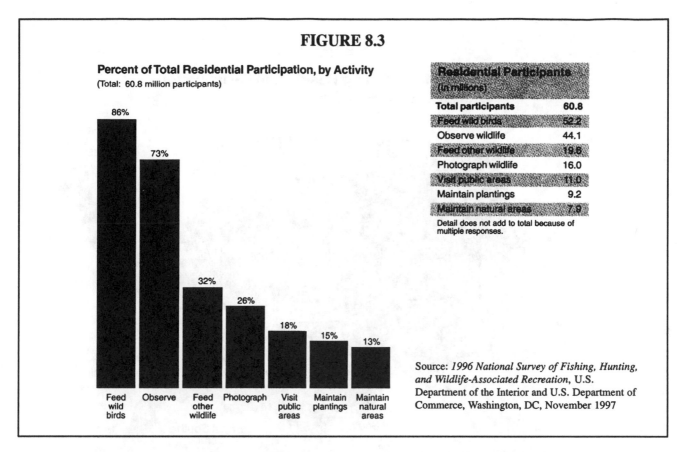

FIGURE 8.3

Percent of Total Residential Participation, by Activity
(Total: 60.8 million participants)

Activity	Percent
Feed wild birds	86%
Observe	73%
Feed other wildlife	32%
Photograph	26%
Visit public areas	18%
Maintain plantings	15%
Maintain natural areas	13%

Residential Participants (in millions)	
Total participants	60.8
Feed wild birds	52.2
Observe wildlife	44.1
Feed other wildlife	19.6
Photograph wildlife	16.0
Visit public areas	11.0
Maintain plantings	9.2
Maintain natural areas	7.9

Detail does not add to total because of multiple responses.

Source: *1996 National Survey of Fishing, Hunting, and Wildlife-Associated Recreation*, U.S. Department of the Interior and U.S. Department of Commerce, Washington, DC, November 1997

was for equipment; 32 percent, trip-related; and 11 percent, other.

Among the 76 million people who enjoyed wildlife-watching activities in their own communities (residential), 86 percent fed the birds, 73 percent observed wildlife, 32 percent photographed wildlife, and 18 percent visited public areas, such as parks. Another 15 percent maintained plantings for wildlife, while 13 percent maintained natural areas for the primary purpose of benefiting wildlife. (See Figure 8.3.) Among those who took trips away from home for the primary purpose of observing, feeding, or photographing wildlife, 97 percent observed, 51 percent photographed, and 42 percent fed the animals.

Residents from the west-north-central area of the country (35 percent) were most likely to enjoy local wildlife activities (Figure 8.4). Residents of the mountain states (16 percent) were most likely to travel to participate in wildlife activities (Figure 8.5). Almost equal proportions of males and females enjoyed wildlife-watching activities.

Whale-Watching

Whale-watching has become increasingly popular in recent years. The whales support an industry pouring millions into coastal economies. The Whale and Dolphin Conservation Society, based in Bath, England, reported that, in 1994, 5.4 million people in 65 countries went on whale-watching expeditions, and the number grows by 10 percent each year. Two-thirds of whale-watching is done in the United States. Worldwide, the activity generates more than $500 million in revenue.

Whale-watching in the United States brought an estimated $37.5 million in direct revenues and another $155.5 million in associated businesses. In southern New England alone, tourists pay more than $21 million each year to visit whales in their natural environment. Humpback, Fin, Minke and, occasionally, Orca or Pilot whales frequent these waters. The highly endangered North Atlantic Right whale can sometimes be spotted.

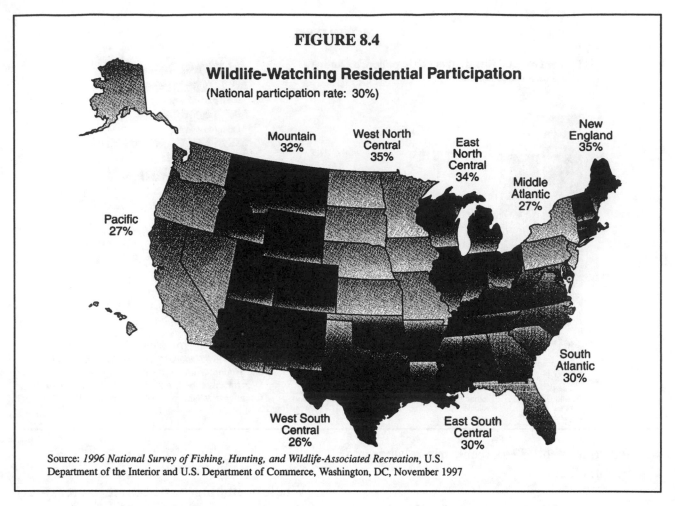

FIGURE 8.4

Wildlife-Watching Residential Participation
(National participation rate: 30%)

Mountain 32%

West North Central 35%

East North Central 34%

New England 35%

Middle Atlantic 27%

Pacific 27%

South Atlantic 30%

West South Central 26%

East South Central 30%

Source: *1996 National Survey of Fishing, Hunting, and Wildlife-Associated Recreation*, U.S. Department of the Interior and U.S. Department of Commerce, Washington, DC, November 1997

The California Gray whale, now removed from the endangered species list, is the star of the West coast's whale-watching industry. Commercial whale-watching vessels (Figure 8.6) also serve as forums for educational outreach and scientific research.

"CANNED HUNTING"

The first arrow flew and landed in a ram's rear, causing him to jump and briefly run. I figured this was a bad shot; I had always heard that experienced bow-hunters aimed for a quick kill. I soon deduced that the hunter's priority was not a quick kill; it was an intact upper body and head for his trophy. The hunter's apparent criterion in aiming was to avoid damaging the part of the animal he would hang on his wall.
— An investigator, The Humane Society of the United States

In the past decade, a controversial form of commercial exploitation of wildlife, known as canned hunting, has swept across the country. Beginning in Texas, canned hunting can now be found in most states. A 1994 Humane Society investigation found there may be as many as several thousand canned-hunting facilities in the United States.

In a canned hunt, the "hunter" pays a set fee and steps into an enclosure where an animal — boar, ram, bear, lion or tiger, zebra, buffalo, rhinoceros, or antelope — is confined. The hunter then kills the animal with the weapon of his choice. The animals are easily cornered. Some have been domesticated or raised in facilities where they have become friendly to humans, even walking up to them.

No federal laws restrict canned hunts. Wisconsin and California are the only two states that have laws governing canned hunts. Investigations re-

136

FIGURE 8.5
Nonresidential Wildlife-Watching Participation
(National participation rate: 12%)

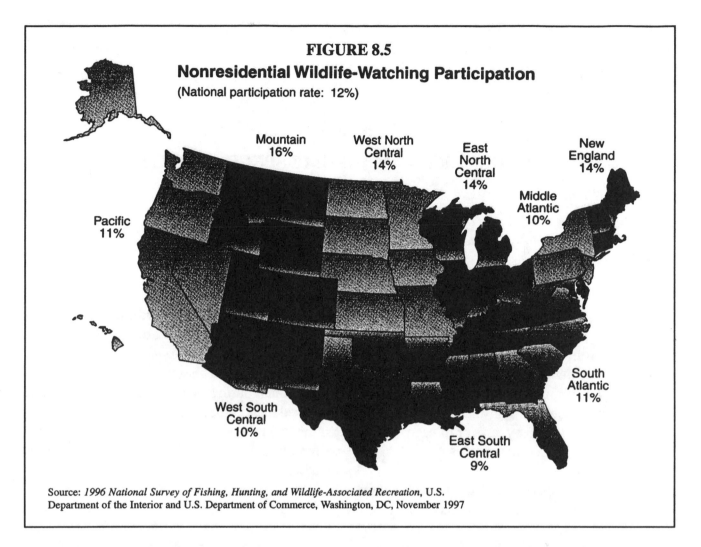

Mountain
16%

West North
Central
14%

East
North
Central
14%

New
England
14%

Middle
Atlantic
10%

Pacific
11%

South
Atlantic
11%

West South
Central
10%

East South
Central
9%

Source: *1996 National Survey of Fishing, Hunting, and Wildlife-Associated Recreation*, U.S.
Department of the Interior and U.S. Department of Commerce, Washington, DC, November 1997

veal that zoos across the nation have sold animals they consider surplus either directly to canned-hunt facilities or to dealers who sell animals to auctions patronized by canned-hunt organizers. Some pressure has been exerted on zoos to acknowledge their responsibility for the animals they discard.

FIGURE 8.6

William Roesler

Whalewatching, one example of the non-consumptive use of wildlife, earns millions of dollars for both the east and west coasts.

137

CHAPTER IX

THE ROAD TO RECOVERY — HOW SOME SPECIES HAVE REBOUNDED

Nature does require
Her times of preservation which, perforce,
I her frail son, amongst my brethren mortal,
Must give my tendence to.
— Shakespeare, *Henry VIII*

Preserving habitat is an important key to species survival. Some endangered species do not need much help from human beings — if the threat is removed, they can recover on their own. Sometimes they simply need to be left alone. For example, most species of fish that are being over-fished can be protected by laws or rules that forbid catching or harvesting that species.

Sometimes a species cannot survive without greater help. In those cases, habitats can be protected by setting aside specific *reserves* where people are not allowed to hunt, put up buildings, or otherwise "civilize" the area. Also, a habitat may need to be restored by correcting or undoing the damage already done. Survival centers, such as zoos and national parks, are often useful in allowing animals to breed. In these settings, people can study the animals to better understand their needs and how to help them survive.

THE HISTORY OF THE PROTECTION OF SPECIES

The idea of conserving nature has a long history. The earliest human beings survived, in part, by killing animals, and they undoubtedly associated the animals they hunted and the kinds of places or habitats where these animals were most abundant.

One of the oldest examples of human understanding of this relationship comes from 242 B.C.E. (before the Common Era), when the Indian emperor, Asoka, created nature reserves in Asia. Marco Polo reported that Asian ruler Kublai Khan (1215-1294) banned the hunting of certain birds and mammals during their reproductive periods and increased their numbers by planting food and protecting cover areas for the species that he wanted to hunt. In South America, during the reign of the Inca kings, seabirds were protected.

The story of Noah's Ark put forward the idea of human beings taking responsibility for ensuring the survival of animal species. The ark was designed to take in seven pairs of each species; three is generally recognized as the minimum number needed to guarantee survival.

An animal's habitat is very dependent on the condition of the soil. Today, soil erosion usually follows deforestation, overgrazing, fire, and overuse. The Chinese have known this for a very long time; the 67th commandment of Taoism reads, "Thou shalt not burn the pastures and the mountain forests."

Until the seventeenth century, kings and princes enacted measures generally intended to retain exclusive rights to the hunting of species that were rare or sought after. At the same time, the elimination of species that terrorized human beings became a national cause. In France, wolf-hunt regiments flushed out and killed the wolves. The state even posted recipes for poisonous baits. In the nine-

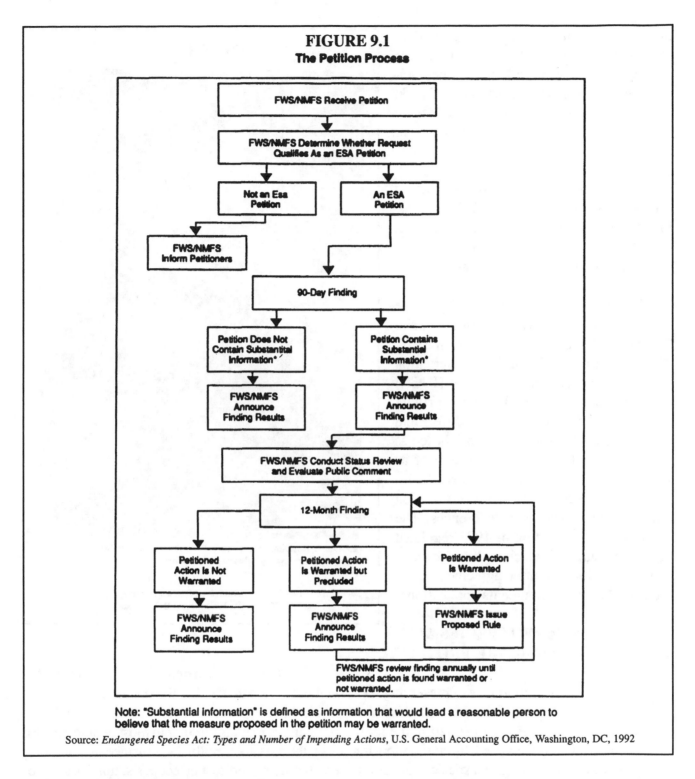

FIGURE 9.1
The Petition Process

FWS/NMFS Receive Petition

FWS/NMFS Determine Whether Request Qualifies As an ESA Petition

Not an Esa Petition

An ESA Petition

FWS/NMFS Inform Petitioners

90-Day Finding

Petition Does Not Contain Substantial Information*

Petition Contains Substantial Information*

FWS/NMFS Announce Finding Results

FWS/NMFS Announce Finding Results

FWS/NMFS Conduct Status Review and Evaluate Public Comment

12-Month Finding

Petitioned Action Is Not Warranted

Petitioned Action Is Warranted but Precluded

Petitioned Action Is Warranted

FWS/NMFS Announce Finding Results

FWS/NMFS Announce Finding Results

FWS/NMFS Issue Proposed Rule

FWS/NMFS review finding annually until petitioned action is found warranted or not warranted.

Note: "Substantial information" is defined as information that would lead a reasonable person to believe that the measure proposed in the petition may be warranted.

Source: *Endangered Species Act: Types and Number of Impending Actions*, U.S. General Accounting Office, Washington, DC, 1992

teenth century American West, ranchers and farmers and government officials killed wolves because they feared the animals threatened their livestock.

In the mid-nineteenth century, many governments became more aware of the need to protect nature without getting any advantage from it other than the conservation of wildlife. In 1864, the first

work on the protection of species, G.P. Marsh's *Man and Nature,* appeared in London.

In 1861, painters of the Barbizon School established the first French nature reserve, covering nearly 3,458 acres of forest at Fountainebleau. Three years later the American government set aside the Yosemite Valley in California as a national reserve. (It became a national park in 1890.) Wyoming's Yellowstone Park was created in 1872 to provide the public a leisure area and was the first U.S. national park. South Africa set up the Sabi Game Reserve in the Transvaal in 1898 as a reserve for hunting game.

In 1895, the first international meeting for the protection of birds was held in Paris, France, leading to new laws in several countries. In 1922, the International Council for the Protection of Birds was founded.

The first international conference for the protection of nature was held in 1913, and the International Office followed in 1928. The International Union for Conservation of Nature and Natural Resources (IUCN) was founded in 1946. In 1961, private sources created the World Wildlife Fund (WWF). The Chinese panda was chosen as the WWF symbol, not only because of its great popularity, but also to reaffirm the international character of nature conservation independent of political differences. The Washington Convention of 1973 regulated trade in endangered species, although many countries did not sign the agreement, leaving no means to guarantee its application.

FIGURE 9.2

Florida scrub jay populations are being protected through the habitat conservation planning process currently being implemented in the Southeast.
USFWS

Source: *The Road Back — Endangered Species Recovery*, U.S. Fish and Wildlife Service, Washington, DC, no date

THE ENDANGERED SPECIES ACT OF 1973 — A LANDMARK PROTECTION*

Recognizing the importance of preserving species diversity, Congress passed the Endangered Species Act of 1973 (ESA; PL93-205), the most far-reaching law ever enacted by any nation for the preservation of endangered species. Under the act, the secretary of the interior, acting through the U.S. Fish and Wildlife Service (FWS), oversees the protection and conservation of all forms of fish, wildlife, and plants found to be in serious jeopardy. The secretary of commerce, acting through the National Marine Fisheries Service (NMFS), is given similar authority for most marine life.

Under the law, a listed life form is protected without regard to whether the species has any commercial or sport value. This includes not only the birds and mammals familiar to most people but also invertebrates like mollusks, crustaceans, and others. It does not protect insect pests, nor does it protect endangered or threatened plants growing on private property; it protects them only on federal land. After passage of the ESA, the FWS was inundated with species petitions for listing — approximately 24,000 petitions were received in the first two years after passage.

*For further "pro and con" discussion of the ESA, see Chapter X and XI.

The Listing Process

In order to list a species, the FWS follows a legal process that begins when a person or organization petitions to list a species. (Figure 9.1 shows the petition process.) Within 90 days, the FWS or NMFS determines whether there is adequate biological data to make a decision. At the point of 90-day findings, 65 percent of petitions are found to have adequate information; 35 percent do not.

FIGURE 9.3
ALONG THE CLINCH RIVER IN SOUTHWESTERN VIRGINIA

Source: *The Road Back — Endangered Species Recovery*, U.S. Fish and Wildlife Service, Washington, DC, no date

For those petitions presenting adequate biological data, FWS/NMFS must make a 12-month finding as to whether the action is warranted. At that point, the FWS/NMFS generally finds that more than half the petitions warrant protection. If action seems warranted, the petition then proceeds to a discussion regarding listing and designation of critical habitat (see below). This critical habitat includes the areas of land, water, and air space specially needed by the species for breeding, resting, and feeding. The ESA gives the government and its agencies the power to do whatever is necessary to protect a species. Once the species is able to survive on its own, it may be removed from the list.

The Endangered Species List

When government biologists decide that a species is becoming dangerously close to extinction, they put the animal on the Endangered Species List. Once an animal species is on the list, it receives special protection. In 1976, the federal government listed 178 species of plants and animals. Since then, that figure has climbed steadily. As of December 1997, in the United States alone, 343 animals and 553 plants were listed as endangered, and 115 animals and 115 plants were threatened. (See Table 1.2, Chapter I.) Another 3,600 species are being studied to see if they need to be added to the list.

The U.S. Fish and Wildlife Service has divided the United States into eight regions. While the endangered and threatened species are located throughout the country, about one-third are located in the South, and about one-third are located in the West.

After a species is listed, its condition and situation are reviewed at least every five years to decide how much longer it will need government protection. The FWS then prepares a "recovery plan" that shows how the species will be protected. Of greatest importance, perhaps, is the fact that the ESA provides federal money to prevent extinction of endangered species. The FWS spends approximately $19 million every year on recovery pro-

141

grams for endangered wildlife.

The number of species being added to the federal list is likely to continue growing. Since the mid-1980s, the candidate species from which future listings will be selected has remained at more than 3,500 species. Over the past two decades, an average of 34 new species per year have been afforded protection under the ESA. While vertebrate species dominated the list during the first years of the act, plant species (48 percent) and invertebrates (13 percent) now comprise a much greater proportion of the listed species.

These species are politically more difficult to defend than mammals, which are more appealing to most Americans. This raises questions about the continued feasibility of a species-by-species preservation strategy. The Clinton Administration is now struggling under intense legal and political pressures to decide which species to protect first.

For its supporters, the Endangered Species Act has proved to be one of the most effective conservation laws ever enacted by any nation. Many Americans believe that the Endangered Species Act has saved many species from extinction. An estimated 40 percent of those species on the list are stable or increasing in number. Unfortunately, money to carry out the programs has become harder to find.

FIGURE 9.4
ALONG THE CLINCH RIVER IN SOUTHWESTERN VIRGINIA, ONE YEAR LATER

Source: *The Road Back — Endangered Species Recovery*, U.S. Fish and Wildlife Service, Washington, DC, no date

Opposition to the Act

Opponents of the ESA believe the law is inefficient, stifles economic growth by curbing development, and sometimes violates private property rights. They further charge that, in many instances, environmental protection results in the loss of jobs and business profits.

The Fifth Amendment of the U.S. Constitution states: "... nor shall private property be taken for public use, without just compensation." This means the government must pay a citizen if it needs land for public use. Opponents of the ESA believe that the federal government should reimburse property owners if their property is diminished by any government regulation, including the ESA.

The simple fact is, very few species are ever removed from the endangered species list, and almost none are "recovered." Continually, however, there are additions to the

142

FIGURE 9.5

An enclosure of the Rio Primate Center in Brazil where endangered primates are bred in captivity (photo by R.A. Mittermeier).

Source: *Conserving the World's Biological Diversity*, prepared and published by the International Union for Conservation of Nature and Natural Resources, World Resources Institute, Conservation International, World Wildlife Fund-US and the World Bank, Gland, Switzerland and Washington, DC, 1990

list. The candidate species list indicates that the number of domestic species whose habitats are protected will more than triple from 962 to between 3,100 and 3,600 in coming years. Unless the ESA is amended, this will cause a tremendous increase in the amount of private property that is restricted under the Act....

It is simply impossible to save every declining species, and it seems blatantly unfair to force a few individuals to endure great economic hardships to save obscure species toward which most Americans are indifferent....

The best way to ensure a proper balancing of costs and benefits in species protection is to require the federal government to compensate landowners whose property it devalues through ESA's land use restrictions.... Requiring the government to compensate landowners ... would force regulators to consider the technical practicability of recovering a species, the species' biological and aesthetic significance, and other costs and benefits of saving the species. These deliberations would result in much more sensible decisions about which species to protect and in which locations. (Thomas Lambert, *The Endangered Species Act: A Train Wreck Ahead*, Center for the Study of American Business, 1995)

Some experts believe the ESA is an unworkable law, addressing processes that have no bearing on the disappearance of species. Furthermore, for many species, extinction is inevitable given the scale and pace of human alteration of landscapes, and no herculean human efforts can stop its course. Many scientists report that rare species are typically listed for protection so late along the slide to extinction that their populations have already become perilously small. In addition, the listing process is far too slow. In fact, some species are believed to have become extinct while federal authorities deliberated.

Even some supporters of the ESA believe that the two decades since passage of the act have been marked by glaring examples of dysfunction in the branches of the government charged with implementing the act. Others blame budget cuts for the seeming inability of the ESA to fully carry out its mandate. The program is severely short of money and overwhelmed by a backlog of hundreds of imperiled species — and by many lawsuits demanding actions to save them.

Some observers believe that although the ESA is needed, it has failed in its central mission and that more, not less, must be done to enforce the law or supplement it. The Wilderness Society, an environmental group, believes that

> We must realize that the Endangered Species Act, even strengthened and fully funded, is necessary but not sufficient to

conserve biological diversity overall. We must complement the Act with a biodiversity program that is ecosystem- and landscape-based and with a policy framework that encourages sustainable development.

An Alternative Approach

Such alternatives to the species-by-species approach have been variously termed the habitat, the ecosystem, the coarse-filter, or the community approach. The fundamental feature common to these approaches is to focus preservation efforts on ecologically important habitats or ecosystems. By focusing on habitat protection, rather than individual species recovery, species would be protected before they reach critically low population sizes. (For

---

TABLE 9.1

SELECTED FEDERAL LAWS AFFECTING THE NATIONAL PARKS

General Park Administration

Equal Employment Opportunity Act of 1972
Land and Water Conservation Fund Act of 1965, as amended
National Park Service General Authorities Act of 1970 (PL 91-383)
Occupational Safety and Health Act of 1970, as amended

Cultural Resources Management/Protection

American Indian Religious Freedom Act of 1978
Antiquities Act of 1906
Archeological and Historic Preservation Act of 1974 (PL 93-291)
Archeological Resources Protection Act 1979, as amended
Historic Sites, Buildings and Antiquities Act of 1935
Native American Graves Protection and Repatriation Act
National Historic Preservation Act

Natural Resources Management/Protection

Clean Air Act
Clean Water Act
Comprehensive Environmental Response, Compensation, and
   Liability Act of 1980, as amended
Endangered Species Act of 1973, as amended
Mining in the Parks Act of 1976 (PL 94-429)
National Environmental Policy Act of 1969, as amended

Visitor Services/Safety

Americans with Disabilities Act of 1990
Architectural Barriers Act of 1968, as amended
Resource Conservation and Recovery Act of 1976
Safe Drinking Water Act
Solid Waste Disposal Act
Toxic Substances Control Act

Source: *National Park Service — Difficult Choices Need to Be Made on the Future of the Parks,* U.S. General Accounting Office, Washington, DC, 1995

---

information on ecosystem conservation approach, see below.)

DELISTED AND DOWNLISTED SPECIES

Species are removed from the Endangered Species list for three reasons: 1) the species has become extinct, 2) the species has recovered, or 3) the original information was wrong. As of January 1998, 27 species that had been on the Endangered Species List had been taken off, or *delisted*. Of those delisted, seven species were removed from the list because they became extinct, 11 species were delisted because they were considered recovered, and nine species were delisted because the original data was in error. The U.S. Fish and Wildlife Service reports that although only a few species have been removed from the list, nearly 41 percent of the listed species are either stable or improving.

Removing species has been a lower priority than adding new ones. In May 1998, Interior Secretary Bruce Babbitt proposed delisting or downlisting another 28 animals and plants, the first mass removals since the ESA's enactment in 1973.

Extinct, Recovered, and Downlisted Species

Of the species on the endangered species list, seven were delisted due to extinction. They include the Tecopa pupfish, the Longjaw cisco, the Blue pike, the Santa Barbara song sparrow, Sampson's pearly mussel, the Amistad gambusia, and the Dusky seaside sparrow. The first four were already extinct by the time they were listed on the first endangered species list in 1973.

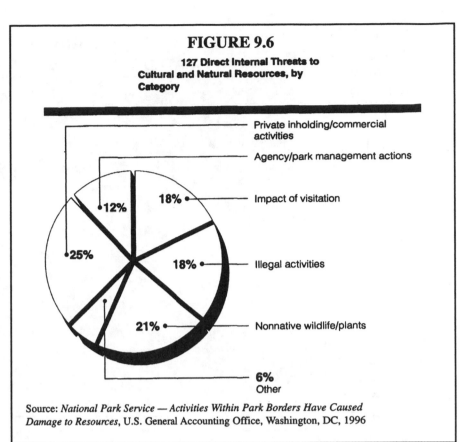

FIGURE 9.6

127 Direct Internal Threats to Cultural and Natural Resources, by Category

Private inholding/commercial activities — 18%

Agency/park management actions — 18%

Impact of visitation — 12%

Illegal activities — 18%

Nonnative wildlife/plants — 21%

Other — 6%

25%

Source: *National Park Service — Activities Within Park Borders Have Caused Damage to Resources*, U.S. General Accounting Office, Washington, DC, 1996

According to the FWS, 11 species were delisted due to recovery. Among them were the Brown pelican, the Palau fantail flycatcher, the Palau ground-dove, the Palau owl, the American alligator, the Rydberg milk-vetch, and the Gray whale. The Arctic peregrine falcon, the Red kangaroo, the Western gray kangaroo, and the Eastern gray kangaroo also recovered.

Species that have stabilized or increased in number may be reclassified from endangered to threatened status. Twenty-two species have been downlisted from endangered to threatened status. Some of the best known are the American alligator, the Gray wolf, the leopard, the Arctic peregrine falcon, the snail darter, and the Bald eagle.

Local Recoveries

In 1994, 14 years after being declared an endangered species and 11 years after being presumed "extinct," the Palos Verdes Blue butterfly reappeared in San Pedro, California. The butterfly's survival is believed to be due to the California gnatcatcher (Chapter V), which also lived in the area and was, until recently, protected there. By preserving the habitat of one species, another species that shares the habitat also benefited.

After a 50-year absence, Black bears have re-established themselves in Big Bend National Park, Texas, and in other parts of West Texas. The bears were eradicated decades ago, primarily because of efforts to dispose of predators that endangered livestock. Park officials report between eight and 12 bears in the park and numerous others in the area surrounding the Davis Mountains. The colonization is remarkable in that it is occurring without human assistance. The bears are believed to have moved from northern Mexico, which has seen a resurgence of Black bears since they became a protected species in the 1980s.

HABITAT CONSERVATION PLANS (HCPs)

Endangered and threatened species live and roam wherever they find suitable habitat, without regard to who owns it. Many landowners fear that they could be denied the use of their land because of the national interest in conserving a species that may inhabit their property. Recognizing that concern, the Congress amended the ESA in 1982 to allow for the creation of Habitat Conservation Plans (HCPs). HCPs are partnerships drawn up by people at the local level, working with either the FWS or the NMFS, depending on the species involved.

FIGURE 9.7
CONFISCATED MOSS AT OLYMPIC NATIONAL PARK

Source: *National Park Service — Activities Within Park Borders Have Caused Damage to Resources*, U.S. General Accounting Office, Washington, DC, 1996

The HCP process allows some individuals of a species to be "taken" under an "incidental take permit" as long as the activity will not significantly reduce the chances of survival and recovery of a wild species. Included in the process is a "no surprises" policy that assures a landowner or developer that no additional future requirements will be imposed for a species covered by an HCP.

Although the tool has been around since 1982, it was little used before 1992, with only 14 permits issued. Between 1992 and 1996, the number soared to more than 190, covering 4.4 million acres, with another 200 HCPs under consideration. HCPs have become an important tool for wildlife conservation. Figure 9.2 shows the Florida scrub jay, which is protected by an HCP in the southeast United States. Figures 9.3 and 9.4 show an area along the Clinch River in Virginia before and after intervention. Protection of this habitat spared species of endangered mussels and fish.

In 1997, after debate and negotiation for over a decade, preservationists and developers settled upon an HCP for San Diego that is regarded by some experts as a possible national model. Under the plan, specific undeveloped sections of land were permanently set aside for protected natural habitat, while other open land was set aside for unrestricted development. As much as possible, the land set aside for natural preservation will be contiguous (be connected). The plan pleased preservationists because species will be protected; developers were pleased that unrestricted development could proceed in defined areas without costly legal challenges by preservationists.

FIGURE 9.8
Historic Rock Art Used for
Target Practice, Arches National Park

Source: *National Park Service — Activities Within Park Border Have Caused Damage to Resources*, U.S. General Accounting Office, Washington, DC, 1996

CAPTIVE BREEDING

For some species, such as the California condor, the Florida panther, or the Black-footed ferret, captive breeding offers the greatest hope for survival. The goal of breeding endangered animals in captivity is to eventually return the species to the wild. The Red and Gray wolves are good examples of species that have been reintroduced into the wild as a result of an intensive captive-breeding program. Figure 9.5 shows a center in Brazil where primates are bred.

THE NATIONAL PARK SYSTEM

Since Congress established Yellowstone National Park as the first national park in 1872, the United States has created a system of national parks occupying millions of acres of land. Today, the 80-million-acre National Park System (NPS) encompasses more than 369 parks, monuments, preserves, memorials, historic sites, recreational areas, seashores, and other units spread from Alaska to the U.S. Virgin Islands to American Samoa. The NPS draws more than 300 million visitations each year. In addition to preserving habitats that range from arctic tundra to tropical rainforest, the system protects representatives of more than half of North America's plant species and a large proportion of the continent's animal species.

The park system is administered by the National Park Service (NPS), established in 1916, which employs over 12,000 permanent personnel and almost twice as many temporary or seasonal workers. The park service both provides for the public's enjoyment of the lands entrusted to its care and protects its lands so they will not be impaired for future generations. Balancing these objectives shapes the debate over how best to manage the national park system.

Working closely with the U.S. Fish and Wildlife Service, the NPS is committed to the protection and restoration of endangered species. James

Ridenour, director of the NPS, named three measures that the NPS takes to protect animals: 1) educates park visitors about species loss; 2) enforces rules of the Endangered Species Act; and 3) provides a protected and undisturbed habitat for animals.

The national parks have played an important role in the return of species. For example, Red wolves and Peregrine falcons have been sheltered across the country in national parks. More than 130 federally listed endangered species are found in national parks. Some species appeared in many of the parks, but approximately 74 species were found in one park alone.

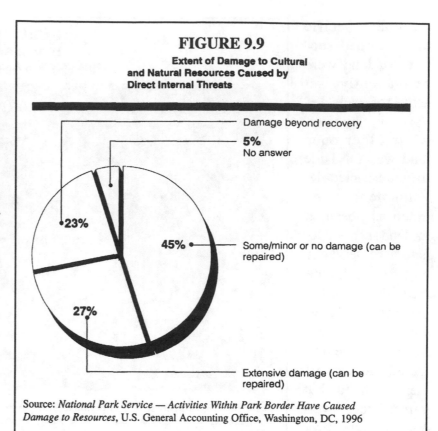

FIGURE 9.9

Extent of Damage to Cultural and Natural Resources Caused by Direct Internal Threats

Damage beyond recovery

5%
No answer

23%

45% Some/minor or no damage (can be repaired)

27%

Extensive damage (can be repaired)

Source: *National Park Service — Activities Within Park Border Have Caused Damage to Resources*, U.S. General Accounting Office, Washington, DC, 1996

Critical Habitats

Many parks contain critical habitats. A *critical habitat* is an area necessary to a particular species, and that animal is specially protected within this habitat. The Endangered Species Act directs the National Park Service to designate critical habitat for endangered and threatened species "when prudent and determinable." Sometimes parks play a major part in taking care of areas that animals need, such as wetlands, tidal and beach areas, swamps, and estuaries (areas where saltwater mixes with freshwater, often the home of many fish and bird species).

The NPS may sometimes find formal designations of critical habitat not prudent because disclosing the exact location of a rare species may make it more vulnerable to collectors, vandals, or curiosity seekers. A designation of critical habitat does not create a wildlife refuge or wilderness area, nor does it close the area to human activity. It applies only to federal agencies if they propose to fund, authorize, or carry out activities that may adversely modify areas within critical habitat. Activities are not restricted unless direct harm to listed wildlife would result.

Problems in the Park System

In 1995, in response to financial crises in many of the nation's parks involving federal budget cuts for park maintenance, the Congress studied the condition of U.S. parks. It reported that the level of visitor services is deteriorating. Visitor services have been cut back, and the condition of many trails, campgrounds, exhibits, and facilities is declining. Included in their findings were

• The elimination of lifeguards at some beaches,

• Museum closings,

• A reduction in operating hours and shortening of open seasons,

• Backlogs of calls for health and safety needs.

At Ellis Island, 32 of 36 buildings were found to be seriously deteriorated. At many parks, officials claim that due to lack of money to maintain records, they lack information on the condition of wildlife within the parks.

The Park Service estimates that the backlog of deferred maintenance rose from $1.9 billion in 1988 to more than $4 billion in 1997. To further complicate the issue, the number of parks has been expanding — 31 parks have been added to the system in the past 10 years.

Another challenge to park management is the increasing number of federal laws that apply to parks. However, funding is not provided to cover the expenses incurred in implementing the laws, such as the Clean Air Act, regulations set by the Environmental Protection Agency (EPA), the Occupational Safety and Health Administration, and others (Table 9.1). Park managers report that meeting such requirements diverts money from day-to-day operating activities. At Glacier National Park, for example, federal requirements for lead paint removal, asbestos removal, surface water treatment, wastewater treatment systems, and accessibility for disabled visitors required park managers to divert funds from other park needs.

Another factor eroding the parks' operating budgets is the rapidly growing visitation, an average of 27 percent per year since 1985. Increases in use drive up costs of waste disposal, general maintenance, road and trail repair, payroll, and utilities.

In 1996, in response to the deterioration in the national park network, Congress studied the threats to the park service and determined that those threats were of two origins, either outside of or from within park boundaries. In a study of the internal activi-

FIGURE 9.10
Arches National Park's Delicate Arch, Where Limits Are Being Considered on the Number of Visitors

Source: *National Park Service — Activities Within Park Border Have Caused Damage to Resources*, U.S. General Accounting Office, Washington, DC, 1996

ties that threatened national parks, the U.S. General Accounting Office (GAO) studied eight of the national parks. The GAO found 127 internal threats to the natural and cultural resources. Most of the threats fell into one of five categories (Figure 9.6):

- The impact of private inholdings (private property within park borders) or commercial development within the parks (25 percent), such as caused by active oil and gas sites or groundwater contamination from homes on lakes;

- Encroachment by nonnative species (21 percent);

- Damage by illegal activities (18 percent), such as poaching or the commercial sale of wild species (Figure 9.7 shows moss confiscated at Olympic National Park);

- Adverse effects of visitation (18 percent), such as traffic congestion, deterioration of vegetation, and trail erosion; and

- Unintended harm by park management actions (12 percent).

Park managers estimated that about 82 percent of the threats have caused more than minor damage to the parks' resources. According to the managers, permanent damage to cultural resources has occurred, such as looting at archaeological sites, bullets fired at historic rock art (Figure 9.8), the deterioration of historic structures, and vandalism of historic cemeteries. Almost one-fourth of the threats caused irreversible damage. Twenty-seven percent of the damage was extensive but repairable, while 45 percent was less serious. (See Figure 9.9.)

Park managers reported that some action was taken in 82 percent of the threats identified. However, they noted that in many cases, steps were taken toward mitigation (lessening the damage), but insufficient funding and staffing often hampered completing those actions. To reduce erosion and damage to sensitive soils, managers installed ropes and rails along hiking trails and erected signs explaining what damage could occur from off-trail walking. Managers are also studying ways to establish "carrying capacities" for frequently visited attractions. This initiative by the NPS stemmed from visitors' comments about the need to preserve the relative solitude at the Delicate Arch at Arches National Park (Figure 9.10).

Difficult Choices for the Future of the Parks

The congressional review determined that since increases in appropriations are unlikely in today's tight budget climate, hard choices lie ahead concerning the future of the national parks. These choices include:

- Generating more income within the parks through higher fees or the involvement of the private sector;

- Limiting the number of parks within the system;

TABLE 9.2		
Type	Number	Acreage
National Wildlife Refuges	482*	88,501,817
Waterfowl Production Areas	166**	1,936,210
Coordination Areas	51***	315,639
TOTAL		90,753,666

Source: *Refuge 2003: A Plan for the National Wildlife Refuge System*, U.S. Fish and Wildlife Service, Washington, DC, 1993

- Reducing the level of visitor services and expectations, such as closing some parks to the public, or limiting the hours or days open, or the number of visitors allowed.

Some parks have raised entrance fees, in general about 5 percent over the last year, although some of the most popular sites experienced a doubling of fees. Fees have been instituted at some areas that were previously free. "Free use of public land is the essence of the American West," some critics of the new policy countered. Despite some protests, however, most recreational users, the largest use of the parks, seem willing to pay.

At the end of the first year of the fee trial, the NPS collected $3.8 million from recreational users. Visitor use is increasing, rather than decreasing, in most of the new fee areas. Although the number of visitors declined in Yellowstone, Yosemite, and the Grand Canyon, where the fee doubled to $20, park officials attribute the decline to a drop in foreign visitors, kept away by the strong dollar.

Another plan being considered is to establish official corporate sponsors of the NPS, much as is done with the Olympic games. Under the plan, about 10 sponsors a year would be chosen, raising $100 million per year, 8 percent of the NPS annual budget.

150

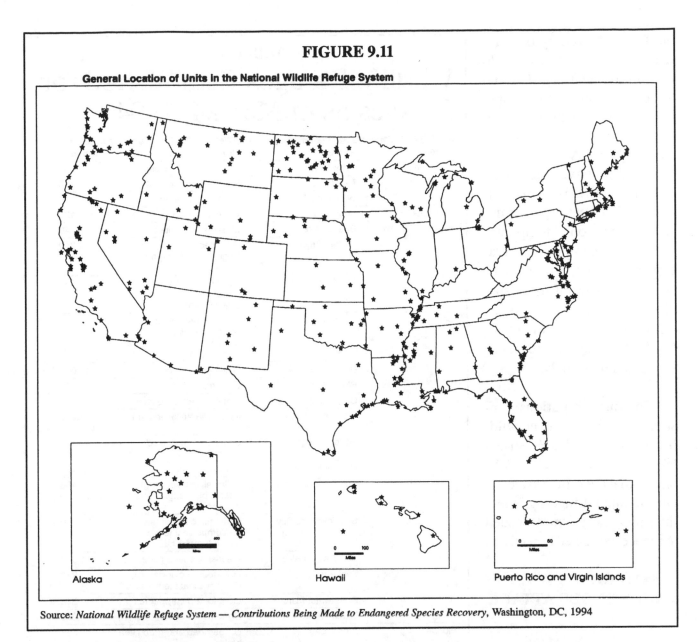

FIGURE 9.11

General Location of Units in the National Wildlife Refuge System

Alaska

Hawaii

Puerto Rico and Virgin Islands

Source: *National Wildlife Refuge System — Contributions Being Made to Endangered Species Recovery*, Washington, DC, 1994

THE NATIONAL WILDLIFE REFUGE SYSTEM

The National Wildlife Refuge System is the only network of federal lands and waters protected and managed principally for fish and wildlife. The refuge system now includes nearly 91 million acres of land and waters (Table 9.2). About 4 percent of the total U.S. land base and 14 percent of the lands owned or managed by the federal government are included in the system. Figure 9.11 shows the location of units in the National Wildlife Refuge System, and Table 9.3 lists the refuges by state and species for which the refuges were established.

The first unit of what would later become the Refuge System was the Pelican Island Bird Reservation in Florida, established in 1903 to protect the dwindling populations of wading birds in Florida. Today, refuges in Alaska — 77 million acres — account for the majority of acreage in the Refuge System. The remaining 499 refuges are widely distributed across all 50 states and five U.S. territories. Approximately one-third of the acreage is wetland habitat, reflecting the importance of wetlands for wildlife survival.

Virtually every species of bird in North America has been recorded in the refuge system, but the wide variety of wildlife also includes over 220 mammals, 250 reptiles and amphibians, and 200 fish species. Of the more than 900 species listed under the Endangered Species Act, 24 percent live and/or have habitat on national wildlife refuges. Many other listed species use refuge lands on a temporary basis for breeding or migratory rest-stops. Figure 9.12 shows the types of listed species found on refuges. As the figure shows, more than two-thirds of the species are plants, birds, and mammals.

Funding limitations constrain efforts to manage wildlife refuges. The U.S. Fish and Wildlife Service (FWS) claims that the refuge system's current annual funding is less than half the amount needed to meet established objectives.

AMERICA'S WILD LANDS UNDER ATTACK

In wildness is the preservation of the world.
— Henry David Thoreau

Since the passage of the Wilderness Act in 1964 (PL 88-577), 630 areas have been designated wilderness, a total of more than 103 million acres or nearly 161,000 square miles. Unlike national parks, which are intended for use by large numbers of visitors, wilderness areas are supposed to be pristine, with limited access and no amenities. The number of people using the areas has been growing in recent years, to 17 million "visitor days" (one person in the area for 12 hours) in 1995, up from 15 million in 1989.

TABLE 9.3

Wildlife Refuges Established for Species as of May 24, 1994

State	Refuge	Primary species	Acreage
Alabama	Blowing Wind Cave	Indiana bat, gray bat	264
	Fern Cave	Indiana bat, gray bat	199
	Watercress Darter	Watercress darter	7
Arkansas	Logan Cave	Ozark cavefish	124
Arizona	Buenos Aires	Masked bobwhite quail	113,940
	Leslie Canyon	Gila (Yaqui) topminnow, Yaqui chub, Peregrine falcon	1,240
	San Bernardino	Gila (Yaqui) topminnow, Yaqui chub, Yaqui catfish, beautiful shiner	2,369
California	Antioch Dunes	Lange's metalmark butterfly, Antioch Dunes evening-primrose, Contra Costa wallflower	55
	Bitter Creek	California condor	14,054
	Blue Ridge	California condor	897
	Castle Rock	Aleutian Canada goose	14
	Coachella Valley	Coachella Valley fringe-toed lizard	3,276
	Ellicott Slough	Santa Cruz long-toed salamander	127
	Hopper Mountain	California condor	2,471
	Sacramento River	Valley elderberry longhorn beetle, bald eagle, least bell's vireo	6,458
	San Francisco Bay	California clapper rail, California least tern, salt marsh harvest mouse	21,200
	San Joaquin River	Aleutian Canada goose	1,638
	Seal Beach	Light-footed clapper rail, California least tern	911
	Sweetwater Marsh	Light-footed clapper rail	316
	Tijuana Slough	Light-footed clapper rail	1,023
Florida	Archie Carr	Loggerhead and green sea turtles	51
	Crocodile Lake	American crocodile	6,560
	Crystal River	West Indian manatee	66
	Florida Panther	Florida panther	23,379
	Hobe Sound	Loggerhead and green sea turtles	980
	National Key Deer	Key deer	8,196

Continued on following page.

However, many visitors to wilderness areas, as well as park managers note the intrusion of civilization in the form of cellular phones, snowmobiles, and aircraft.

True wilderness remains for most humans a place to go only occasionally, or never at all. In 1997, the Wilderness Society, an environmental advocacy organization, listed "America's 10 Most Endangered Wild Lands." The 10 locations were chosen based on their natural resources, national significance, and the immediate threats to their integrity. Most of the sites are wildlife reserves.

Among the 10 most harmed locations were the Arctic National Wildlife Refuge (Alaska), Klamath Basin National Wildlife Refuge (Oregon/California), Snoqualmie Pass (Washington), Boundary Waters Canoe Area (Minnesota), and the Grand Staircase/Escalante National Monument (Utah). Also included were Owyhee Canyonlands (Idaho), Okefenokee National Wildlife Refuge (Georgia/Florida), Cabeza Prieta National Wildlife Refuge (Arizona), the Whitney Estate in New York, and California's Mojave Desert.

Many other national parks and monuments are suffering. More than five million people visit the Grand Canyon each year. On a busy day, 6,500 vehicles compete for 2,000 parking spaces. By 2001, at the Grand Canyon and Zion and Yosemite National Parks, park officials will require visitors to use mass transit. Federal restrictions have been set on aircraft flights over and near the Grand Canyon.

TABLE 9.3 (Continued)

State	Refuge	Primary species	Acreage
	St. Johns	Dusky seaside sparrow (extinct)	6,255
Hawaii	Hakalau Forest	Akepa, akiapolaau, 'o'u, Hawaiian hawk, Hawaiian creeper	16,515
	Hanalei	Hawaiian stilt, Hawaiian coot, Hawaiian moorhen, Hawaiian duck	917
	Huleia	Hawaiian stilt, Hawaiian coot, Hawaiian moorhen, Hawaiian duck	241
	James C. Campbell	Hawaiian stilt, Hawaiian coot, Hawaiian moorhen, Hawaiian duck	166
	Kakahaia	Hawaiian stilt, Hawaiian coot	45
	Kealia Pond	Hawaiian stilt, Hawaiian coot	691
	Pearl Harbor	Hawaiian stilt	61
Iowa	Driftless Area	Iowa pleistocene snail	507
Massachusetts	Massasoit	Plymouth red-bellied turtle	184
Michigan	Kirtland's Warbler	Kirtland's warbler	6,530
Mississippi	Mississippi Sandhill Crane	Mississippi sandhill crane	19,308
Missouri	Ozark Cavefish	Ozark cavefish	40
	Pilot Knob	Indiana bat	90
Nebraska	Karl E. Mundt	Bald eagle	19
Nevada	Ash Meadows	Devil's hole pupfish, Warm Springs pupfish, Ash Meadows amargosa pupfish, Ash Meadows speckled dace, Ash Meadows naucorid, Ash Meadows blazing star, Amargosa niterwort, Ash Meadows milk-vetch, Ash Meadows sunray, spring-loving centaury, Ash Meadows gumplant, Ash Meadows ivesia	13,231
	Moapa Valley	Moapa dace	32
Oklahoma	Oklahoma Bat Caves	Ozark big-eared bat, gray bat	658
Oregon	Bear Valley	Bald eagle	4,178
	Julia Butler Hansen Refuge for Columbian White-tailed Deer (also in Washington)	Columbian white-tailed deer	1,978

Continued on following page.
Continued on following page.

ZOOS

Although zoos (zoological parks) have often had a bad reputation among many animal lovers who object to capturing and confining wild animals in cages and unnatural conditions, zoos have played a role in the survival of some species. One

153

of the biggest challenges has been getting animals to reproduce in captivity. Ling Ling, a rare panda bear, a gift from the People's Republic of China to the United States, made headlines each time she expected a baby. The nation was saddened each time she lost one and finally mourned her death in 1993.

A New Role — a New Philosophy — for Zoos

At one time, zoos kept animals closely caged and in conditions that many people felt were unnatural and unhealthy for the species. Today, many zoos have been redesigned and rebuilt to house the animals in areas very similar to their natural habitats. In addition, for many species, a zoo may be the only place where a particular animal may ever be seen because the species is dying out. Many zoos have developed public education programs tying zoo exhibits to the natural ecology and have become homes for endangered species. Many zoos have evolved from being "menageries" for the pleasure of humans to being living museums and ecological conservation centers for species.

The Bronx Zoo in New York is pioneering new efforts to extend its expertise into field study. Zoos and aquariums constitute an extraordinary base of data for field conservation operations. The aim is to apply expertise on animal health, nutrition, handling, and reproduction to the needs of animals in the wild. With habitats for large animals becoming increasingly degraded, Bronx Zoo veterinarians are closely monitoring animal health in the field. "It's a good indication of environmental degradation," said Dr. William Karesh, a Bronx-based veterinarian.

The resources of society, in this case the zoo, are being focused on preservation. Because con-

TABLE 9.3 (Continued)

State	Refuge	Primary species	Acreage
	Nestucca Bay	Aleutian Canada goose	399
South Dakota	Karl E. Mundt	Bald eagle	1,044
Texas	Attwater Prairie Chicken	Attwater prairie chicken	7,984
	Balcones Canyonlands	Black-capped vireo, golden-cheeked warbler	7,905
Virginia	James River	Bald eagle	4,147
	Mason Neck	Bald eagle	2,276
Virgin Islands	Green Cay	St. Croix ground lizard	14
	Sandy Point	Leatherback sea turtle	327
Washington	Julia B. Hansen Refuge for Columbian White-tailed Deer (also in Oregon)	Columbian white-tailed deer	2,777
Wyoming	Mortenson Lake	Wyoming toad	1,776
Total acreage			**310,110**

Note: This list does not include refuges which were originally established for other purposes and later added specific lands for listed species.

Source: *National Wildlife Refuge System — Contributions Being Made to Endangered Species Recovery*, U.S. General Accounting Office, Washington, DC, 1994

servation does not occur in a social and economic vacuum, Bronx-based conservationists are working with national governments, local politicians, and international aid agencies to preserve habitat and protect animals. Their goal is to transfer technology and expertise to developing countries so that they can develop their own conservation efforts.

Ethical Questions Faced by Zoos

For many people, keeping animals captive is an ethical problem. In order to provide living conditions similar to a species' natural habitat and fitting to that species' instincts, zoo managers often face tough scientific and moral questions. Zoos are obligated to enrich an animal's environment in ways that permit the animal to engage in a variety of natural activities.

Although many species will not likely survive without captive breeding programs, some species pose both a danger to humans and huge expense to keep them captive. Male (bull) elephants, for example, are extremely difficult and dangerous to handle. Only a small number of facilities are equipped with expensive, specialized elephant-care pens to contain them. Even there, the bulls are often dangerous to each other, to handlers, and to visitors, killing an average of two keepers per year in North American facilities. The Los Angeles Zoo, one of America's leading zoos, will no longer accept the bulls. If such facilities choose not to maintain the elephants, where will they live instead, and without a large enough number of males for genetic diversity, can the species survive?

What about feeding live prey animals to zoo carnivores? Few people are concerned about feeding live fish or insects to carnivorous species, but what about feeding a live rabbit or deer to a tiger? Captive-bred California condors, which are carrion eaters destined to be released into the wild, must learn to hunt meat and are fed sheep carcasses. Zoo managers report that the public seems to enjoy seeing a bear work on a chicken carcass, but how will they accept feeding live prey to animals that catch their food live in the wild and are healthier when they can do so in captivity?

Many people also question the use of animals in circuses and rodeos. They claim the animals are often subjected to cruel treatment for the purpose of entertaining humans.

FEDERAL LANDS

The federal government owns about 650 million acres, approximately 30 percent of the nation's total surface area. Four federal land management agencies — the Department of Agriculture's Forest Service and the Department of Interior's Bureau of Land Management (BLM), Fish and Wildlife Service (FWS), and National Park Service (NPS) — manage about 95 percent of this land; the Department of Defense manages the remainder. These four agencies manage about 623 million acres — 27 percent of the approximately 2.3 billion acres in the United States. The percentage

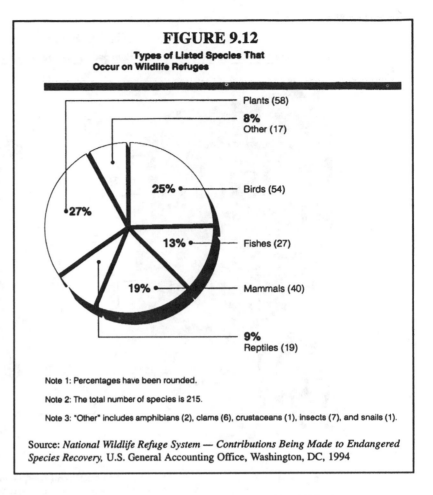

FIGURE 9.12
Types of Listed Species That Occur on Wildlife Refuges

Plants (58)
8% Other (17)
25% Birds (54)
27%
13% Fishes (27)
19% Mammals (40)
9% Reptiles (19)

Note 1: Percentages have been rounded.

Note 2: The total number of species is 215.

Note 3: "Other" includes amphibians (2), clams (6), crustaceans (1), insects (7), and snails (1).

Source: *National Wildlife Refuge System — Contributions Being Made to Endangered Species Recovery*, U.S. General Accounting Office, Washington, DC, 1994

of each state's total acreage managed by these agencies varies widely — from less than 1 percent in Iowa to about 81 percent in Nevada. Figure 9.13 shows the approximate percentage of federal land in each state. Large percentages of many western states are owned by the federal government.

Federal lands contain a significant portion of the nation's wealth of natural resources, approximately 38 percent of the nation's forests, 54 percent of grazing lands, and the sources of many of the nation's rivers.

Legislation to Protect Federal Lands

Over the past 30 years, Congress has enacted a number of laws to protect natural resources on federal, state, and private lands. Among other things, these laws affect what can be done in connection with the air, water, soils, plants, and animals. In addition, the use of some federal lands is regulated by law or administrative restrictions. Most of the

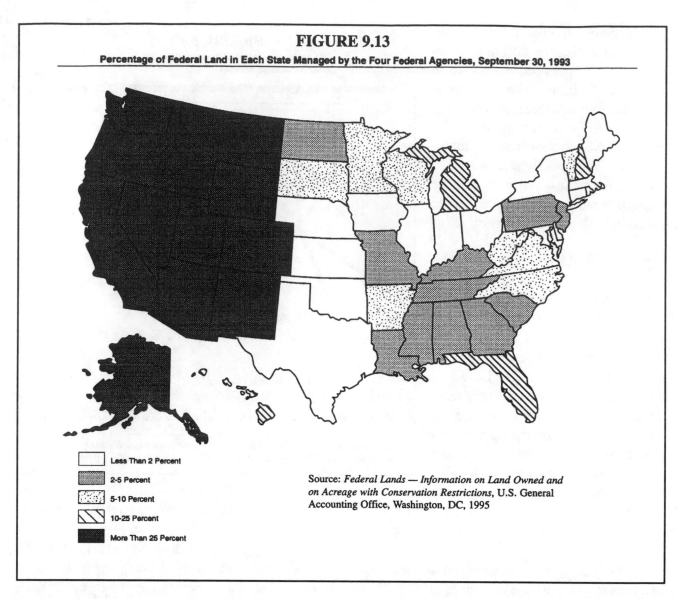

FIGURE 9.13

Percentage of Federal Land in Each State Managed by the Four Federal Agencies, September 30, 1993

Less Than 2 Percent

2-5 Percent

5-10 Percent

10-25 Percent

More Than 25 Percent

Source: *Federal Lands — Information on Land Owned and on Acreage with Conservation Restrictions*, U.S. General Accounting Office, Washington, DC, 1995

federal acreage with conservation restrictions is located in 13 western states. Figure 9.14 shows the percentage of land in each of those states restricted for conservation purposes. The acreage with conservation restrictions is expected to change in future years as congressional decisions are made about additional land for such things as wilderness and national parks. Despite legislation and the efforts of a number of federal agencies to protect U.S. natural resources, ecological conditions on many federal lands have declined.

To date, Congress has designated 103 million acres of land as wilderness (see above). Even though land may have a restriction that sets it aside for conservation purposes, this does not preclude all activities within the designated areas. For example, the "wilderness" designation generally allows, among other things, the existence of administrative structures, the development of minerals, access to private lands within the wilderness, the grazing of livestock in instances where rights were previously established, and use of nonmotorized recreational vehicles.

Under the Wild and Scenic Rivers Act of 1968 (PL 90-542), Congress has set aside 1 million acres of federal acreage along rivers. A principal protection afforded by a "wild and scenic river designation" is the ban on water resource projects to divert or hinder the flow of water, such as dams.

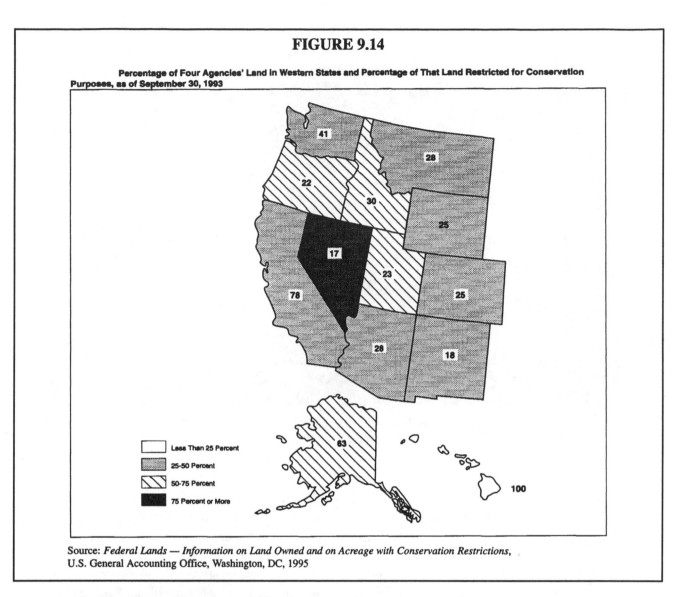

FIGURE 9.14

Percentage of Four Agencies' Land in Western States and Percentage of That Land Restricted for Conservation Purposes, as of September 30, 1993

Less Than 25 Percent
25-50 Percent
50-75 Percent
75 Percent or More

Source: *Federal Lands — Information on Land Owned and on Acreage with Conservation Restrictions*, U.S. General Accounting Office, Washington, DC, 1995

ECOSYSTEM CONSERVATION REPLACES SPECIES-BY-SPECIES CONSERVATION

The History of U.S. Land Management

During the United State's first century as a nation, the federal government viewed its land management role as temporary. At that time, the federal government owned about 80 percent of the nation's surface area. Beginning in 1785, the government began to survey and sell its vast land holdings to new states, settlers, and railroad companies, opening the American frontier. By the end of the nineteenth century, the federal government had transferred most of its generally productive lands in the eastern, southern, far west, and midwestern United States to private ownership. It also gener- ally allowed private uses on the remaining federal lands.

After several decades of rapid development and unrestricted use, many of the nation's lands and natural resources were significantly degraded. Responding to growing concerns, Congress began to redefine the federal government's role in land management from temporary to permanent reten- tion and active stewardship.

Over the past 30 years, increasing scientific and public concern about the declining condition of the nation's resources led Congress to enact a number of laws to protect resources on both federal and nonfederal lands. As a result, the current land man- agement framework has evolved into a complex collection of agencies, land units, and laws. In

FIGURE 9.15

Boundary Between Yellowstone National Park and Targhee National Forest

Source: *Ecosystem Management — Additional Actions Needed to Adequately Test a Promising Approach,* U.S. General Accounting Office, Washington, DC, 1994

many instances, this complexity has resulted in duplications, omissions, and confusion about the various laws and authorities. The effects of these different missions and requirements are sometimes easily seen where two agencies' lands are next to one another. For example, Figure 9.15 shows the difference between Yellowstone National Park, where timber harvesting is prohibited, and Targhee National Forest in Idaho, where large areas of trees have been removed through clearcutting.

Such declines in land quality have required federal land managers to reduce levels of timber harvests, livestock grazing, recreational activities, and other uses on some land units. These reductions, in turn, have had adverse economic effects on some nearby communities whose economies are highly dependent on uses associated with federal lands. These adverse effects have created intense conflicts over federal land management.

As a result of continuing declines in natural resources and conflict between environmentalists and industry, many officials and scientists have come to agree that land management must no longer be focused on individual land units or individual natural resources or species but, rather, on whole ecosystems (see below). Furthermore, many agency officials, scientists, and policy analysts agree that ecosystem management will generally fall short of its goal if it is limited to activities on federal lands. The Clinton Administration, agreeing with many conservation biologists, has adopted a strategy of focusing first on federal lands.

Conservation in the Twenty-First Century — Ecosystem Management

The U.S. Fish and Wildlife Service defines ecosystem management as "protecting or restoring the function, structure, and species composition of an ecosystem, recognizing that all components are interrelated."

In 1993, Secretary of the Interior Bruce Babbitt reassigned research and monitoring programs from eight agencies within the Department of the Interior to form a new agency, the National Biological Service (NBS). This agency is responsible for gathering, analyzing, and disseminating biological information necessary for stewardship of the nation's resources. As a result, the NBS conducted the first study of ecosystems in the United States, finding many U.S. ecosystems imperiled. (For information on the study, see Chapter III.) In 1996, the NBS was integrated into the United States Geological Service (USGS) as the Biological Resources Division (BRD).

Researchers have found that communities of plants and animals, which can include humans, are interdependent and interact with their physical environment (soil, water, and air) to form distinct ecological units — ecosystems — that span federal and nonfederal lands. As a result, a growing number of officials, scientists, and natural resource policy analysts believe that a broader approach is needed to manage natural resources. They believe that maintaining or restoring ecosystems, rather than individual resources or species, would better address declining ecological conditions and ensure long-term sustainable land use.

In 1993, the White House Office on Environmental Policy, created by President Bill Clinton, established the Interagency Ecosystem Management Task Force to implement an ecosystem approach to environmental management. Since that time, all four of the primary federal land management agencies have independently announced that they are implementing an ecosystem approach to managing their lands and natural resources. The Clinton Administration's budget proposals initially included $700 million for ecosystem management initiatives, including four pilot projects — the old-growth forests of the Pacific Northwest; south Florida, including the Everglades and Florida Bay; the urban watershed of the Anacosta River in Maryland and the District of Columbia; and Alaska's Prince William Sound. However, the conservative Congress that came into office in 1994 cut budgets, which have largely sidelined such efforts.

In 1992, more than 100 world nations met in Rio de Janeiro in Brazil for a conference on the environment, the Earth Summit. One of the agreements reached was a pact to save species, habitats, and ecosystems. Although many countries signed the treaty, President George Bush did not, fearing that the treaty might be harmful to business interests in the United States. Nonetheless, many other nations agreed to safeguard natural ecosystems and to protect biodiversity. In 1994, President Bill Clinton signed the treaty.

THE UNITED NATIONS' LIST OF PROTECTED AREAS

The United Nations has set up areas in the world where, like the national parks and refuges in the United States, animals are protected. These protected areas are specially designed to nurture wildlife. Often they consist of a core zone in the center of the area where the animals or plants cannot be disturbed by human beings, construction, hunting, or even sightseers. Around that area are "buffer zones" and other transition spaces that act as shields or a cushioning for the core zone. At the outside rim are areas for managed human living. In 1998, there are 30,000 protected areas in the world covering 13.2 million square kilometers of land, freshwater, and sea. The terrestrial part of the network is far larger than the marine component, and accounts for 11.7 million square kilometers — nearly 8 percent of the world's land area.

Conservation biology theory advocates that protected areas should be as large as possible in order to increase biological diversity. The larger they are, the better they are buffered from outside pressures. The world's largest protected areas are Greenland National Park (Greenland), Ar-Rub'al-khali Wildlife Management Area (Saudi Arabia), Great Barrier Reef Marine Park (Australia), Qiang Tang Nature Reserve (China), Cape Churchill Wildlife Management Area (Canada), and the Northern Wildlife Management Zone (Saudi Arabia).

CHAPTER X

THE ENDANGERED SPECIES ACT HAS WORKED WELL

PREPARED STATEMENT OF BRUCE BAB-BITT, U.S. SECRETARY OF THE INTERIOR, BEFORE THE SENATE COMMITTEE ON ENVIRONMENT AND PUBLIC WORKS, JULY 13, 1995

I would like to ... discuss the Endangered Species Act, one of our nation's most important conservation laws. The stated purposes of this law are relatively simple but far-reaching — to conserve the ecosystems on which endangered and threatened species depend and to provide a program for their conservation, including their recovery. Despite the high level of public support for the Act, the subject of its reauthorization seems to generate much more heat than light.

Recent media coverage has focused almost entirely on either the Act's vaunted success stories (such as bald eagle, gray whale, peregrine falcon, and whooping crane) or on reported "horror stories" (e.g., accounts involving the California fairy shrimp and Stephens' kangaroo rat). While some of these stories are valid, others are clearly exaggerated or false.

What has actually been happening over the past two years, much less publicized, is quiet revolution on the implementation of the Act....

As you are aware, yesterday the President announced an administration proposal to exempt 95 percent of American homeowners from any restrictions on their property imposed by the Endangered Species Act. President Clinton recognized that home ownership and the opportunity for homeowners to use their property free of unnecessary restrictions is essential to the fulfillment of the American dream. The proposal would essentially eliminate restrictions related to the presence of threatened species on tracts of land used for single family residential homes and other activities that disturb five or fewer acres of land....

America has been the world leader in conservation since the days of Teddy Roosevelt. We were the first country to establish national parks, national forests, and national wildlife refuges. We also led the way with other landmark laws to conserve our nation's air, water, and other vital resources. In 1973, Congress continued this tradition by enacting by a nearly unanimous vote, the Endangered Species Act. This remarkable law, regarded as the world's most important wildlife conservation statute, reflects the deep respect and appreciation Americans hold for our precious natural resources, as well as an understanding that the fate of people and wildlife alike is linked to the well-being of the environment around us.

In a sense, the Act is a measure of the planet's life support system, and therefore our own. It serves as an emergency protection for the diversity of animals and plants essential for many purposes, most notably medicine, agriculture, and ecological resilience. As the rate of species loss rises, so do the stakes for all of us. Extinction is not a controlled experiment, but an irreversible process. Put another way, endangered means that there is still time, but extinction is forever. The Act is our safety net.

... These objectives include, but are not limited to, expanding the role of states: reducing socioeconomic effects of listing and recovery; ensuring that best available peer-reviewed science is the bases of all ESA decisionmaking; and increasing cooperation among federal agencies....

Ultimately, the changes that have already been adopted in the administration's strategy recognize that the central goal of the act is protection of habitat for threatened and endangered species; that the most valuable habitat usually supports a rich mixture of species; and that the efforts to protect such habitat inevitably will involve weighing costs and benefits....

Our approach to the Endangered Species Act is intended to recognize trade-offs and balance decisions, taking the long-term view. If sound science and wise management of our natural resources guide our actions, we will benefit not only threatened and endangered species, but the human species as well.

PREPARED STATEMENT OF DR. MICHAEL T. CLEGG, CHAIRPERSON OF THE NATIONAL RESEARCH COUNCIL'S COMMITTEE ON SCIENTIFIC ISSUES IN ENDANGERED SPECIES ACT, BEFORE THE SENATE COMMITTEE ON ENVIRONMENT AND PUBLIC WORKS, JULY 13, 1995

In broad terms, [the National Research Council's Committee on Scientific Issues in the Endangered Species Act] were asked whether the Endangered Species Act conforms to contemporary scientific knowledge about habitat, risks to species and identifying species, subspecies, and other biological groups below the species level. We also were asked to consider whether the Act conforms to what we know about the factors needed for recovery of endangered species, possible conservation conflicts between endangered species, and the timing of key decisions under the act.

The 1973 Endangered Species act and its amendments constitute the broadest and most powerful law in this nation to protect endangered species and their habitats. The survival of species such as the whooping crane, American peregrine falcon, southern sea otter, and blackfooted ferret attests to the act's success. But it is also a controversial law, particularly in cases where its implementation has delayed or prevented public and private development and other economic activities. Many of these conflicts have played out in the public-policy arena and in the courts.

... our committee finds that there has been a good match between science and the Endangered Species Act. Given new scientific knowledge, we simply recommend changes to improve its effectiveness.

The ultimate goal of the Endangered Species Act is to ensure the long-term survival of a species. We all know that species extinctions have occurred since life has been on Earth. But the current rate of extinction is among the highest in the entire fossil record, in large part because of human activity. The introduction of non-native species and especially the degradation and loss of habitat are causing extinctions at a rate that many scientists consider a crisis.

The relationship between vanishing habitats and vanishing species nationwide is well-documented. Consequently, protecting species in the wild most often means conserving the habitats where they live and breed. The act's emphasis on protecting habitat reflects current scientific understanding of this crucial relationship.

We endorse the regional bases, negotiated approaches to the development of habitat conservation plans provided for by the 1982 amendments to the act. Although difficult to negotiate, because they require agreement among many contending parties, such plans are already in use in several regions of the country to protect endangered and threatened species. The U.S. Fish and Wildlife Service should provide guidance on obtaining the necessary biological data and other information to help develop these plans.

... We realize that detailed information needed to designate critical habitat for a given species often is lacking. Just because a species occurs within a habitat does not necessarily mean that it requires that habitat for survival. To complicate matters, the absence of a species from a given habitat does not mean that the habitat is not critical to the survival of the species. These uncertainties, combined with public concern over economic consequences, often make designating critical habitat both controversial and arduous. This can delay or even prevent protection.

To avoid such situations, we recommend that when a species is listed as endangered, a core amount of survival habitat should be protected as an emergency, stop-gap measure without reference to economic impact. This survival habitat should be able to support either current populations or the population necessary to ensure short-term survival for a period of 25 to 50 years. When the required recovery plans are adopted or the required critical habitat is identified and designated, the survival-habitat protections should automatically expire.

Shrinking amounts of available habitat are creating conflicts between what is needed to protect different species in the same region, though such conflicts have been rare in the past. The most effective way to avoid conflicts is to maintain protected areas large enough to allow for the existence of a diverse array of habitats within a single area....

... We hope that our recommendations can help make the implementation of the act more effective at protecting endangered species, more predictable, and less disruptive for everyone. We believe that there is a common ground for a more enlightened and cooperative public conservation policy.

PREPARED STATEMENT OF JANE LUBCHENCO, DEPARTMENT OF ZOOLOGY, OREGON STATE UNIVERSITY, BEFORE THE SENATE COMMITTEE ON ENVIRONMENT AND PUBLIC WORKS, JULY 13, 1995

The Endangered Species Act of 1973 was a remarkable piece of legislation. Now, twenty-two years later, the time has come to revisit the ESA and to reconsider its goals and the mechanisms for achieving them. This task is one of the most important challenges.... The responsibility of safeguarding the nation's biological resources is profound. The challenge is also fundamentally different from many of the other important responsibilities of Congress. Most policies formulated at one point in time can be altered at a later date. However, because the loss of a species is irreversible, many of the consequences of a poorly conceived ESA cannot be reversed.

Jurassic Park notwithstanding, species cannot be brought back to life, nor can most of their important functions be replaced. Losing species means losing genes, losing potentially important chemicals for medicine, or losing life-supporting ecological services. The permanency of extinction and the folly of squandering the natural biological capital on which we all depend should prompt a profound sense of responsibility and a suitably careful approach. Few bad decisions will have such irreversible consequences.

The task of reauthorization should take full advantage of the substantial, recent advances in science. We are fortunate to have access to a wealth of scientific information, information that can be used effectively to meet the daunting responsibility of safeguarding the nation's biological resources for coming generations.

Together, these reports provide unequivocal testimony to strong consensus within the scientific community, strong consensus about the importance of preserving the nation's biological resources, strong consensus about the critical importance of these resources to people, and strong consensus about the dual need to protect both species and habitats.

People depend upon biological resources in myriad and generally unappreciated ways. Even the much-maligned "creepy, crawly critters" or even the simply plain organisms may be bountiful sources of useful products like medicines....

Species provide much more than "goods" such as medicines, food and genes; they also provide "services" to people. Intact ecosystems with their full component of species provide many essential services which we take for granted. Old growth forests and wetlands purify water and detoxify pollutants; kelp forests and salt marshes provide nursery ground for fishes and protect shores from erosion during storms. Other "ecosystem services" include the provision of fertile soil, pollination for crops, and control of pests and pathogens. These ecosystem services are provided free of charge. They are not included in our economic valuation systems. They are not easily replaced. These services are of obvious importance to people and warrant strong protection.

In some cases, protection of individual species through the ESA has had the added benefit of protection of the ecosystem in which the species lives and therefore both other species and the ecosystem. For example, protection of the northern spotted owl has probably resulted in protection of some 280 other species of plants and vertebrates, as well as protection of watersheds that provide clean drinking water for cities and spawning grounds for salmon.

The increase in scientific understanding of species and ecosystems over the past two decades strongly reinforces the original goals of the ESA. Thus, in addition to ethical and moral reasons to protect species and habitats, it is in our own best interests to do so. Protection of species benefits us all. New information also provides guidance about how to achieve this protection in more efficient and effective ways.

... Throughout human history, parents have looked to the younger generation as the hope for the future, the hope for continuing the good things we have begun and for correcting our errors. Now, however, the next generation may not be able to undo our most egregious and short-sighted mistakes. As E.O. Wilson has said, loss of biodiversity is the folly least likely to be forgiven us by future generations.

PREPARED STATEMENT OF WILLIAM ROBERT IRVIN, DEPUTY VICE PRESIDENT, CENTER FOR MARINE CONSERVATION, BEFORE THE SENATE COMMITTEE ON ENVIRONMENT AND PUBLIC WORKS, JULY 13, 1995

Maintaining a strong ESA is important to our nation because, in a very real sense, the ESA protects the United States. Nearly half of our prescription medicines are derived from plants and other wildlife. You may have heard of the rosy periwinkle, a flowering plant native to Madagascar. This innocuous plant, grown in nurseries but nearly extinct in the world, is used to produce the drugs Vincristine and Vinblastine, which achieve a 99 percent remission rate in children suffering from leukemia....

The ESA's role in protecting biological diversity is also essential to agriculture. The world relies on only about 20 of the approximately 250,000 identified plant specimens for 90 percent of our food supply. Just three species — corn, wheat, and rice — provide half the world's food. This incredibly thin reed on which human survival depends is susceptible to devastating insect infestations and blights. One of the best ways to protect domesticated crops from such disasters is to crossbreed them with wild varieties....

Although the ESA has often been caricatured as a law that costs jobs, it is, in fact, a law that protects jobs. In the Pacific Northwest, the ESA's protection of endangered salmon runs is essential to protecting a commercial and recreational fishing industry providing 60,000 jobs and $1 billion in personal income to the region's economy. Even protecting such unglamorous species as freshwater mussels, 43 percent of which are threatened, endangered, or extinct, protects jobs. Export of mussel shells from the United States to Japan for the cultured pearl industry is worth $60 million annually to the American economy, supporting 10,000 jobs.

In nearly every state, we can find examples of the ESA working to protect endangered wildlife and needs of our nation....

Even in *Noah's Choice*, a book that is critical of the ESA, one finds examples of the ESA successfully balancing the needs of endangered species with the needs of people....

The ESA achieves this balance because Congress and the agencies charged with implementing the law have included a myriad of balancing mechanisms within the law. In virtually every provision of the ESA, social and economic factors are taken into account.

To paraphrase Michael Bean, author of *The Evolution of National Wildlife Law*, the amazing thing about the Endangered Species Act is not how many conflicts there have been, but how few. Perhaps even more amazing is that, despite the heavy consideration given to economic and other concerns under the ESA, the ESA has been quite successful in its central mission, saving species from extinction. ... as the National Research Council concluded in its recent study, *Science and the Endangered Species Act*, "[T]he ESA has successfully prevented some species from becoming extinct. Retention of the ESA would help to prevent species extinction."

... some fundamental principles should be kept in mind, against which any ESA reauthorization legislation should be measured.

First, we should not profligately spend our children's inheritance. Conserving species benefits future generations as well as ourselves. These benefits may not always be quantifiable in monetary terms. Long-term benefits to future generations must not be sacrificed for short-term economic gains.

Second, an ounce of prevention is worth a pound of cure. Conserving species before they are on the brink of extinction offers more and better opportunities to balance species conservation against economic and other considerations, helping avoid conflicts.

Third, we must put our money where our mouths are. Sustained and adequate funding of historically underfunded endangered species conservation programs is essential. Similarly, greater incentives should be provided to private landowners to encourage endangered species conservation on their properties.

Fourth, we must keep our eyes on the ball. The purpose of the ESA is to conserve threatened and endangered species and the ecosystems upon which they depend. While it is important to make the ESA flexible, effective conservation of species and their habitats must remain the fundamental goal of the law.

... the ESA was never intended to solve all our wildlife conservation problems. Instead, the ESA was intended as a safety net, protecting species from extinction when other measures have failed. Thus, in addition to making the ESA itself more proactive, it is essential that all our wildlife conservation laws and policies, particularly those governing management of public resources such as federal lands and marine resources, must be more proactive in conserving wildlife.

CHAPTER XI

THE ENDANGERED SPECIES ACT HAS NOT WORKED WELL

STATEMENT OF R.J. SMITH, SENIOR EN-VIRONMENTAL SCHOLAR, COMPETI-TIVE ENTERPRISE, BEFORE THE SENATE COMMITTEE ON ENVIRONMENT AND PUBLIC WORKS, AUGUST 3, 1995

Our efforts and other efforts to protect property rights and to require compensation for property owners whose land or property is taken by the government for the purposes of the act, are in no manner whatsoever an effort to gut the act or to harm wildlife or habitat. It is instead a rational and carefully considered effort to make the act work for both people and for species.

Many of the most remarkable conservation success stories of this century were achieved through the full and willing cooperation of private landowners who had no fear of maintaining species or habitat on their lands because they do not face the loss of the use of their lands or the economic value of their property as a result of their good stewardship....

Most landowners were more than willing to help. There was no downside. If the ducks utilized the nest boxes, the landowners would not be prevented from using their lands, harvesting their trees or crops, or operating vehicles within a half mile radius of the nest side....

Similar efforts have worked for a wide range of species which can benefit from additional or improved nest sites and natural habitat or in degraded habitat.

They all worked ... because the presence of the species or its habitat was not a liability to the landowner. Unfortunately, the ESA works in precisely the opposite and wrong manner. The better steward a landowner is the more wildlife habitat he maintains on one's land, the more likely it is that you will be rewarded by the loss of the use of or the economic value of your lands and property....

Now that is the worst possible way to encourage landowners to help protect endangered species and habitat. In fact, it does just the opposite. It encourages them to get rid of wildlife habitat, to sterilize their lands. It creates the "shoot, shovel and shut up syndrome."

Because of the way the act operates, it has become a disaster. It harms people and their property, and it harms species and habitat. It is bad for people and it is bad for species. Over the past half year a vast amount of time and effort has gone into efforts to find or create positive incentives to place into the Endangered Species Act in order to eliminate many of the unintended consequences of the act, to end the fear and loathing that so many landowners increasingly have for the act, and to prevent or curtail the acts of habitat sterilization.

But this is largely an illusory and self-defeating effort. While many of these new devised incentives are promising and very innovative, they may have little if any positive effect. The one incentive that will work is to remove the perverse incentives, the disincentives in the act. Remove the penalties for having wildlife and habitat on one's lands. Stop regulatory takings of private lands. Stop making stewardship a liability. Work with the nation's private landowners instead of against them. If you do take their lands, then pay them compensation, precisely as you do with their lands that are taken for any other public good.

... private landowners are not afraid of wildlife on their lands. They are afraid of the Feds on their lands. Eliminate that fear and they will once again be willing to help protect wildlife and habitat. In most cases, I believe landowners will not require costly incentives. Removal of the underlying fear of loss of their lands will again make many of them willing to share their lands with species and habitat.

In conclusion,... by removing the sword of Damocles from the head of private landowners, we can make private landowners look at the Fish and Wildlife Service again the same way they viewed the Soil and Conservation Service and the USDA's Conservation Reserve Program. The American people will benefit, and the American wildlife will benefit.

STATEMENT OF THE GRASSROOTS ESA COALITION FOR INCLUSION IN THE RECORD OF PROCEEDINGS OF THE HEARINGS OF THE SENATE COMMITTEE ON ENVIRONMENT AND PUBLIC WORKS, JUNE 3, 1995

... The old law has been a failure for endangered species and for people. It has not led to the legitimate recovery of a single endangered species while costing billions of dollars and tremendous harm. The old way destroyed trust between people and our wildlife officials. We need to reestablish trust so we can conserve wildlife — no program will succeed without the support of our farmers, our ranchers, our citizens.

The old law failed because it is based on flawed ideas. It is founded on regulation and punishment. If you look at the actual law by section you see it is all about bureaucracy — consultation, permits, law enforcement ... there isn't even a section of the law called "conservation," "saving" or "recovery."

It is a bureaucratic machine and its fruits are paperwork and court cases and fines — not conserved and recovered endangered species. What the Grassroots ESA Coalition and all Americans want to see is a law that works for wildlife, not one that works against people.

The future of conservation lies in establishing an entirely new foundation for the conservation of endangered species — one based on the truism that if you want more of something you reward people for it, not punish them. The debate that will unfold before the public is one between methods of conservation.

The old way is shackled to the idea that Washington bureaucrats can come up with a government solution through national land use control. Its supporters do not want to acknowledge that the law has failed because doing so would mean an end to the influence and power they have under the old system.

The Coalition sees a new way that can actually help endangered species because it stops punishing people for providing habitat and encourages them to do so. It creates an opportunity for our officials — for government — to reestablish trust and work with and earn the support of citizens. The Grassroots ESA Coalition is working to promote this new way.

If you think that government bureaucracy works, that welfare stops poverty and does not need reform or that the DMV and Post Office operate the way they should, then the old endangered species program is for you. If you do not, and you want to conserve endangered species without wasting money, intruding on people's lives and causing more pain and problems, then the Grassroots ESA Coalition is for you.

We therefore support repealing current law and replacing it with an Endangered Species Act based upon these principles:

- Animals and plants should be responsibly conserved for the benefit and enjoyment of mankind.

- The primary responsibility for conservation of animals and plants shall be reserved to the States.

- Federal conservation efforts shall rely entirely on voluntary, incentive-based programs to enlist the cooperation of America's landowners and invigorate their conservation ethic.

- Federal conservation efforts shall encourage conservation through commerce, including the private propagation of animals and plants.

- Specific safeguards shall ensure that this Act cannot be used to prevent the wise use of the vast federal estate.

- Federal conservation decisions shall incur the lowest cost possible to citizens and taxpayers.

- Federal conservation efforts shall be based on sound science and give priority to more taxonomically unique, genetically complex and more economically and ecologically valuable animals and plants.

- Federal conservation prohibitions should be limited to forbidding actions intended to kill or physically injure a listed vertebrate species with the exception of uses that create incentives and funding for an animal's conservation.

STATEMENT OF SENATOR DIRK KEMPTHORNE (R-ID) BEFORE THE SENATE COMMITTEE ON ENVIRONMENT AND PUBLIC WORKS, JUNE 3, 1995

I envision an Endangered Species Act that treats property owners fairly and with consideration and that recognizes private property rights and minimizes the social and economic impacts of this law on the lives of its citizens …

This Act in its present course of heavy regulations and putting people and their communities at risk will not work. To single out individual communities to carry the brunt of recovery when the entire national community is the beneficiary is wrong. But to also say that extinction of a species is no big deal and just the luck of the draw for that particular species, and that we won't lift a human finger to help is equally wrong. And the proponents of each of those two extremes probably deserve each other on some remote island where the only way they can survive is to help one another.

So what's right? To reform the Endangered Species Act and to use good science that makes good public policy decisions with innovation and incentives and, where necessary, public financial resources to do what we as a human race, the stewards of this environment, can to benefit not only other species, but ourselves as well. I try to refrain from calling one group environmentalist, because we'd all better be environmentalists because this is all we have.

Is the term "probusiness environmentalist" an oxymoron? Well, it better not be, because without a healthy economy you won't have the resources you need to conserve the rare species among us... As Charles Mann and Mark Plummer said in their book, *Noah's Choice*, and I quote, "If we want truly to improve the lot of endangered species we should stop shooting for the stars, because the arrows will fall back to our feet. By aiming a little closer we might shoot farther in the desired direction." And I will add, and hit the target more often.

PREPARED SUBMISSION OF MICHAEL D. CRAPO (R-ID) TO THE SENATE COMMITTEE ON ENVIRONMENT AND PUBLIC WORKS, JUNE 3, 1995

The goals of the ESA, protection of threatened or endangered species, can be achieved without sacrificing jobs or unduly burdening our economy.

Unfortunately, the ESA has not been successful in accomplishing any of these goals. In the twenty-two years since the ESA was enacted some 1,450 species and subspecies have been listed as either endangered or threatened. Almost 4,100 others are current candidates for listing. In these twenty-two years, only nineteen species have been delisted.... Seven species have become extinct, and only four have been recovered under the definitions set by the Department of Interior.

Not only have species suffered under the implementation of the Act, but jobs have also been lost, the economic livelihood of thousands of families have been jeopardized, private property rights have been eroded, and cities and states have been exposed to unnecessarily increased costs. Each endangered species listing can trigger millions of dollars of federal spending — and even a greater burden on local and private citizens.

One recent study found that the recovery plans for just 388 endangered species — 25,000 pages of bureaucratese — will cost the U.S. Government over $880 million. Instead of fostering a process which brings interested and affected parties together to promote the well being and recovery of a species, the current system forces opposing opinions to take adversarial positions. It is time to change the implementation of the Act to take it back to its original goal, that of species preservation.

... We have an historic opportunity to craft a strong bill to protect and restore threatened and endangered species and preserve private property and water rights while sustaining strong resource-based economies. We must no longer approach the issue by pitting endangered species against jobs and families.

The [reforming] guiding principles

(1) Make the ESA more compatible with private property rights and free market forces. It's time to end the unreasonable curtailment of private property rights....

(2) Refine the ESA's definition of species and eliminate the use of questionable science in endangered species classification.

(3) Improve and streamline the regulatory process and enhance state, local and citizen participation. The private citizen often feels that they have no voice in ESA regulations and policies.

STATEMENT OF SENATOR KAY BAILEY HUTCHISON (R-TX) BEFORE THE SENATE COMMITTEE ON ENVIRONMENT AND PUBLIC WORKS, MARCH 7, 1995

Endangered species protection, if it is a worthwhile goal for society, that society at large, not just the men and women who produce our food and clothing, must fairly share the burden and the cost of species protection....

The Federal Government will only be able to protect species under the Act with proper direction from Congress and with full support of the public. By restricting land and water use through additional listings, the Fish and Wildlife Service is undermining public support for the Act and is actually harming the cause of protecting species from extinction....

The listing of the Arkansas River Shiner as an endangered species in Texas, Oklahoma, and Kansas is not necessary. There is a shiner population in the Pecos River of New Mexico that is not at risk and others may be established ...

Listing the shiner could have profound impact on the Panhandle's surface and groundwater supply. Water from the Ogallala Aquifer serves the citizens of Amarillo and the surrounding areas. If the shiner is listed, use of the aquifer could be cut back, causing severe difficulties to the region's agricultural economy. Similarly, use of surface water is essential to the farming communities surrounding Amarillo and Lubbock; limitations on surface water use could also harm their economies.

Water is scarce in the Panhandle. We cannot afford to give fish bait more protection than people, but if the shiner is listed, it would have more right to the water than the Panhandle farmers and ranchers and the people of Amarillo, Texas....

I am discouraged to hear that some people may be planning to cast the endangered species debate as an effort to help only large landowners. I don't need to talk about constitutional rights to tell you how wrong that is. In Texas, 3,000 people turned out to talk about critical habitat designation in towns where no more than 1,000 people live. That's not the turnout you get for an issue that only affects the rich.

...The Fish and Wildlife Service has had adequate time to carry out its primary responsibilities under the Act. It has overzealously enforced the Act by expanding the definition of a harm beyond Congress' intent, listing species without regard to water supplies necessary for the health and safety of the people and proposing habitat without taking economic concerns into account unless it was forced to do so by the people.

When those agencies lost sight of Congress' intentions and lost their common sense, only Congress and the President can set them straight. Now is the time for Congress to review their actions and exercise its legislative power to revise their instructions. Let's call a time-out on listings until we can put endangered species protection back on track.

STATEMENT OF KENNETH W. PETERSON, CHAIRMAN, BOARD OF SUPERVISORS, KERN COUNTY, CALIFORNIA

The citizens of Kern County support the preservation of America's rich natural heritage. But the Endangered Species Act is not achieving this aim. Instead, the state and federal governments are using the Act to dictate the uses of private land, to extort land and money from property owners, and to drive the cost of many local public works to prohibitive extremes. The agencies which apply and enforce the Act have almost become a law unto themselves, assuming powers never intended by the Act and, in my view, never granted by the Constitution. In very few cases are any endangered species recovering. Humans, however, are reeling from the impact.

There is wide agreement that the Act is broken and it needs to be fixed. Unless Congress pulls this misguided vehicle off the road by stopping further listings until we can agree how to repair it, this assault on our land, our rights, and our livelihoods will continue.

... the Environmental Protection Agency recently issued a biological opinion preventing valley farmers from controlling rodents such as rabbits, squirrels, and gophers with chemicals since these rodenticides could also affect the San Joaquin kit fox and the tipton kangaroo rat. That means that farmers who may never have seen evidence of a kit fox or a rat on their land must stand by and watch as more common pests ravage their crops. On farmer lost $40,000 of melons last spring to rabbits after that decision. The California Department of Food and Agriculture estimates crop losses in Kern County alone will total $73 million each year. And foregoing commonly used, low-risk rodenticides also increases the public health risk of rodent-transmitted diseases.

... Why have the courts been so prominent in shaping endangered species law? Perhaps it is because the original Act was not written clearly enough. There are no clear-cut scientific standards for reaching species and habitat decisions or evaluating recovery plans. There aren't any deadlines for consultations or recovery plans. And there is virtually no reckoning of the economic costs involved or any requirement that the public should pay the costs of achieving public aims like preserving species. In Kern County, many are asking, "How much is enough? When does it end?"

... it's been said that when you don't know where you're going, any road will get you there. I don't think the government really knows where it wants to go with the Endangered Species Act.

IMPORTANT NAMES AND ADDRESSES

American Association of Zoological
Parks and Aquariums
7970 Old Georgetown Rd.
Bethesda, MD 20814
(301) 907-7777
FAX (301) 907-2980

American Ornithologists' Union
730 11th St. NW
Washington, DC 20001-4521
(202) 357-2051
FAX (202) 628-4311

Animal Protection Institute
2831 Fruitridge Rd.
Sacramento, CA 95820
(916) 731-5521

Animal Welfare Institute
P.O. Box 3650
Washington, DC 20007
(202) 337-2332
FAX (202) 338-9478

Biological Resources Division (BRD)
— USGS
U.S. Dept. of the Interior
12201 Sunrise Valley Dr.
Reston, VA 22092
(301) 317-3819

Center for Marine Conservation
1725 DeSales St., Suite 600
Washington, DC 20036
(202) 429-5609
FAX (202) 872-0619

Defenders of Wildlife
1101 14th St. NW, Suite 1400
Washington, DC 20005
(202) 682-9400
FAX (202) 833-3349

Environmental Defense Fund
1875 Connecticut Ave. NW, Suite
1016
Washington, DC 20009
(202) 387-3500
FAX (202) 234-6049

Friends of the Earth
1025 Vermont Ave. NW, 3rd Floor
Washington, DC 20005-6303
(202) 783-7400
FAX (202) 783-0444

Greenpeace U.S.A.
1436 U St. NW
Washington, DC 20009
(202) 462-1177
FAX (202) 462-4507

Human Ecology Action League
P.O. Box 49126
Atlanta, GA 30359
(404) 248-1898
FAX (404) 248-0162

Humane Society of the United States
2100 L. St. NW
Washington, DC 20037
(202) 452-1100
FAX (202) 778-6132

Izaak Walton League of America
707 Conservation Ln.
Gaithersburg, MD 20878-2783
(301) 548-0150
FAX (301) 548-0146

Marine Mammal Commission
1825 Connecticut Ave. NW
Washington, DC 20009
(202) 606-5504
FAX (202) 606-5510

National Audubon Society
1901 Pennsylvania Ave., #1100
Washington, DC 20006
(202) 861-2242
FAX (202) 861-4290

National Wildlife Federation
1400 16th St. NW
Washington, DC 20036
(202) 797-6800
FAX (202) 797-6646

Natural Resources Defense Council
1200 New York Ave. NW, Suite 400
Washington, DC 20005
(202) 289-6868
FAX (202) 289-1060

Nature Conservancy
1815 North Lynn St.
Arlington, VA 22209
(703) 841-5300
FAX (703) 841-1283

People for the Ethical Treatment of
Animals (PETA)
501 Front St.
Norfolk, VA 23510
(757) 622-7382
FAX (757) 622-0457

Rachel Carson Council
8940 Joans Mill Rd.
Chevy Chase, MD 20815
(301) 652-1877
FAX (301) 451-7179

Sierra Club
408 C St. NE
Washington, DC 20002
(202) 547-1141
FAX (202) 547-6009

Union of Concerned Scientists
1616 P St. NW, #310
Washington, DC 20036
(202) 332-0900
FAX (202) 332-0905

U.S. Fish and Wildlife Service
Endangered Species Office
Main Interior Building
Washington, DC 20240
(703) 358-1711

The Wilderness Society
900 17th St. NW
Washington, DC 20006
(202) 833-2300
FAX (202) 429-3958

Wildlife Management Institute
1101 14th St. NW, Suite 801
Washington, DC 20005
(202) 371-1808
FAX (202) 408-5059

World Wildlife Fund
1250 24th St. NW
Washington, DC 20037
(202) 293-4800
FAX (202) 293-9211

Worldwatch Institute
1776 Massachusetts Ave. NW
Washington, DC 20036
(202) 452-1999
FAX (202) 296-7365

RESOURCES

The National Park Service of the United States Department of the Interior provides a variety of materials on public lands and on matters concerning wildlife, including *Refuges 2003* (1993), which documents the loss of habitat for many species of wildlife. The Department of the Interior also publishes the semi-monthly *Endangered Species Technical Bulletin* newsletter, which tracks the status of listed endangered and threatened species. The National Biological Service, of the U.S. Department of Interior prepared *Our Living Resources* (1995), a compilation of data on species and ecosystems and the first report of that agency on the status of U.S. wildlife. The *1996 National Survey of Fishing, Hunting and Wildlife-Associated Recreation* (1997), prepared by the Department of the Interior and the Bureau of the Census, was the source of information and tables on wildlife as recreation. The U.S. Forest Service prepared the exhaustive report, *Species Endangerment Patterns in the United States* (1994).

The U.S. Fish and Wildlife Service published *Endangered and Threatened Wildlife and Plants* (1994) and *The Road Back — Endangered Species Recovery* (1997). The U.S. Department of Commerce is responsible for the *Marine Mammal Protection Act of 1972: Annual Report* (1997) and *Our Living Oceans* (1993). The U.S. General Accounting Office (GAO) monitors governmental activity and prepares briefing reports on various environmental topics for Congress, including energy, pollution, federal lands, species loss, and national parks, which were important in the preparation of this book. *Every Species Counts: Research on Threatened, Endangered, and Sensitive Animals* (1992), prepared by the U.S. Department of Agriculture, was also useful.

The Environmental Protection Agency (EPA) monitors the status of the environment. Agency publications include *Progress in Ground-Water Protection and Restoration* (1990), *National Air Pollution Emission Trends, 1990-1994* (1995), and *Constructed Wetlands from Wastewater Treatment and Wildlife Habitat* (1993).

The now-defunct Office of Technology Assessment (OTA), a former analytical support agency of the United States Congress, provided outstanding resource information for Congress and the public on a variety of scientific and technological issues including *The Greenhouse Trap: What We're Doing to the Atmosphere and How We Can Slow Global Warming* (1991),

Changing By Degrees: Steps to Reduce Greenhouse Gases (1991), *Wastes in Marine Environments* (1987), and *Acid Rain and Transported Air Pollutants* (1984).

The Endangered Species Handbook (1990), published by the Animal Welfare Institute, provides a complete overview of species loss. Its *Flight to Extinction* (not dated) discusses losses of exotic birds to trade. The Institute's *America Leads the World in Preventing the Extinction of Species* (not dated) provides updates on recent successes in saving threatened species. Its *Whales vs. Whalers 1971-1995* (1996) documents the whaling industry during that time period.

The Endangered Species Coalition, a private conservation agency, publishes a wide range of publications on wildlife and the environment, including *The Endangered Species Act: A Commitment Worth Keeping* (The Wilderness Society, 1992) and *The Endangered Species Act: A Record of Success* (1995). The Wilderness Society published *Beyond the Endangered Species Act: Conservation in the 21st Century* (1992). The National Research Council of the National Academy of Sciences published *Science and the Endangered Species Act* (1995), a history and analysis of the Endangered Species Act. The Natural Resources Defense Council, a national non-profit environmental organization, prepared *Testing the Waters: Who Knows What You're Getting Into?* (1996).

Conserving the World's Biological Diversity, prepared by the International Union for Conservation of Nature and Natural Resources (IUCN), World Resources Institute, Conservation International, World Wildlife Fund, and the World Bank (1990), is a detailed resource on world ecology. The *1997 Red List of Threatened Plants*, the result of a 20-year study by the IUCN, is an invaluable tool to understanding the status of plant species.

The United Nations Environment Programme (UNEP) provided *Global Biodiversity* (1993), and the Environmental Investigative Agency published *CITES — Enforcement not Extinction* (1994) on world trade in wildlife. Information Plus thanks the National Sporting Goods Association, which maintains data on recreational participation and sales, for the use of information from their survey on recreational participation. Information Plus especially appreciates permission to use Mr. William Rossiter's photographs of whales and whale-watching tour boats.

INDEX

Acid rain, 26-35
Adventure vacationing, 130-131
Alaska, 95-96
Alligators, 74-75
Amazon rain forest, 47
Amphibians, 100-102
Apes, 123-125
Aquaculture, 72
Aquatic life, 30-31
Aquatic species, 52ff
Asia, 124-126
Balcones Canyonlands Conservation Plan, 51
Bald eagle, 80-82, 121
Bald Eagle Protection Act, 81
Bears, 90-92
Bighorn sheep, 105-106
Biological diversity (biodiversity), 6, 12, 15-16, 26, 36
Biosphere, 2
Birds, 32-33, 77ff
Bison, 104-105
Black-capped Vireo, 84
Black-footed ferret, 98-99
Buffalo, see Bison
Butterflies, 99-100
California condor, 88-89
California gnatcatcher, 84-85
Canada, 18, 35
Canned hunting, 136-137
Captive breeding, 147
Carbon cycle, 24
Carbon dioxide, 22-23
Cats, 79-80
Cheetah, 98
China, 63, 125
Chinese medicine, 124
Chloroflourocarbons (CFCs), 23
Cichlids, 69-70
Clean Air Act, 35
Clear-cutting, 42
Climate, 19-23, 28-29
Condor, See California condor
Convention on the International Trade in Endangered Species (CITES), 114, 116, 123, 125, 127-128
Coral reefs, 71-72
Critical habitat, 148
Critical loads, 32
Crocodiles, 118
Cyanide fishing, 71-72
Dams, 60-63, 74
DDT (dichloro-diphenyl-trichloroethane), 6, 54, 80, 87
Deforestation, 40, 42-43
Dodo bird, 77
Dolphins, 73-75, 115
Driftnets, 71
Ecosystems, 2
Elephants, 122-123
Endangered species
    definition of, 3
    listed, 4, 11

Endangered Species Act, 50-51, 64, 70, 76, 88, 93, 139-144, 160-169
Endangered Species List, 87, 141-142
Environmental ethics, 6
Environmental factors, 19ff
Evolution, 19
Exotic birds, 117-121
Extinction rates, 4, 79
Exxon Valdez, 53, 80
Falconry, 88
Farm Bill of 1990, 56
Federal Insecticide, Fungicide, and Rodenticide Act, 80
Federal lands, 155-157
Ferrets, see Black-footed ferret
Fertilizers, 56
Fish, 66-72
Fish consumption advisories, 58-59
Fishing, 134
Florida Everglades, 48
Florida panther, 94, 97-98
Food chain, 58
Forests, 40-47
Fox hunting, 106-107
Fur trade, 123
General Agreement on Tariffs and Trade (GATT), 128-129
Global warming, 21-26, 39
Golden-cheeked warbler, 84
Grassland birds, 85
Greenhouse effect, 20-23
Habitat, 6-7
Habitat Conservation Plans (HAPs), 146-147
Herpetofauna, 90ff
Hunting, 132-134
"Indicator species," 6
Indonesia, 120
Insects, 90ff
Integrated Pest Management (IPM), 55
Intergovernmental Panel on Climate Change (IPCC), 21-22
International Whaling Commission (IWC), 111-112
Introduced species, 59-60
Jaguar, 99
Lacey Act, 75-76, 126-127
Lake Erie, 53
Lemurs, 101
Logging, 42-43
Long-line fishing, 71
Magnuson Act, 68, 75, 76
Mammals, 90ff
Manatees, 63-64
Mangroves, 48-49
Marine Mammal Protection Act, 76
Mass extinctions, 7-8
Medicinal plants, 44-46
Mediterranean Sea, 53
Mercury, 57
Methane, 22
Moths, 99-100
Mussels, 72, 74

National Acid Precipitation Assessment Program (NAPAP), 33-34
National Park Service, 147, 149
National Park System, 147-150
National Wildlife Refuge System, 15-152
Nitrogen, 27, 34
North American Breeding Bird Survey, 83
North American Free Trade Agreement (NAFTA), 18, 128-129
Northern spotted owl, 84-86
Ocean dumping, 57, 61
Oil spills, 53-54, 80-81
Overfishing, 67-69
Ozone, 58
Pandas, 91-93
Passenger pigeon, 77-78
Penguins, 81
Peregrine falcon, 86-88
Pesticides, 54-56
Plants, 36ff, 50-51
Population, 9, 11-12
Primates, 90ff, 123-125
Protected areas, 159
Recreation, 130ff
Red-cockaded woodpecker, 86-87
Reptiles, 117
Research animals, 104, 107-109
Rhinoceros, 115-117
Salmon, 70-71
Salton Sea, 23-24
Sea level, 23-24
Sea lions, 65-66
Seals, 65-67
Sea turtle, 64-65
Sharks, 74-75, 113-114
Siberian tiger, 95, 98
Songbirds, 82-85
Species diversity, See Biological diversity
Theft, timber, 43
Threatened, definition, 3
Trade in wild animals, 110ff
Turtle-excluder device (TED), 76
United Nations Economic Commission (UNEC), 31
Water pollution, 53-59
Wetlands, 47-51
Whales, 74-75, 110-112, 114
Whale-watching, 135-136
Whooping crane, 87-88
Wild and Scenic Rivers Act of 1968, 156
Wild Bird Conservation Act (1992), 118
Wild, Free-Roaming Horses and Burros Act, 103
Wild horses, 102-104
Wildcrafting, 43-44
Wilderness Act of 1964, 152
Wilderness areas, 152-153
Wildlife-watching, 134-136
Wolves, 92-96
World Trade Organization, 129
Yellowstone National Park, 94, 105
Zoos, 153-155